Conserving Wildlife

International Education and
Communication Approaches

Conserving Wildlife

International Education and
Communication Approaches

■■
■■

Edited by

Susan K. Jacobson

COLUMBIA UNIVERSITY PRESS   NEW YORK

Columbia University Press
New York   Chichester, West Sussex
Copyright © 1995 Columbia University Press

Library of Congress Cataloging-in-Publication Data
Conserving wildlife : international education and communication
approaches / edited by Susan K. Jacobson.
    p.   cm. — (Methods and cases in conservation science)
    Includes bibliographical references and index.
    ISBN 0-231-07966-4. — ISBN 0-231-07967-2 (pbk.)
    1. Wildlife conservation—Study and teaching—Activity programs.
2. Wildlife conservation—Citizen participation.   3. Wildlife
conservation—Case studies. I. Jacobson, Susan Kay. II. Series.
QL83.15.C65   1995
333.95′16—dc20   94-37275

∞   CIP
Casebound editions of Columbia University Press books are
printed on permanent and durable acid-free paper.

Printed in the United States of America
c 10 9 8 7 6 5 4 3 2 1

Contents

∷

List of Figures   ix

List of Tables   xi

About the Editor   xiii

About the Contributors   xv

Acknowledgments   xxi

Introduction: xxiii
Wildlife Conservation Through Education
Susan K. Jacobson

PART 1: CONSERVING NATURAL AREAS   1

1. A Systems Model for Conservation Education in Parks: 3
    Examples from Malaysia and Brazil
    Susan K. Jacobson and Suzana M. Padua

2. Appealing to the Heart as Well as the Head: 16
    Outback Australia's Junior Ranger Program
    Stuart Traynor

3. Monitoring Awareness and Attitude in Conservation Education: 28
    The Mountain Gorilla Project in Rwanda
    William Weber

PART 2: PROTECTING DECLINING SPECIES   49

4. Reversing Population Declines in Seabirds on the North Shore   51
    of the Gulf of St. Lawrence, Canada
    Kathleen A. Blanchard

5. Golden Lion Tamarin Conservation Program: A Community   64
    Educational Effort for Forest Conservation in Rio de Janeiro
    State, Brazil
    Lou Ann Hollingsworth Dietz and Elizabeth Yoshimi Nagagata

6. Marketing the Conservation Message: Using Parrots to   87
    Promote Protection and Pride in the Caribbean
    Paul J. Butler

7. Comprehensive Approaches for Saving Bats   103
    Patricia A. Morton and Mari J. Murphy

PART 3: TARGETING RESOURCE USERS   119

8. Integrated Crane Conservation Activities in Pakistan:
    Education, Research, and Public Relations   121
    Steven E. Landfried, Muhammad Mumtaz Malik, Ashiq Ahmad,
    and A. Aleem Chaudhry

9. Education to Promote Male-Selective Harvest of Grizzly Bear   156
    in the Yukon
    Bernard L. Smith

PART 4: PROGRAMMING FOR SCHOOLS   175

10. The Global Rivers Environmental Education Network   177
    William B. Stapp, Mare M. Cromwell, and Arjen Wals

11. Engaging Students in Wildlife-Focused Action Projects in   198
    Florida: A Thirty-five-Year Perspective
    William C. Hammond

12. A Zoo with Class in Victoria, Australia   219
    Greg Hunt

PART 5: INVOLVING COMMUNITY GROUPS   233

13. Multilevel Conservation and Education at the Community   235
    Baboon Sanctuary, Belize
    Robert H. Horwich and Jonathan Lyon

14. Les Mielles: A Conservation Opportunity in the United Kingdom   254
    Michael Romeril

15. Conservation and Local Naturalist Guide Training Programs   263
    in Costa Rica
    Pia Paaby and David B. Clark

References   277

Index   289

Figures

Intro.1. *Effective wildlife conservation programs rely on (1) public educa-*   xxiv
tion and participation, (2) ecological research and management, and (3) appro-
priate legislation and enforcement.

1.1. *Systems model for the planning, implementation, and product evalua-*   4
tion of conservation education programs.

1.2. *Location of programs in Sabah, East Malaysia, and eastern Brazil.*   5

2.1. *The Junior Ranger Program was conducted in the vast Northern Terri-*   17
tory of Australia.

3.1. Rwanda. *Volcanos National Park is located in northern Rwanda.*   29

3.2. Forest value (if can't be cut). *Survey results concerning noncon-*   34
sumptive values of the forest of Volcanos National Park.

3.3. Animal value (if can't be hunted). *Survey results concerning non-*   34
consumptive values of the wildlife of Volcanos National Park.

3.4. Virunga forest impact on water supply. *Survey results concern-*   35
ing the role of the Virunga ecosystem in water catchment.

3.5. *Survey results concerning whether the Volcanos National Park should be*   36
opened for agricultural exploitation.

5.1. *Model for development of a conservation education project.*   66

5.2. Do you recognize this animal (golden lion tamarin)? *Recogni-*   78
tion of a tamarin from a photograph, before and after two years of educational
activities.

5.3. In what size groups does this (tamarin) live? *Responses given be-*   79
fore and after two years of educational activities.

5.4. Is the golden lion tamarin beneficial? *Responses given before and*   80
after two years of educational activities.

5.5. What would you do if you found a little monkey in the   81
woods? *Responses given before and after two years of educational activities.*

5.6. What would you do if you found a little bird in the   83
woods? *Responses given before and after two years of educational activities.*

5.7. What would you do if you found a snake in the woods? *Res-*   83
ponses given before and after two years of educational activities.

5.8. Where did you see or hear of the golden lion tamarin? *Re-*   84
sponses given by adults of the municipality of Silva Jardim after two years of edu-
cational activities.

8.1. *Siberian crane-migration route through northern Pakistan.*   124

9.1a. *Side views of adult female, adult male, subadult female, and subadult*   164
male grizzly bears.

9.1b. *Front views of adult female, adult male, subadult female, and sub-*   165
adult male grizzly bears.

9.2. *Adhesive sticker distributed to hunting guides to provide a checklist of*   167
identifying characteristics of adult male grizzly bears.

9.3. *Example of text from the booklet Hunt Wisely: A Guide to Male-Selec-*   168
tive Grizzly Bear Hunting.

10.1. *The National Sanitation Foundation Water-Quality Index.*   181

10.2. *Basic elements of the original Interactive Water-Monitoring Program*   184
for schools.

10.3. *GREEN-EcoNet Computer Conference discussion.*   192

12.1. *Summary of teachers' comments relating to the value of the Zoologi-*   229
cal Board of Victoria Education Service classroom programs.

13.1. *Composite map of the Community Baboon Sanctuary (CBS).*   238

13.2. *Aerial photograph of the central portion of the CBS.*   239

13.3. *Lyon discussing land ownership boundaries with participating sanctu-*   243
ary landowners.

13.4. *Administrative and management structure of the CBS.*   245

13.5. *A typical poster exhibit in the CBS Museum.*   248

13.6. *A CBS Museum exhibit room.*   249

13.7. *Fallet Young, the CBS's first manager, and Reuben Rhaburn, the first*   250
assistant manager and present committee member, lecturing on a section of the
CBS interpretive trail.

13.8. *Map of Belize indicating community conservation sites.*   251

14.1. *Les Mielles development plan.*   256

14.2. *A Les Mielles Visitor Interpretation Center in a converted and restored*   259
nineteenth-century Martello tower.

15.1. *Location of La Selva Biological Station in Costa Rica.*   264

Tables

Intro.1. Elements Leading to Successful Conservation Education   xxxii
and Communication Programs

Table 3.1. Rwandan Perceptions of Land Issues   32

Table 3.2. Changes in Rwandan Perceptions of Park Conservation   43
Values (1979–1984)

Table 3.3. Relationship Between Attendance at a Conservation Edu-   44
cation Program and Perceptions of Park Conservation Values in the
Virunga Region

Table 3.4. Ranked Perceptions of Priority Problems at Different   47
Levels in Ruhengeri Prefecture

Table 4.1. Changes in Knowledge of Wildlife Laws: Percentages of   60
Heads-of-Households Correctly Stating the Legal Status of Select Seabirds

Table 4.2. Changes in Attitudes About Wildlife Laws: Percentages   61
of Heads-of-Households that Believe Hunting Should Be Allowed

Table 5.1. Survey About Fauna and Flora   69

Table 6.1. Forestry and Wildlife Division Questionnaire   94

Table 8.1. Representative Questions from 1983 Crane Hunter Ques-   130
tionnaire, Jurram Valley, North-West Frontier Province, Pakistan

Table 9.1. Constraints Associated with an Educational Program to   162
Promote Male-Selective Hunting of Grizzly Bears

Table 9.2. Details of Educational Interventions in the Grizzly Bear   166
Harvest Management Program, 1989–1992

Table 15.1. Organization of the Local Naturalists' Training Course   266
at the La Selva Biological Station, Puerto Viejo, Costa Rica

About the Editor

■■
■■

Susan K. Jacobson is the director of the Program for Studies in Tropical Conservation and associate professor in the Department of Wildlife and Range Sciences at the University of Florida. She earned her Ph.D. degree in resource ecology and environmental education from Duke University and has published more than sixty journal articles, book chapters, reports, and books dealing with natural resource education and wildlife conservation in Central America, Africa, Southeast Asia, and the United States.

About the Contributors

∷

ASHIQ AHMAD graduated from Peshawar University with M.S. degrees in zoology and forestry. He later received an M.S. degree in resource management from Edinburgh University. He worked for twenty-five years at the Pakistan Forest Institute in Peshawar as researcher and wildlife instructor. Presently he serves as conservation director for WWF-Pakistan. Ashiq has pioneered crane migration research throughout Pakistan. He is the author of more than thirty-five scientific articles and technical reports and is a frequent presenter at international conferences.

KATHLEEN A. BLANCHARD is executive vice president of the Quebec-Labrador Foundation (QLF), a nonprofit U.S. and Canadian conservation organization, and a cofounder of QLF's Atlantic Center for the Environment. Her work in seabird conservation has won national awards and earned international recognition. She is an adjunct professor in wildlife at McGill University's Macdonald College and has served on the boards of several North American conservation and environmental education organizations. She holds Ph.D. and M.S. degrees from Cornell University and a B.A. from the University of Pennsylvania. She has lectured widely in North America and abroad.

PAUL J. BUTLER served ten years as conservation adviser to Saint Lucia's Forestry Department. Today he works with RARE Center for Tropical Conservation, a U.S. agency providing conservation assistance to the islands of the Caribbean. The conservation marketing campaign has been featured in *Newsweek* magazine, *American Birds,* and *Wildlife Conservation.* It also has been the subject of several television documentaries, including an Audubon Special entitled "Caribbean Cool."

A. ALEEM CHAUDHRY   has M.S. degrees in zoology from Punjab University and in forestry from Peshawar University. He also has a Ph.D. in wildlife management from the University of Edinburgh. Chaudhry worked as a forester in the Punjab and later as a researcher for the Pakistan Forest Institute. Since 1986 he has been responsible for the development of crane migration research and wildlife ecology and management projects as director of the Punjab Wildlife Research Center at Faisalabad.

DAVID B. CLARK   is the codirector of the La Selva Biological Station, Organization for Tropical Studies, in Costa Rica. He has been involved in more than sixty tropical field biology courses at different levels and in the development of the local naturalist program. He earned his Ph.D. degree in zoology at the University of Wisconsin, Madison.

MARE M. CROMWELL   is program coordinator of the GREEN Project. She has worked with water-quality projects for more than six years in the Great Lakes and Chesapeake Bay regions. She currently advises GREEN water-quality programs worldwide. She has developed curricular and instructional materials concerning rain forest awareness, watershed studies, and computer conferencing. She holds an M.S. degree in natural resources with a focus in environmental education from the University of Michigan.

LOU ANN HOLLINGSWORTH DIETZ   is senior program officer and coordinator of environmental education for the World Wide Fund for Nature Brazil Program. She earned her M.A. and Education Specialist degrees in instructional design and technology and educational systems development from Michigan State University. She has been actively involved for the last twenty years in the development, implementation, and evaluation of conservation projects in Brazil.

WILLIAM C. HAMMOND   has taught for thirty-three years, recently retiring as director of Curriculum Services and Environmental Education for the Lee District schools in Florida. He serves as President of Natural Context, an international consulting firm, presenting speeches, workshops, and seminars. He is the author of books and articles in the fields of environmental education, creative management "the natural way," personal creativity, and journal keeping, while continuing to teach and learn. Presently he is completing a dissertation entitled "Environment Action Theory and Practice within the Public Schools" at Simon Fraser University in Canada.

ROBERT H. HORWICH,   president of Howlers Forever, received a Ph.D. in ethology in 1967 from the University of Maryland. Following postdoctoral work in India with the Smithsonian Institution, he became a researcher for the

Brookfield Zoo. He has studied infant development in birds and mammals since 1962, including developing a method for reintroducing endangered cranes. He has studied primates in India and Central America since 1967 and has worked on community sanctuaries since 1984.

GREG HUNT earned a B.S. diploma in education and currently is the principal of Melbourne's Zoo Education Service, perhaps the world's largest school education service based in a zoo. He has a science/zoology background and is president of the Victoria Association for Environmental Education and vice president of the Australian Association for Environmental Education.

STEVEN E. LANDFRIED received a B.A. degree in history from Lawrence University in Appleton, Wisconsin, and graduated from the University of Wisconsin-Madison with M.S. and Ph.D. degrees in curriculum and instruction. He has served as public affairs officer for the International Crane Foundation from 1979 to 1981 and has worked on crane research and conservation education projects for the International Affairs Office of the U.S. Fish and Wildlife Agency since 1980. He has written more than twenty-five articles and has contributed to numerous international conferences—most recently as a leading proponent of avian satellite tracking. During the school year, he is the coordinator of the Alternative Learning Program at Stoughton High School in Stoughton, Wisconsin.

JONATHAN LYON, a doctoral student at Pennsylvania State University, is studying the effects of soil acidity on root growth of forest trees in the northeastern United States. He has researched prairie and wetland restoration in Wisconsin and studied land use, tree phenology, and rain forest succession following slash-and-burn agriculture at the Community Baboon Sanctuary in Belize. He has been working on community sanctuaries since 1985.

MUHAMMAD MUMTAZ MALIK graduated with a B.S. degree in forestry from Forest College, Peshawar University, and later received an M.S. degree in wildlife biology from the University of Montana. He worked as a researcher with the Pakistan Forest Institute for five years. He has served in the Forest Department of the North-West Frontier Province (NWFP) for about eighteen years. Malik currently is the conservator of wildlife in the NWFP—where he has pioneered practical crane conservation programs. His doctoral project in wildlife sciences at the University of Montana is pending.

PATRICIA A. MORTON is the former education director for Bat Conservation International and is now a research associate at the International Center for Bat Research and Conservation at Texas A & M University. She has an M.S. degree in zoology from the University of Wisconsin. She has written many articles on conservation education about bats and has developed educational projects and campaigns for the United States, Mexico, and Central and South America.

MARI J. MURPHY has been editor of Bat Conservation International's quarterly magazine, *BATS,* since 1985. She has written numerous articles for the magazine and designed many educational and promotional materials for the organization.

ELIZABETH YOSHIMI NAGAGATA, a biologist and native of Rio de Janeiro, became involved in conservation in 1984 as an intern in the Golden Lion Tamarin Conservation Project. She assisted for two years in the development of the project's education effort and assumed responsibility for program coordination from 1986 to 1989. She is currently completing an M.S. degree in the evaluation of environmental education programs, at Michigan State University, and remains involved in training Brazilian environmental educators.

PIA PAABY is currently teaching conservation biology at the School for Field Studies at the Center for Sustainable Development. She taught tropical limnology at the University of Costa Rica, School of Biology, and also, in cooperation with the Organization for Tropical Studies, coordinated and taught several graduate and undergraduate level courses in tropical population ecology for international students. Additionally, she planned and organized the local naturalist program. She earned her Ph.D. degree in environmental studies at the University of California, Davis.

SUZANA M. PADUA worked in the field of visual communications until 1988 when she established the environmental education program for the Black Lion Tamarin Project at the Morro do Diabo State Park. She completed her M.A. degree in Latin American studies at the University of Florida in 1991, and is now president of IPÊ, Instituto de Projetos e Pesquisas Ecológicas, in São Paulo, Brazil, and director of Brazil Programs at Wildlife Preservation Trust International.

MICHAEL ROMERIL is the conservation officer for Jersey, Channel Islands. Employed in the island's Planning Department, he is responsible for all nature conservation matters on the small island, which is subject to considerable recreation and tourism pressures. For a number of years he has advised the United Nations Environment Program and the World Tourism Organization on tourism and environmental issues, as well as representing both organizations at international conferences and workshops. Romeril also serves as vice president (former chairman) of the Institution of Environmental Sciences.

BARNEY L. SMITH is currently the management biologist responsible for public involvement programs with the Fish and Wildlife Branch of the Yukon Department of Renewable Resources. In this role he is liaison with public boards and councils established to ensure cooperation between Yukon First Nations and the Government of the Yukon in fish and wildlife management, and community groups in collaborative management programs. Between 1978 and 1990, Barney was the management biologist responsible for research and management programs for three bear species in the Yukon. He holds an M.S. degree in rural extension studies from the University of Guelph (1992), where he explored collaborative strategies to promote local conservation of wildlife, and a B.S. degree from Simon Fraser University (1978) where he studied marine and terrestrial ecology, and communications.

WILLIAM B. STAPP is a professor of resource planning and conservation in the School of Natural Resources. He has served as president of the North American Association for Environmental Education, and as the first director of the Office of Environmental Education for UNESCO. He is the author of many papers, chapters, and books on environmental education, including the *Field Manual for Water Quality Monitoring.* He has been particularly active in environmental education programs with a community problem-solving focus. He has worked in all regions of the world and is recognized as a foremost leader in the field of environmental education, having received numerous awards for his work.

STUART TRAYNOR is education officer for the Conservation Commission of the Northern Territory. He moved to central Australia eighteen years ago after completing a biology degree and diploma in education at the University of Sydney. He taught in high schools for nine years and then joined the Conservation Commission to establish its environmental education program. He has published a number of articles and booklets on environmental education, flora, and fauna.

ARJEN WALS currently serves as a consultant to GREEN and as the director of networking for the Caretakers of the Environment International. He is active in environmental education research in the Department of Agricultural Education at Wageningen Agricultural University in The Netherlands. He earned his Ph.D. degree in natural resources from the University of Michigan and has published several articles on action research in environmental education, computer networking in environmental education, and watershed monitoring programs for secondary schools.

WILLIAM WEBER has worked for the past twenty years on conservation issues in Africa. He has conducted pioneering research on socioeconomic and political factors in conservation; designed and implemented several highly successful field projects, including the ecotourism and educational components of the Mountain Gorilla Project in Rwanda; and made important contributions to the ongoing debate on integrated conservation and development policies and practices. He continues to write and speak on these issues, while also coordinating a forty-six-country research and conservation program as director of conservation operations for the Wildlife Conservation Society.

Acknowledgments

■■
■■

I thank the chapter authors for their valuable contributions and their undaunting perseverance through various revisions. I am deeply indebted to Curtis Gentry for his tireless and insightful editorial assistance and for shepherding the book through its final throes of publication. I am grateful to Sarah Webb Miller and Linda Fallon for secretarial assistance, and to Eleta Vaughan and Kristy Wallmo for indexing help. Many students and faculty at the University of Florida provided critical review of a number of the chapters: Lori Ames, Lyn Branch, Laura Brandt, Susan Canfield, Elizabeth Chick, Ginger Clark, Laurie Collins, Don Jackson, Wanda Jones, Meryl Klein, Kurt Leuschner, Jennifer Liebertz, Susan Marynowski, Sarah Miller, Robert Redick, Kenneth Rice, Claudia Rocha, Wendy Rose, Andrew Seidl, Luis Suarez, and Janna Underhill. I thank the Department of Wildlife and Range Sciences' chairpersons—Michael Collopy, George Tanner, and Patricia Werner—for their collegiality and commitment to scholarship.

I am grateful to Ed Lugenbeel and the staff at Columbia University Press for their help and patience, and to John Robinson for initial encouragement in this undertaking. The University of Florida Program for Studies in Tropical Conservation, the Pew Charitable Trusts, and my husband, Jeff Hardesty, provided support in many ways and forms. In honor of my parents, Betty and Perry Jacobson, proceeds from the sale of this book will be used to support conservation education activities.

Introduction: Wildlife Conservation Through Education

■■
■■

Susan K. Jacobson

Human needs and aspirations the world over can only be satisfied as environmental awareness leads to appropriate action at all levels of society, from the smallest local communities to the whole community of nations. Appropriate action requires a solid base of sound information and technical skills. But action also depends upon motivation, which depends upon widespread understanding, and that, in turn, depends upon education.
—Mostafa K. Tolba (former director),
United Nations Environment Program

This volume explores fifteen exemplary education and communication programs that have contributed to the conservation of wildlife and natural resources around the world. Practical perspectives such as these are needed as we confront the unabated extinction of animal and plant species and the ever increasing human pressure on tropical and temperate forests, wetlands, and marine environments. The conservation of such ecosystems depends on public participation and support. Developing successful education and communication programs toward this end is an essential aspect of wildlife conservation and resource management. Yet we face a dearth of documented examples of the effective design and implementation of conservation education programs.

Education at all levels must be developed to enable people to understand the interrelationships between humans and the environment. This

Figure intro.1 Effective wildlife conservation programs rely on (1) public education and participation, (2) ecological research and management, and (3) appropriate legislation and enforcement.

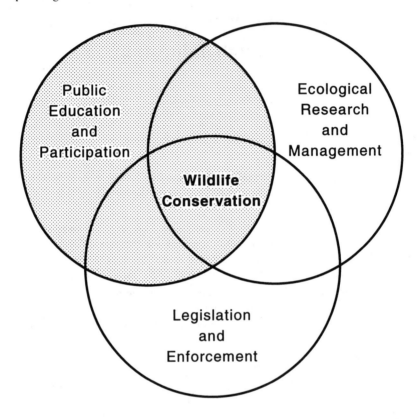

is essential if viable solutions are to be found to challenges facing the conservation of wildlife—encompassing all natural life-forms and areas. The clarion call by members of the World Commission on Environment and Development for a "vast campaign of education, debate, and public participation . . . if sustainable human progress is to be made" continues to echo at meetings such as the 1992 United Nations Conference on Environment and Development. Although conservation education alone will not solve environmental problems, effective education and communication programs are a prerequisite for better natural resource management, and ultimately for safeguarding the biosphere on which we all depend (figure intro.1).

The goals of conservation education are many and usually include:

- increasing public knowledge and consequent support for the development of appropriate environmental management and conservation policies
- fostering a conservation ethic that will enable people to responsibly steward natural resources
- altering patterns of natural resource consumption
- enhancing technical capabilities of natural resource managers
- incorporating resource management concerns into private sector and government policy-making processes

Many conservation education efforts have been aimed at the formal school system and often eclipse programs for adult and youth populations that are carried out informally by nongovernmental organizations, community groups, and resource agencies. These informal programs represent an area of neglect in natural resource education, yet one of enormous potential. Traditional formal educational methods, techniques, and strategies are often not relevant or acceptable outside the classroom. An analysis of case studies of informal education and communication programs from around the world reveals effective alternatives.

Educational programs must guide individuals beyond a general awareness of conservation problems to the commitment and action that eventually will solve these problems. Effective programs must be implemented in a diversity of settings with a variety of audiences. These range from cognitive and problem-oriented programs in schools to activities addressing environmental values and attitudes in communities and better technical training for resource professionals. This volume focuses on informal programs using parks, nature centers, zoos, community organizations, schools, resource agencies, and the media to reach and involve both youth and adults. These programs primarily are instigated in response to local needs and with local participation, where solutions to the challenges of biological conservation and sustainable resource use can be found most visibly. Through the presentation of representative case studies of successful initiatives, this volume provides a much needed analysis of conservation education and communication programming.

TOPICAL EMPHASES

The fifteen chapters provide a synthesis of the extent to which education and communication programs can lead to the conservation of wildlife and sustainable environmental management. The analytical framework of each chapter contributes to a better understanding of the practical design and implementation of activities. Evaluation of the products of the fifteen programs identifies component strengths and priorities for the future. Chapters are grouped by the following topical areas, although many of the programs encompass more than one: (a) conserving natural areas; (b) protecting declining species; (c) targeting resource users; (d) programming for schools; and (e) involving community groups. These studies show how and why programs succeed in achieving conservation goals and demonstrate that comprehensive efforts are necessary and worthwhile to help conserve wildlife and manage natural resources.

CONSERVING NATURAL AREAS

Educational programs associated with the conservation of natural areas can potentially have a large impact on natural resource management. More than 3,500 reserved areas have been established in more than 120 countries (Brown 1988). Since 1970 governments have expanded the networks of protected areas by more than 80 percent, nearly two-thirds of which are in developing countries. Audiences for educational programs associated with protected areas potentially span almost all ages, backgrounds, and cultures.

Although education is often a poor stepchild to other mandates, the effectiveness of park education programs is demonstrated by Jacobson and Padua in chapter 1. They describe the development of school programs at parks in Malaysia and Brazil based on a model for continuous program evaluation—a comprehensive process of planning, implementation, and product assessment. The model presented in this chapter provided a guide for the format of all the chapters that follow.

The Outback Australia Junior Ranger Program described by Traynor in chapter 2 demonstrates the use of protected areas for shaping positive attitudes and behavior of youth. The goal is to produce long-term changes toward a stewardship ethic. In chapter 3 Weber focuses on adult populations surrounding the Volcanos National Park in Rwanda.

His research explores the necessary integration of conservation with economic development in rural areas surrounding parks. Weber demonstrates the importance of baseline information—in this case, survey research data—for providing a benchmark for progress.

PROTECTING DECLINING SPECIES

As we are confronted with the extinction of some seventeen thousand species annually (Wilson 1988), educational programs addressing declining species are especially critical. In chapter 4 Blanchard describes a community education program in rural Canada that contributed to a 90 percent increase in populations of threatened sea birds on the Quebec North Shore. A conservation education program in the Brazilian coastal forest for golden lion tamarins, a squirrel-sized primate whose numbers had declined to four hundred individuals, is described by Dietz and Nagagata in chapter 5. In organizing their educational program, Dietz and Nagagata worked closely with community leaders to develop a variety of projects, ranging from school curricula to activities for farmers and landowners.

On the island of St. Lucia a widespread public education campaign helped lead to the doubling of the endangered St. Lucian parrot population. In chapter 6 Butler describes the results of the program, such as the declaration of the parrot as the national bird and the enactment of important forestry legislation.

Bats are the focus of public education by Bat Conservation International. Disappearing at an alarming rate, bats are responsible for dispersing seeds, pollinating important tropical fruit crops, and controlling insect pests (e.g., a colony of twenty million Mexican free-tailed bats is estimated to eat a quarter of a million pounds of insects nightly). Morton and Murphy, in chapter 7, describe how educational efforts have helped to overcome superstition and relentless persecution of bats in a number of countries from Australia to Costa Rica.

TARGETING RESOURCE USERS

Conservation education programming for resource users presents a challenging arena for resource management. The two chapters in this section demonstrate the difficulty of combining preservation with exploitation of sensitive wildlife resources. Chapter 8, by Landfried, Malik,

Ahmad, and Chaudhry, documents lessons learned in the losing battle
to save populations of Siberian cranes in Pakistan. In chapter 9 Smith
addresses hunter education in Canada to promote a more sustainable
harvest of grizzly bears.

PROGRAMMING FOR SCHOOLS

Most environmental attitudes are formed during childhood. Thus
schoolchildren are an important target for conservation education. The
programs described in this section exemplify an ideal approach—hands-
on, participatory, interdisciplinary—to involve children in the complexities of environmental problem solving. In chapter 10 Stapp, Cromwell,
and Wals describe the evolution of a program to monitor water quality
that has been adopted in more than fifty-five countries. Participating
students are exploring their local rivers, presenting their findings to
government officials, and exchanging data and insights with students in
other cultures throughout the world.

In chapter 11 Hammond describes thirty-five years' experience in
high school "action" projects focused on wildlife. Cadres of schoolchildren helped solve local conservation problems facing Florida's
threatened habitats and endangered animals like bald eagles and manatees. In chapter 12 Hunt describes a zoo education program in Australia
that has reached more than eighty thousand schoolchildren with a
conservation message and their first close look at elusive native wildlife.

INVOLVING COMMUNITY GROUPS

Educational programs involving rural community members are often
multifaceted to address complex issues associated with conservation and
economic development. In chapter 13 Horwich and Lyon describe a
holistic program in Belize that integrates private land management with
a conservation education and ecotourism program. Working with local
farmers, they have developed a low-cost, low-technology approach to
promote community-based conservation.

Romeril discusses in chapter 14 the challenge of maintaining a part
of the Jersey Island, U.K., for the conservation of temperate and
Mediterranean wildlife, as well as cultural history. An effective public
relations and information program has been the key to Jersey's success.
In the final chapter Paaby and Clark combine ecotourism with conserva-

tion in the development of a naturalist guide training program in Costa Rica. They link training and employment of local community members to the maintenance of a private biological reserve. As ecotourism to protected areas in the tropics grows, the successful integration of conservation and development is increasingly critical.

CHAPTER FORMAT

Each case study is presented in the same format to facilitate comparisons and analysis. The format allows examination of the planning, implementation, and assessment of each program. In the section on *Planning,* the authors were asked to describe the major decisions made during their planning and development process. This section includes answers to questions such as:

- What environmental problems or needs did your program address?
- What were your goals and objectives?
- Who was your target audience(s)?
- What resources were available and what constraints did you face?
- Who participated in the planning process and how?
- What alternative methods did you consider in the development of your program?

The *Implementation* section describes the efforts of the program staff in executing the program. Authors discuss answers to the following questions:

- How did your program operate?
- What was its content?
- What approaches or techniques did you use?
- Did you prepare pre- and post-program activities?
- How did the staff and audience participate in the process?
- Was your budget sufficient and consistent?

The *Product* section describes and evaluates the results of the program. The following questions are among the points included in this discussion:

- Did you achieve your objectives? How did you measure this— quantitatively and/or qualitatively?

- Were there secondary or unexpected results?
- What were the long-term effects?
- What modifications or expansions have you made?
- What were the key elements leading to success? Can you provide any general recommendations for conservation education programs?
- How have you disseminated information about your program? Has it been adopted elsewhere?
- What are your program's current or future needs?

ELEMENTS OF SUCCESS

A multitude of innovative and effective conservation education and communication programs can be found around the world. The twenty-five authors contributing to this volume describe exemplary programs spanning five continents. Several potential contributors solicited from underrepresented regions, such as Eastern Europe and Africa, were unable to prepare a manuscript because they lacked time, staff, or resources—obstacles commonly faced by conservation educators worldwide. The programs selected were characterized by the systematic collection of data that enabled the authors to determine approaches and components leading to success. Authors of many of the established programs were able to assess long-term changes in knowledge, shifts in attitudes, or increases in conservation-oriented behaviors in their targeted audiences.

The regions and programs represented in this volume offer insight into the complexity of the problems involved in developing effective conservation education and communication programs. Interdisciplinary and integrated solutions shared by the contributors provide a broad array of approaches for tackling conservation problems in the century ahead. Table intro.1 outlines some of the key elements that led to the successful planning, implementation, and evaluation of the programs described in this volume. Each chapter provides rich details, both common and unique, weaving a tapestry of the art and science of effective education and communication programming for wildlife conservation. The innovative ideas presented here should enhance efforts to improve education and communication programs and stimulate integrated conservation initiatives through better incorporation of these strategies.

Table Intro.1. Elements Leading To Successful Conservation Education And Communication Programs

PLANNING
- Have clear program goals
- Identify measurable and realistic objectives
- Adopt an interdisciplinary approach
- Determine target audiences and *involve* them in the process
- Assess participants' social/educational/economic backgrounds
- Ensure program relevance to local populations
- Build necessary government/organization/industry/community support
- Maintain a budget plan
- Develop a sustainable internal/organizational plan
- Plan for potential problems and resolution of conflicts

IMPLEMENTATION
- Follow an integrated approach
- Use existing organizations and groups effectively
- Encourage active/voluntary participation
- Involve reluctant participants creatively, e.g., reaching parents through children
- Be sensitive to the audience
- Provide direct contact with the environment/resource
- Use key ecosystems/resources/species in programs effectively
- Select appropriate educational media
- Use media, especially mass media, efficiently
- Focus on economic/cultural values
- Provide conservation incentives
- Maintain informality/entertainment value of the program
- Stay flexible

PRODUCT EVALUATION
- Evaluate program components continuously
- Use more than one method of evaluation
- Collect effective feedback for program modification/creation of new programs
- Link the program with other conservation components, e.g., economic and cultural incentives
- Transfer programs to local control and support
- Develop long-term plans for sustainability
- Disseminate program results widely

Conserving Wildlife

International Education and
Communication Approaches

PART ONE

Conserving Natural Areas

1

A Systems Model for Conservation Education in Parks: Examples from Malaysia and Brazil

⬛

Susan K. Jacobson and
Suzana M. Padua

Conservation education programs in parks in developing countries are a recent phenomena. Many of the park systems are relatively new, and limited resources and personnel have generally not been directed toward public education efforts. Yet park programs are especially needed in developing countries which are often rich in biological diversity. Programs can help foster more favorable attitudes toward conservation, augment limited school curricula, promote sustainable natural resource management, and increase a park system's flow of benefits to the public by serving as an educational resource.

We describe the development of two conservation education programs using national parks in Malaysian Borneo and central Brazil. The two programs targeted local primary schools and were designed using a comprehensive evaluation model (Jacobson 1986, 1991). The model provided a basis for making decisions during program planning and implementation, as well as in the assessment of products and outcomes, thus providing evaluation from the inception to the completion of the programs. This "womb to tomb" systematic approach provided feedback for continual improvement while the programs were being developed and allowed staff and administrators to judge the programs' merits upon completion (figure 1.1).

PLANNING

The planning stage for the programs included the collection of data to formulate the programs' goals and objectives, to identify potential participants, to determine types of activities that could be developed, and to ascertain available resources for implementing these activities. At this stage, local culture, history, and geography, as well as the parks' ecology and regional natural resource use, were reviewed with local residents to ensure the design of well-integrated materials. In rural areas of many developing countries, park programs to complement primary school curricula are important because the majority of children do not attend secondary school. Moreover, primary school teachers often have only a secondary education, and advanced training for teachers, particularly in the sciences, is rare. Hence the environmental expertise of park staff or researchers can be especially valuable to the communities residing near protected areas.

Research also indicates that parks, as well as other informal settings, offer opportunities to enhance environmental learning beyond formal education. Occasional visits to natural areas, in contrast to daily school attendance, offer novel, thought-provoking experiences, usually stimulating students' curiosity and interest. This, in turn, facilitates informa-

Figure 1.1 Systems model for the planning, implementation, and product evaluation of conservation education programs.

tion processing by assisting coding, memory storage, and retrieval of information (Koran and Longino 1983). Furthermore, outdoor educational experiences offered in parks can provide physical, emotional, and spiritual benefits, as well as intellectual growth (e.g., Miles 1986/87; Grumbine 1988). The combination of cognitive and affective changes that can be achieved at a park visit may eventually promote behavioral changes (Hungerford and Volk 1990); this is especially important when building support for biological conservation in communities bordering parks.

The school program for Kinabalu Park in Malaysian Borneo was developed in 1985. Kinabalu Park encompasses the tallest mountain in Southeast Asia (4,101 m), and protects a great diversity of plants and animals, including orangutans, clouded leopards, and more than fifteen hundred species of orchids (Jacobson 1990). The program for Morro do Diabo Park in Brazil was established in 1989 following the same model. This park protects some of the last remaining Atlantic forests of interior Brazil, and is home to several endangered species, including the black lion tamarin (*Leontopithecus chrysopygus*). This charismatic monkey was used as a focal, or target, species and mascot for the educational program (figure 1.2).

During the planning stage, the needs of the parks, teachers, and students were assessed. Kinabalu Park has a government mandate to provide education "for people to appreciate and enjoy what the parks stand for and offer," and to "be coordinated with the State's educational

Figure 1.2 Location of programs in Sabah, East Malaysia, and eastern Brazil.

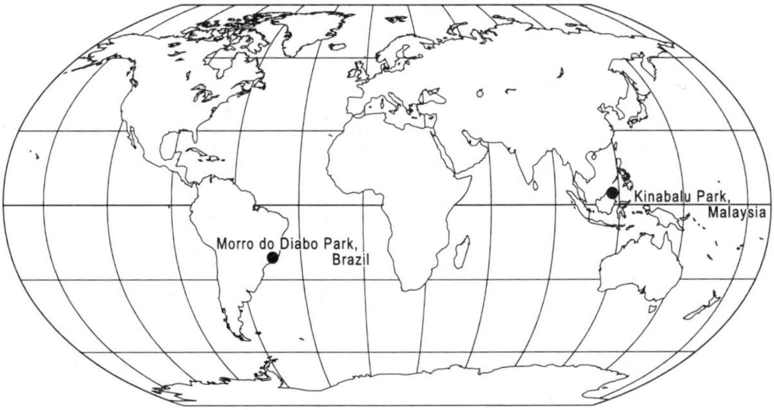

system in environmental subjects" (Jenkins et al. 1976). In spite of this charge, no programs involving the schools had been developed. The educational program at Morro do Diabo Park was neither mandated nor funded within the park system; no structured activities nor personnel had been allocated for this purpose. Few local students had visited the park before 1989. In both programs the teachers' needs were assessed by visits to the local schools and through interviews with educators invited to visit the parks. On the basis of teacher and student interviews, students' educational needs included becoming more aware of their natural environment and more informed in preparation for making decisions about the wise use of Malaysia's or Brazil's natural resources.

From these needs, three goals for the programs emerged: (1) to introduce students to the parks and to the parks' values and benefits; (2) to present students with basic ecological principles in the field in order to complement their school curricula; and (3) to increase student interest in the natural world. From the activities that were ultimately designed, an interdisciplinary approach touching on science, art, mathematics, and other subjects was developed. This holistic approach was emphasized further in the Brazil program where special courses were developed for local teachers of all subjects. In order to later assess whether the programs were successful, measurable aims were specified during planning. Objectives incorporated changes in both knowledge and skills of the students. For example, students would be able to achieve the following tasks after attendance at a program: (1) list benefits of the park; (2) explain several ecological principles; (3) identify several common plants and animals in the park and their adaptations to the environment; and (4) become interested enough in nature to continue environmental activities at their schools and homes.

The planning stage also involved inventories of the specific resources and constraints of the physical and social environment, as well as the limitations of the institutions involved with the programs. In each case it was necessary to examine the park systems, the schools, and other resources available in Malaysia and Brazil. The most critical resources of the parks were the personnel involved. In Malaysia four park naturalists and park rangers with ecological training specific to Kinabalu Park, along with a park ecologist and a research scientist, were available to help develop and implement the program. The facilities at the park included a sixty-seat auditorium, laboratory, herbarium, mountain garden collection, and library. The resources at Morro do Diabo were more

Mt. Kinabalu, 4,101 meters high, figures prominently in the local, traditional religion (*photo by S. Jacobson*).

limited; two park employees and four local high school students were trained as nature guides to assist with the school program. The training was direct and hands-on, and included participation in the design of the program's activities. Three nature trails and a visitor center were created specifically for the educational program. Student learning activities were developed to involve all five senses and stimulate curiosity. Each activity or stage was pilot-tested in order to assess its effectiveness and to make modifications.

Both parks' initial budgets for the programs were minimal, so the staff had to work with materials that were on hand. In order to garner additional resources, grant proposals were sent to institutions with conservation concerns. External funding helped to purchase items that were difficult to obtain. The Brazilian education staff acquired a television and video set, a bus, and funding for promotional materials and stipends for nature guides and other professionals who helped launch the program.

The school resources included the curricula, teacher input, and student interests. The headmasters and teachers from the local school systems were interviewed to determine what materials and methods would best suit their curricular needs. The Kinabalu program targeted students aged ten to thirteen by augmenting their existing curriculum. The Morro do Diabo program was designed for all grades, with different activities appropriate for each age group. Community-oriented activities also were designed to increase the effectiveness and support of the programs as a whole. Because these were new programs, both in Malaysia and Brazil, it was important to involve the school systems, as well as the students' families, in the parks' conservation awareness activities. At Kinabalu Park we determined that local schoolyards would be suitable environments for extending student exposure to the concepts emphasized during their park visit. Post-program activities were implemented at the schools under the teachers' guidance. The need for a teacher's guidebook to provide background information about the park's ecology, as well as detailed instruction concerning the students' activities at the park, also became evident. This was especially critical for teachers who had never been to the park. By identifying these and other resources and constraints, the scope of the programs was delineated. In the Brazilian program the education staff gave a slide show at the local schools before the students visited the park. This was helpful to prepare the students with basic knowledge, expose them to ecological values, and also suggest appropriate behavior while at the park. Post-visit strategies were also implemented at the Brazil schools, although these were mainly developed by the local teachers with the occasional guidance by the park education staff.

PROCESS

Various evaluation methods were used to assess student learning and interest as the programs were developed. Six school groups participated in the pilot program at Kinabalu Park. At the Morro do Diabo Park, activities were evaluated each time they were created or modified for different grade levels. In both programs, after a slide presentation about the values of the park and conservation, the students were divided into groups of ten to fifteen to participate in a series of activities along nature trails. They experienced guided walks to identify and discuss local plant and animal species and their adaptations to the environment. They filled in check-off identification sheets, made leaf and bark rubbings to explore the diversity of vegetation through visual representation, and engaged in activities designed to use all five senses. Games

Students explore the montane vegetation of Kinabalu Park (*photo by S. Jacobson*).

were created for students to find signs of animals, as well as to identify them through their sounds or movements. Students studied decaying logs to understand the process of decomposition, soil formation, and nutrient cycling. At the park program's end, the students and teachers filled out questionnaires, commenting on each of the activities and their relevance to their curricula. They further were encouraged to make suggestions for future improvements in the program.

Once the program was developed at Kinabalu Park, a follow-up activity worksheet was created for students to complete in their schools and homes. The purpose of the worksheet was to reinforce what the students had learned at the park, to encourage them to explore the natural world around them, and to share information with their families. Additionally, a ten-item activity list was developed. On completion of nine of the activities, students became "Junior Rangers," and received a certificate, ecology book, and badge from Kinabalu Park. The activities included drawing or writing about plants and insects around the students' school and home; listing the animal life that fed or took shelter in a local tree; constructing a food web; identifying environmental problems at their school, such as litter or water pollution, and their

possible solutions; listing the six parks in Sabah, Malaysia; and interviewing adults to learn about their local natural history. The teachers
were provided with a discussion guide of potential answers. It was the
teachers' responsibility to review the answers with the students and to
notify the park staff of the names of successful students who were to
receive "Junior Ranger" awards.

The Brazilian program had follow-up activities that involved parents
and other community members. With the park and the local natural
environment as the main themes, these activities included art exhibits,
music festivals, plays, T-shirt design competitions, as well as various
other contests. The prizes were usually donated by the community store
owners, lawyers, doctors, bankers, and other professionals who were
also invited to serve on the juries of these competitions. In this way all
social strata were encouraged to participate in activities designed to
foster increased concern for the regional natural environment. The
local radio station was willing to publicize these activities, providing
opportunities for the education staff to send conservation messages to
home audiences.

In order to assess the effectiveness of the school programs, we
developed questionnaires to survey students' opinions of the activities
and to measure changes in knowledge. A sixteen-item test was designed
for Kinabalu Park and a nineteen-item test for Morro do Diabo to assess
students' knowledge and attitudes of the park and basic ecological
concepts related to the program's objectives. The tests required students
to list the park's values, to explain some ecological processes, to identify
several common plants and animals, and to express specific attitudes
toward various wild animals. These tests were given to the students
both before and after the program to evaluate their cognitive and
affective achievements relating to the concepts the programs addressed.
Their scores were expected to improve after exposure to the park
activities. Pilot tests were conducted several times to eliminate ambigu-
ities and problem questions.

At Kinabalu Park, with the completion of the revised student booklets, the teacher's guidebook, a follow-up worksheet, and the outcome
test, the modified program was ready to be implemented. The park staff
met again with the headmasters of the local schools to arrange programs
for the primary grades. The teachers were given copies of the program
materials and requested to give the pre-program tests to their students.
At the Morro do Diabo Park, the program's implementation and im-

Kinabalu Park staff collecting dipterocarp seeds for an educational presentation (*photo by S. Jacobson*).

provements had to rely more heavily on the park staff. This was because of the novelty of the program, not only for the students but for the teachers as well. However, teachers were eager to participate and learn more about the local natural environment. They recognized the park's potential to serve as an educational resource and used the didactic materials prepared for them for this purpose. All teachers received a set of hand-outs on the regional history, geography, ecology, and park's natural resources. Banks and local business offices donated a number of copies of these materials so all teachers and school directors could have access to the information. In this way the lack of park resources was compensated for by community involvement, which increasingly contributed to the support of the programs.

During the Process stage the programs were continually evaluated and then modified accordingly. These modifications reflected the park staff's growing knowledge derived both from conducting the trial programs and from the feedback of students and teachers. The staff's knowledge of park ecology relevant to the program, and awareness of logistical factors such as timing, weather, scheduling of schools, and equipment, all increased and could be incorporated into the final program.

PRODUCT

The effectiveness of the programs was determined by a process of continual evaluation, from inception to outcome. The evaluation of the programs' products used a number of techniques. A written evaluation provided input from students and teachers concerning their opinions and suggestions about the program activities. The teachers also were asked about the usefulness of the teacher's guidebook and other materials furnished. The formal cognitive and affective test given before and after the program assessed the change in students' knowledge and their attitudinal shifts about the parks and the natural environment relative to the objectives of the programs. At Kinabalu Park, the results for the school groups tested showed significantly improved scores after the students participated in the program ($t = 1.93$, $P < 0.05$; $t = 5.53$, $P < 0.001$).

The school program at Morro do Diabo incorporated an experimental design in the product evaluation: 144 students from fifth to eighth grades were randomly assigned to a treatment group, whose members were to be exposed to the program, or to a control group. Both groups of students answered a written questionnaire on three different occasions: pre-test, post-test, and a retention test (thirty days after the post-test) to measure the students' retention of information. The treatment groups performed significantly better than the control groups, and information was retained for more than a month (F = 98.29, $P < 0.05$). Boys scored higher than girls in the pre-test, indicating greater prior knowledge about the environment. However, girls showed greater improvement and scored similarly to boys on the post-test and on the retention test. Differences also existed among grade levels; all tested grades showed significant differences from pre-tests to post-tests among the experimental groups, but the more advanced grades scored consistently higher.

We also used unobtrusive measures to assess student outcome from the programs. At Kinabalu Park the willingness and success of 72 percent of the students to complete the follow-up "Junior Ranger" activities and worksheets indicated a high level of continued student interest in their natural environment. At Morro do Diabo, only 3 of 144 students did not want to visit the park again, and 100 percent of those who did wished to bring a relative to the park. Students also showed an increased interest in the environment while still at the park. They

A school group about to leave the Morro do Diabo Park on the program bus which displays the environmental education logo depicting the black lion tamarin (*photo by S. Padua*).

continued with activities and discussed the results many hours after the program was completed.

In addition to measuring the programs' effectiveness in achieving their objectives, we also kept a careful record of the number of schools and students involved in the programs in order to justify the budget. After completing the pilot programs, the results were presented to the park administration. The staff made recommendations concerning the printing of booklets and badges and noted the constraints of the programs owing to budgetary and personnel limitations. At this point the park administrations could make decisions about the merits of expanding the programs. They also could use this information to involve other governmental departments, such as the education ministry, in the programming. The park administrations perceived that the educational programs enhanced their management objectives. The increased awareness of the environment that resulted from the programs seemed to contribute to a decrease of threats such as hunting and timber cutting in the Morro do Diabo region, although this was not formally evaluated. Additionally, the local community's involvement was demonstrated when they helped extinguish a forest fire that threatened the park, and pressured the local government to relocate the city's garbage dump away from the park. This type of community involvement had never occurred before the educational program, although threats to the park were continuous since the park's creation in 1942.

The program at Kinabalu Park was designed specifically to augment the school science curriculum; however, both teachers and students noted in their written evaluations that it also helped in other subjects. They found that the measurements of plants and animals taught mathematics; leaf rubbings and "Junior Ranger" activities involved art; the climatic information pertained to geography; the recording of observations assisted in language training; and the exploratory blindfold walk and listening exercises increased students' overall awareness of their five senses in interpreting the world around them. The parks' staff found from the questionnaires that the wide range of activities, from leaf rubbings to peering through a magnifying glass, succeeded in offering a variety of approaches to learning. In noting their preference, individual students and teachers applauded the diversity of activities.

The significant results of these studies show that students achieved

An exploratory interpretive center at the Morro do Diabo Park provides close-up views of wildlife and sensory exhibits (*photo by S. Padua*).

positive knowledge and attitudinal gains through the informal educational programs at the parks. Furthermore, the parks seemed to benefit from the involvement of students, who encouraged their families and other community members to participate in conservation initiatives. With increasing population pressure on natural resources, park protection and conservation increasingly depend on public awareness and community participation. These studies provide a practical example of how park personnel and teachers can effectively use the park environment for student learning. Toward this end we found the systems evaluation approach a useful model to conceptualize, develop, implement, and assess an extracurricular conservation education program. Partnerships between schools and parks, as well as with other informal settings, are critical for enhancing environmental learning and the conservation of natural areas.

Acknowledgments

Many people in Kinabalu and Morro do Diabo parks worked on the development of the school programs. We are especially grateful to L. Ali, F. Liew, R. Sidek, A. Phillips, G. Sinit, H. Peter, M. Zaini, F. Tan, A. Gunsalam, and T. Yussup at Kinabalu Park, and the education team at Morro do Diabo. The administrators, headmaster, teachers, and students of SRK Don Bosco school in Sabah and the Teodoro Sampaio and Mirante do Paranapanema schools in Brazil kindly participated in these studies. Support was also provided by the Forestry Institute of São Paulo, Shell Foundation, Apenheul Zoo, Canadian Embassy in Brazil, Fanwood Foundation, U.S. Fish and Wildlife Service, Whitley Animal Protection Trust, Wildlife Preservation Trust International, World Wildlife Fund, and the University of Florida Program for Studies in Tropical Conservation. We thank C. Gentry for his insightful review of this manuscript and graphical expertise, and S. W. Miller for secretarial assistance. Some of the material in this chapter has been presented in Jacobson and Padua (1992) and is reprinted by permission of the Association for Childhood Education International, Wheaton, Maryland.

2

Appealing to the Heart as Well as the Head: Outback Australia's Junior Ranger Program

■■
■■

Stuart Traynor

This chapter explores a government conservation agency's attempt to develop an educational program that appeals to the heart as well as the head: the Junior Ranger Program in Australia's Northern Territory. I also outline the development of programs to promote pro-conservation behavior among young Aboriginal people in outback areas. Large areas of outback Australia are now being returned to Aboriginal ownership. Educational programs are thereby needed to help a new generation of Aboriginal people manage their land and conserve wildlife populations.

PLANNING

Approaches to the environment in Australian schools tend to be left-brain dominated. In other words, teaching strategies emphasize facts, figures, concepts, and skills rather than feelings, values, and behavior. The importance of increasing people's knowledge and understanding of environmental issues is unquestionable. However, increased knowledge about the environment does not automatically result in behavior that is

Figure 2.1 The Junior Ranger Program was conducted in the vast Northern Territory of Australia.

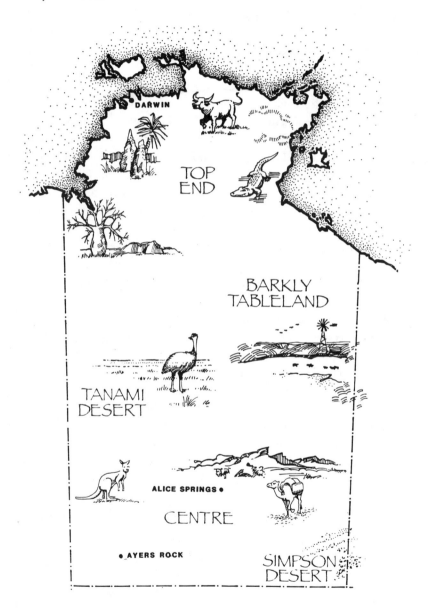

environmentally responsible. Affective and social factors also must be addressed since people's behavior depends not only on their skills and knowledge but also on their feelings, motivation, and commitment. In 1990 the Conservation Commission of the Northern Territory (CCNT) initiated a new environmental education program with a strong emphasis on affective and social factors.

Australia's Northern Territory is roughly one-seventh the size of the United States—1.3 million square kilometers. It is a mostly semiarid landscape with a population of only 175,000 people. The main towns are Darwin (pop. 78,000), located on the northern coast, and Alice Springs (pop. 25,000) in Central Australia (see figure 2.1). Cattle grazing, mining, and tourism are the major industries. The Conservation Commission is responsible for the conservation and protection of the natural environment. This includes establishing and managing national parks and reserves; conserving flora, fauna, and land resources; and monitoring the impact of development on the environment. Under the government's *Conservation Commission Act of 1980* the CCNT also is required to undertake scientific research and assist in education relating to the environment.

Since its formation in 1980 the CCNT has been aware that achieving its goal of conservation and ecologically sustainable development requires the support and involvement of the whole community. Consequently, it has placed a high priority on providing information to the public through booklets, posters, park signs, pamphlets, and ranger-guided tours. However, in more recent years the Commission has given more attention to community education programs aimed at shaping positive attitudes and behavior. It was from this perspective that the territorywide Junior Ranger Program was created in 1990. The aim was to establish a program for young people that would impact specifically on their values and their motivation to act. We wanted to provide young people with positive experiences in the natural environment on a regular basis since people who have enjoyable and memorable experiences with nature are more likely to become protective of it (Hungerford 1989). We also wanted to provide role models who could inspire young people to adopt environmentally responsible life-styles and behavior.

Initial planning of the Junior Ranger Program came from the top administrator of our organization. Rangers had been conducting activities at the Yulara School near Ayers Rock since 1986, and participating

Nine- and ten-year-old Junior Rangers collecting bush tucker (wild passionfruit, *Capparis spinosa*) (*photo by S. Traynor*).

students had been rewarded with Junior Ranger badges and certificates. The Northern Territory government's minister for conservation had been impressed with our activities during a visit to the Rock. In January 1990 he discussed the development of a territorywide Junior Ranger Program with the director of the CCNT and its senior education officer. Planning thus began with the knowledge that (1) the program would have the government's full support, and (2) the necessary financial resources would be made available. The only constraint was that the program would be designed to operate within the existing staffing arrangements of the CCNT.

Initially we planned to link groups of keen young people with particular national parks. We intended that they would become actively involved in the management of the park and its wildlife. However, we soon realized that this proposal was not the best option because it would limit the number of young people who could participate. It would also place undue pressure on the park rangers whose enthusiasm for the scheme and ability to entertain the Junior Rangers varied considerably.

Thus this model was abandoned in favor of a scheme that would give young people a choice of after-school and weekend activities with different rangers, CCNT scientists, and technical officers. These activities would include almost the whole range of the Commission's areas of responsibility: park management, wildlife management and research, land care, and bushfire control.

IMPLEMENTATION

The program began five months later in May 1990 with upper primary and junior secondary students from five participating schools. It was expanded to fifteen schools in 1991 and twenty schools (with a total of four hundred students) in 1992. As well as operating in the major Territory towns, a special program has been organized for young people on far-flung cattle stations and other isolated localities using the two-way radio network of the Alice Springs School of the Air. Activities are generally conducted outside of school hours and are designed to supplement the school's existing programs of environmental education.

All the activities emphasize having a good time with people who can act as positive role models. You might find our Junior Rangers conducting a mammal survey with a park ranger at night or setting crocodile traps in Darwin Harbor. You might find them birdwatching at the local sewerage ponds or with a CCNT scientist learning about captive-breeding and reintroduction programs for endangered animals. You may see them involved in feral animal control in a coastal wetland or on a bush tucker expedition in search of edible native plants. You might just find them sitting around a campfire, making billy tea and damper, discussing conservation issues.

There is an informality to the sessions that distinguishes them from normal school activities. We have operated on the premise that if the Junior Rangers don't have a good time, then we are hardly likely to win their hearts.

The Junior Ranger Program is coordinated by the Commission's two education officers, one based in Darwin and the other in Alice Springs. A fair bit of travel, by both road and commercial aircraft, is required to get to some of the Junior Ranger groups because of the Territory's large land area and sparse population. The cost of the program is difficult to itemize because Junior Ranger activities are usually organized to coincide with other aspects of the CCNT's work program. However, a reasonable estimate would be approximately U.S. $13,000 for travel and

A bird-watching trip at the Alice Springs sewerage ponds for Junior Rangers and their families from outlying cattle stations (*photo by S. Traynor*).

accommodations and a further U.S. $4,000 for equipment, materials, and other incidental expenses.

In addition, a twelve-page monochrome magazine called the *Junior Ranger Review* is produced four times a year. Four thousand copies of each edition are printed, and it is distributed free of charge through all national parks and CCNT offices. It contains a blend of local nature stories and environmental news, as well as lift-out activity sheets to help young people explore their local environment on their own time. Three-quarters of the cost is covered by sponsorship from a large, nonprofit medical insurance fund. The magazine includes prominent acknowledgment of their financial support and carries their logo and corporate message.

PRODUCT

No formal evaluation has yet been set up to measure the effectiveness of this program. This is partly because of the realities of life in outback Australia and the fact that the program is seeking to produce long-term changes in behavior. People's behavior is influenced by a complex mixture of personal, social, and economic factors, and it is not clear which variable or variables are most influential. However, we have found the Hines et al. (1986/87) model of responsible environmental behavior very useful. Their model incorporates those factors known to be associated with environmentally responsible behavior. These include three cognitive factors: knowledge of environmental issues, knowledge of action strategies, and skills in taking action. However, abilities alone are not sufficient to result in action. A person must also have a desire to act. The model demonstrates that this is affected by a number of personality factors: one's attitudes toward the environment and toward taking action; the degree of responsibility one feels toward the environment; one's degree of commitment; and one's perception of whether one has the ability to change things.

Our Junior Ranger Program aims to impact these personality factors. We see it as a program that appeals to the heart, as well as the head. Initial indications are that we are on the right track. Interest from the young people involved has remained high and more schools are wanting to participate than we can currently accommodate. The dropout rate, over the seven-month period that the program operates each year, is fairly low. When young people do drop out, it seems to be because of conflict with other activities, such as sports, rather than dissatisfaction with the Junior Ranger Program. However, it is clear that the program appeals more to younger people (aged nine–twelve) than to junior high school students (aged thirteen–fifteen). Also, more girls are involved than boys; in 1991, 70 percent of the participants were female.

The high demand to expand the program further has the potential to overwhelm us. We are trying to target the groups in our community to whom we feel the program can be most beneficial. In particular, two years into its implementation, we decided to target Aboriginal children in Central Australia who are not demonstrably conservationists and can be quite destructive toward wildlife, especially birds.

In designing an educational program for these children, their social and cultural background needed to be considered. Aboriginal people comprise approximately one-quarter of the Northern Territory population. Two-thirds of them live in remote communities away from the major towns. Aboriginal people have a youthful population structure with more than half their number being under the age of twenty.

Anthropologists estimate that Aboriginal occupation of Australia may go back as far as fifty thousand years. Before European settlement of the

Junior Rangers check their water transpiration bag on a bush survival activity during an overnight camp in the sand dunes (*photo by S. Traynor*).

country in 1788, the Aboriginal people had attained their own equilibrium with the Australian environment and had a great love for the land, which was vividly described by Strehlow (1947). He wrote: "The Northern Aranda clings to his native soil with every fibre of his being." However, their achievement of sustainable utilization should not be confused with the contemporary concept of conservation. Vandenbeld (1988) says: "There is a tendency to overestimate the Aboriginal people as the original conservationists . . . perhaps in a reaction against the original underestimation of them as the miserablest people on earth." Aboriginal people certainly had an intricate knowledge of the environment, but survival, not conservation per se, was their aim. "And like all hunter-gatherers, survival meant leaving something for tomorrow. They had a complex system of proscriptions, the effect of which was usually to maintain animal and plant reserves" (Vandenbeld 1988). Low population densities and their husbandry of natural resources ensured that changes to the landscape occurred in a controlled fashion. They moved regularly in response to seasonal changes in food availability, but over relatively short distances. Permanent movement to other parts of the country was not an option because each group remained attached to specific regions. Consequently, they had to maintain their resource base.

Davis (1988) says: "There is no evidence to suggest that Aboriginal people consciously constructed their approach to the natural environment with a conservation ethic." Their worldview was quite different from that of contemporary conservationists. They did not see themselves as managers of the Earth's resources. In fact, one could argue that their worldview was one in which the environment cared for them. Their law required that they perform certain rituals at sacred sites to ensure the abundance of wildlife. The people and the wildlife shared a spiritual bond, and their fortunes were seen as being shared as well. As long as they performed the rituals, everything would be all right and nature would provide for the people.

Regardless of whether or not they were conservationists in our contemporary sense, sound management principles were clearly inherent in Aboriginal tenure of the land. Aboriginal culture is still strong in many parts of Australia, but in central Australia people are not living the way they were before European settlement. We can romanticize the old ways, but life was hard and nature can be cruel in Australia's arid lands. Not surprisingly, people have now opted for a different, more sedentary life-style in permanent communities.

Aboriginal teenagers discussing rabbit control in spinifex grass habitat with Ranger Dennis Matthews (*photo by S. Traynor*).

While this new life-style has helped guarantee food, water, and accommodation, it has also brought environmental problems. The change from a somewhat mobile life-style to permanent campsites has resulted in some land degradation and major litter problems in Aboriginal communities. (Waste disposal was not a problem when the people followed their traditional life-style, as their small numbers, biodegradable garbage, and mobility ensured that nature was able to quickly clean up after them.) In addition, the spread of feral animals across Australia has reduced the availability of native wildlife and plants traditionally harvested by Aboriginal people for food. In fact, Central Australia has a terrible record of mammal extinctions, after little more than a century of European settlement.

On a positive note, just under 50 percent of the Northern Territory has been returned to Aboriginal ownership under the federal government's *Land Rights Act*. But the old way of life in Central Australia is gone, and the clock cannot be turned back two hundred years. Environmental education programs are needed to enable a new generation of Aboriginal people to manage the land and conserve the remaining native wildlife populations.

Following the headway made in urban areas, a trial Junior Ranger Program has now been set up in Kulpiturra, a small Aboriginal outstation on a large expanse of Aboriginal land in Central Australia. Kulpiturra was selected because (1) the community and the local school teacher were very keen to be involved in the program; (2) school attendance is unusually high, and the children value education; and (3) the community is located near a major national park. The park rangers began a program of regular activities in the school covering issues such as wildlife studies, feral animal control, and land management. A number of adults at Kulpiturra attend these activities, and a community barbecue is always held at the school to coincide with the rangers' visits.

Any environmental education program that is antagonistic to experience at home or among peers is not likely to be successful. Consequently, the families are being involved in as many activities as possible in the hope of encouraging a supportive context for the development of pro-conservation behavior. Environmental games and simulations are used whenever possible to illustrate ecological concepts, as well as to make the sessions lighthearted and enjoyable. Overnight camps with the rangers are also popular and are another means of getting families involved.

Time alone will tell if the Northern Territory Junior Ranger Program will bring about any long-term change in environmental behavior. Social psychologist Ajzen (1988) says that much of our behavior is based on the psychological concept of norms: what is accepted, what is expected, traditions, and unwritten rules. Six months after the Kulpiturra program began, one could still see young people littering the countryside or hurling rocks at birds flying by. However, we are not discouraged by this. From the outset we had worked on the assumption that new attitudes are probably caught, rather than taught, and that it would take time for the rangers' attitudes to rub off onto the children. "Generally speaking," says Ajzen, "people intend to perform a behavior when they evaluate it positively and when they believe that important others think they should perform it." It won't happen overnight, but we believe that the rangers have great potential for changing behavior by acting as positive role models.

3

Monitoring Awareness and Attitude in Conservation Education: The Mountain Gorilla Project in Rwanda

██
██

William Weber

The number of conservation initiatives in developing countries has exploded over the past two decades. In line with current models for conservation action, these efforts are also increasingly comprehensive in their approach, and most include an education component (Bruntland 1987; IUCN 1980; McNeely and Miller 1984). This reflects the significance conservationists attach to improved understanding by, and communication with, local populations.

The diversity of approaches to conservation education, however, seems to parallel the diversity of ecosystems and socioeconomic contexts. To a certain degree, this reflects the variability of conditions and the complexity of problems to be confronted across the tropics. Perhaps more commonly, it is also a function of uncertainty and a lack of professional training on the part of those responsible for the conception and implementation of conservation education programs.

The Mountain Gorilla Project (MGP) in Rwanda has received considerable attention for its successful ecotourism program and its crucial role in reversing the decline of the rare and highly endangered mountain gorilla (Weber 1987a, 1989, 1993; Vedder and Weber 1990; Hannah 1992; Wells et al. 1992). Much less attention, however, has been focused on the conservation education component of the project. This chapter attempts to redress that imbalance, through a general description of the MGP education program. More specifically, the central role of attitudinal surveys in the initial design and subsequent monitoring of that program will be assessed.

PLANNING

The Problem

Rising to heights of more than 4,500 meters, the Virunga volcanos extend along a 65-kilometer front to form the international boundary between Rwanda, Zaire, and Uganda (figure 3.1). Covered with a dense mix of montane forest and alpine vegetation, the 420-square-kilometer Virunga reserve system stands out as a natural island in an otherwise completely modified agricultural landscape. It is also the last refuge of the rare and reclusive mountain gorilla (*Gorilla gorilla beringei*).

For most of this century the true nature of the gorilla remained

Figure 3.1 Rwanda.   Volcanos National Park is located in northern Rwanda.

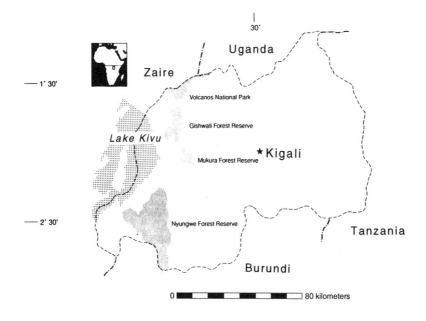

shrouded in mystery. By the mid-1970s, however, the pioneering work of George Schaller (1963, 1964) and Dian Fossey (1970, 1971) had shattered the monster myths and made the mountain gorilla a focus of world attention. Yet just as popular articles, books, and films brought these special creatures and their complex social lives into the general consciousness, it also became clear that their very existence was at risk.

From a total of roughly 450 in 1960, the Virunga gorilla population had crashed dramatically to an estimated 274 individuals by 1973 (Groom 1973; Harcourt and Groom 1972). A combination of poaching and habitat loss appeared to be the most immediate cause of this decline, but no one really knew. More fundamental causes could only be imagined; while efforts had been made to better understand gorilla behavior and sociality, not a single study had ever focused on the more basic problems that confronted their survival.

Interdisciplinary Research

The MGP stemmed primarily from a project initiated in 1978 to better understand the causes of the mountain gorilla's decline and to recommend corrective action (Vedder and Weber 1990; Weber 1979, 1981, 1987b, 1989; Weber and Vedder 1983). The research phase of this effort took an interdisciplinary approach, combining traditional conservation biology with assessments from the socioeconomic and political spheres.

The first step in this process was to determine the current status of the gorilla population by means of a census. This yielded a count of 268 individuals: a possible indication of some stabilization of the total population. More detailed demographic analyses, however, highlighted a continuing decline in the percentage of young gorillas that could only be attributed to poaching and/or other disturbance factors (Weber and Vedder 1983; Vedder 1989a). Further studies showed that although significant gorilla resources had been lost because of forest clearing, if the poaching and other disturbance factors were controlled, sufficient high-quality habitat remained to support a possible return to a 1960 population level of 400 to 500 gorillas (Vedder 1984; Weber and Vedder 1983).

The demographic and ecological viability studies thus indicated the clear potential for reestablishment of the Virunga gorilla population, providing better protection could be assured. Parallel research conducted outside the reserve, however, yielded less encouraging results (Weber 1987b, 1989). Rwanda's 26,000 square kilometers of hills and valleys already supported nearly four hundred people per arable square kilometer in 1979: the highest rural density in Africa. Settlement levels were even higher on the fertile volcanic soils of the Virunga region, and further population growth was fueled by an annual increment of 3.7 percent. As a direct result, the average farm size declined to barely 0.5 hectares per family, fallow cycles were shortened, and long-term productivity was threatened. Adding to this pressure on the land was a lack of nonfarm employment in a rural economy, where 95 percent of the population lived by farming and family income averaged less than $200 per annum (Weber 1981). That more than 50 percent of the original parkland in Rwanda's Volcanos National Park (PNV) had already been degazetted for agricultural use by the early 1970s was understandable against this background; that more would be claimed was a given (Harroy 1981).

Attitudinal surveys. The social science research that went into planning the MGP included a significant effort to better understand attitudinal and awareness factors in the gorilla conservation equation through the use of survey questionnaires.[1] Local farmers living within five kilometers of the PNV were the primary subjects, though urban dwellers and university students from the region also were targeted in parallel surveys.

Background questions revealed a farming population in which a large majority (82 percent) held the equivalent of private ownership rights to their land; the average adult had no more than three years of primary education; and the mean number of children per family was 4.3 (barely half the mean desired number of 8.3 children) (Weber 1989). Further questions addressed Rwandan perceptions of overall land availability (table 3.1). Results showed that barely 40 percent of this group had enough farmland to subdivide among their current children, and only 7 percent felt that there would be enough land for the next generation. Faced with this shortage, a slight majority of the local farmers suggested the traditional Rwandan solution to the problem: emigration. Unfortu-

---

[1] Surveys were conducted randomly by rural sociology students from the University of Rwanda, under the supervision of the author.

nately, regional politics precluded any significant movements into neighboring countries, and parklands were the last internal frontier. Interest-
ingly, university students more rarely cited the emigration option (17
percent) and far more frequently cited the need for improved agriculture (39 percent) or even birth control (30 percent).

With regard to perceived values of the PNV, nearly 60 percent of
the local farmers in 1979 thought that the remaining parkland was
suitable for agriculture (Weber 1989): a belief that ran contrary to
strong empirical evidence that few, if any, crops would do well above
the park's lower limit of 2,700 meters (Delepierre 1982). More realistically, a significant minority (42 percent) of those living in the vicinity of
the PNV also believed that local people needed to hunt and cut wood

Table 3.1. Rwandan Perceptions of Land Issues

QUESTION	FARMERS N = 72 %	NONFARMERS N = 43 %	UNIVERSITY N = 76 %
Own land?			
Yes	82	65	—
No	18	35	—
Land sufficient?			
Yes	80	71	—
No	20	29	
Land enough to subdivide?			
Yes	40	39	—
No	60	61	
Enough land for all Rwandans?			
Yes	9	0	—
No	91	100	
Enough land for next generation?			
Yes		0	—
No		100	
Solution to land shortage?			
Emigration	52	42	17
Intensive agriculture	2	14	40
Birth control	3	11	30
God/government	12	5	1
Other	33	37	37
Don't know	19	16	5

Shown are frequencies of listed responses to questions concerning land issues, for each of three population categories: farmers, nonfarmers, and university students. The figures represent the percentage of respondents of
each population category. (Multiple responses were allowed to the question on the solution to land shortage.)

in the park to satisfy their basic subsistence needs. That such illegal use occurred was regularly confirmed by direct observation.

Perhaps the most revealing line of questioning concerned nonconsumptive values of the forest and wildlife of the PNV (figures 3.2 and 3.3). Asked what value the Virunga forest might have beyond direct exploitation (i.e., cutting or clearing), more than half the local residents (54 percent) were unable to give an answer of any kind. Of those who did, equal percentages (19 percent) cited the forest's role in maintaining a humid regional microclimate and in providing habitat for wildlife. Highly significant differences appeared in the responses of nearby urban residents and university students, especially with regard to their low incidence of nonresponses. Both groups were also much more likely than farmers to note the forest's role in climate regulation. University students alone noted the research and tourism potential of the forest; these values, however, were identified by barely 10 percent of all students.

With regard to wildlife, more than 58 percent of the local farmers failed to perceive a single nonconsumptive value of the animals living in the PNV. That is, if they could not be hunted for their meat or skins, they served no other evident purpose for the majority of people. Still, nearly 40 percent of the population did recognize the potential for wildlife to bring in tourism revenue and jobs—a remarkable finding given that the PNV had earned only a few thousand dollars during the entire year preceding the survey. Majorities among students (71 percent) and townspeople (61 percent) also noted tourism's potential, while smaller numbers cited other values. University students, in particular, recognized the importance of the park's wildlife for the purposes of species preservation (20 percent), research (12 percent), ecosystem maintenance (7 percent), and even aesthetic reasons (8 percent). These values, however, held little meaning for those farmers living closest to the park.

Following from the above, a few more specific questions were asked. The first concerned the role of the Virunga ecosystem in water catchment: specifically, did the forest and other vegetation have a beneficial impact on local water supplies? Here, the farmers (49 percent) were more likely to see the connection than were either the townspeople (37 percent) or students (27 percent), but majorities of each group still failed to recognize this commonly cited value of montane forest conservation (figure 3.4). In the next set of questions, gorillas were the focus

Figure 3.2 Forest value (if can't be cut).   Survey results concerning non-consumptive values of the forest of Volcanos National Park.

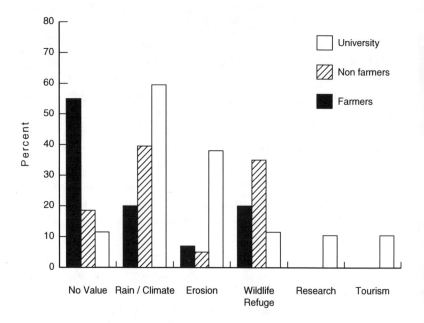

Figure 3.3 Animal value (if can't be hunted).   Survey results concerning nonconsumptive values of the wildlife of Volcanos National Park.

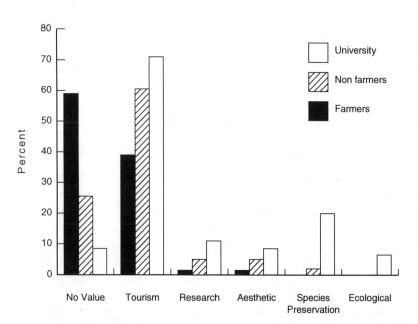

(Weber 1987a, 1981). Two-thirds of the local residents said that they knew what a gorilla was, although 25 percent of those could not describe one in any way. Of those who did, 58 percent referred to them as "humanlike," whereas only 10 percent thought they were "dangerous." Informed that mountain gorillas were only found in the Virungas and that there were barely 260 of them left, an overwhelming 83 percent of the local farmers and 100 percent of the townspeople thought that they should be protected. However, in response to the final question—"Should the PNV be opened for agricultural exploitation?"—a majority (51 percent) of local farmers answered yes (figure 3.5).

Sorting out the contradictions inherent in the last two sets of answers was but one of the many tasks to undertake when the final survey results were tabulated. Clearly, much more information was now available to those of us planning how to make gorilla conservation more effective, including how to design a sound conservation education program. Much of the information, to be sure, pointed toward an uphill battle. Yet there was also solid evidence that we were not dealing with a monolithic Rwandan public, uninterested in all conservation values

Figure 3.4 Virunga forest impact on water supply.   Survey results concerning the role of the Virunga ecosystem in water catchment.

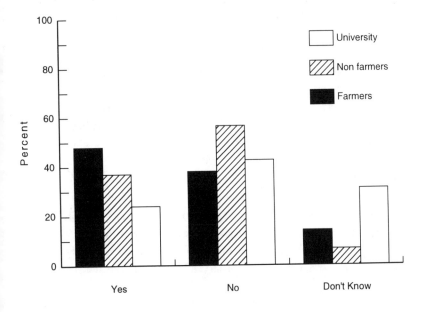

Figure 3.5 Survey results concerning whether the Volcanos National Park should be opened for agricultural exploitation.

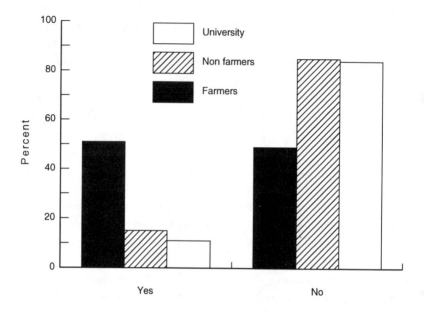

and adamantly opposed to the park, as some had implied. There was even a surprisingly strong vein of support for gorillas. In addition, more detailed analyses of the data revealed an inclination toward conservation on the part of younger, better-educated farmers (i.e., at least a sixth grade education) who represented a growing minority in their communities.

That much said, it was still clear that conservation efforts in Rwanda could not count on any widespread foundation of popular support. More precisely, the set of values that most Westerners brought to African conservation would be given very little weight within the local cultural context. Scientific, aesthetic, or moral reasons for conservation were either not recognized or greatly devalued, and even utilitarian arguments would have to be tailored to local conditions.

The survey results described above were combined with earlier findings from the biological sphere to make the most comprehensive assessment possible of the gorilla conservation picture in 1979. The urgent need to move from assessment to action, however, was dramatically underscored when, in February of that year, the government of

Rwanda once again decided to convert more of the PNV for development purposes. This time, fully one-third of the park—including the
richest gorilla habitat—was to be cleared for an internationally funded
cattle-raising scheme. For the first time, though, an alternative assessment of issues and options was available to decision-makers, in the form
of our study and recommendations. The result was a brief but intensive
period of deliberation and negotiation, following which the cattle project was put on hold,[2] and the Mountain Gorilla Project was born
of necessity.

IMPLEMENTATION

The action phase of the Mountain Gorilla Project[3] began in August
1979. A three-pronged approach was taken, with key activities in the
following sectors: (1) improving park security to deal with the most
immediate problem of poaching; (2) developing a tourism program
centered on the gorillas in order to generate income, employment, and
political support; and (3) creating a conservation education program to
increase public awareness over the long term.

While the anti-poaching and tourism components received the most
funding and attention, the MGP education program operated for ten
years with limited support and less than optimal continuity. However,
the conservation education (CE) program achieved some notable successes in the face of these and other obstacles. This section will describe
the primary initiatives in the education sphere.

The first step in developing the CE program was to draw on the
interdisciplinary research database in order to identify key issues to be
addressed. These fell into three principal categories. First, there was the
need to take what was known about gorilla behavior, ecology, and
endangered status and package this information in an appropriate man-

---

[2] A modification of this project was eventually funded by the World Bank and relocated to the
neighboring Gishwati Forest in northwestern Rwanda. It has resulted in the clearing of more
than 40 percent of that forest and has been sharply criticized for its disregard for attendant
environmental impacts (Vedder 1989a).

[3] The research leading up to the creation of the MGP, as described in this chapter, was supported
by the Wildlife Conservation Society (WCS). The consortium formed to implement the MGP,
however, consisted of the African Wildlife Foundation, the Fauna and Flora Preservation Society,
and the World Wildlife Fund. WCS continued to support regular censuses of the gorilla population.

ner for Rwandan audiences. Second, an emphasis had to be placed on the more utilitarian values of wildlife and park conservation. In the obvious case of tourism, what was being taught would be reinforced by the reality of increased revenue and employment resulting from the MGP tourism component. In the somewhat less tangible realm of water-catchment values, the content of the CE program was paramount. Finally, the case had to be made that a long-term solution to the population-land crisis did not lie in clearing the small relic forest of the Virungas.

The next step was to target certain audiences. Primary among these was the farming population living in the area of the PNV. This population was delimited by a roughly defined 10-kilometer band around the park, within which all elementary schools and social centers were targeted for direct contact of one kind or another. The second group that we decided to focus on was farther away from the park and consisted of the future leaders who would be graduating from the twenty-nine secondary schools and two universities in the country. A third important group was composed of the current elite and decision-makers living in the capital city.

Finally, we needed to decide on appropriate formats for communicating with the selected audiences. Audiovisual presentations were developed for all groups. We had previously helped to produce several French language films on the gorillas for European television, however, and these were available to us in Rwanda. These were excellent for showing gorilla behavior, but they had two shortcomings. First, the majority of rural Rwandans do not speak French and so a fluent Kinyarwanda speaker was needed to provide a running commentary under certain circumstances. Fortunately, the scenes of gorilla social life commanded great attention by all audiences, with or without translation. A more important drawback was that the television films only covered a narrow range of the conservation content desired in the CE program.

To cover a broader content range, we also put together a slide program that explored the more comprehensive set of issues outlined above. The slide program was produced with prerecorded tapes in both French and Kinyarwanda so that they could be shown at times when project personnel were not available. A booklet with both the text and pictures was also produced for teachers and distributed along with the

Mountain gorilla family in the Virunga forest (*photo by Vedder and Weber*).

slide-tape show to every secondary school in the country and every local primary school with electricity (Vedder and Weber 1980). In most instances, however, audiovisual presentations were made by MGP personnel, traveling from site to site in a small, but well-equipped mobile education unit. This direct contact not only assured some quality control, but also permitted lengthy two-way discussions after each show, which was one of the most important elements of the overall program. It was certainly a way to get rapid feedback and new material and approaches for future programs.

Several other formats and media were used in the CE effort. These included more traditional posters and calendars, as well as strategically placed permanent and mobile displays. In addition, project personnel helped to launch a weekly environmental program on the national radio. Most surprising, thanks to the fortuitous occurrence of a national educational reform effort in the early 1980s, we were also able to help shape the environmental curriculum at all levels of the national educational system. This permitted the incorporation of appropriate material in both primary and secondary programs; it also opened the way for conservation content in other disciplines, such as math (e.g., carrying capacities) and history (e.g., the creation of Rwanda's parks) (Minani, personal communication). It should be noted that this is a long-term strategy. The first students exposed to this new curriculum have only just begun to graduate from primary school, and none have finished high school as of 1992.

Throughout the life of the MGP/CE program, the principal focus remained the population living in the shadow of the Virungas. Schools and community centers within walking distance of the park received the most frequent visits and had the greatest exposure to formal presentations. As the program evolved, some more hands-on approaches were added to enhance conservation awareness and support within this population. Direct exposure to gorillas through organized visits was one such approach. Under this program, small groups of students, teachers, or local leaders were taken to visit one of the four families of wild gorillas habituated to regular visits by tourists. These visits were an extremely popular and effective means of expanding interest and support during the first half of the 1980s. By 1986, however, the Office Rwandais du Tourisme et des Parcs Nationaux (ORTPN) put an end to low-cost educational visits on the grounds that these visits were limiting sites for foreign tourists to visit and thereby causing the government to lose precious foreign revenue. Without questioning the importance of the tourism program to the overall gorilla conservation program, this decision has always seemed extremely shortsighted and counterproductive.

Another more participatory approach to education involved the creation of conservation clubs at schools in the vicinity of the PNV. In addition to visits to the park and the gorillas, several of these clubs directly involved themselves with issues within their own communities. Principal among these were tree planting and improved agricultural techniques, such as agroforestry and erosion control (Wilson and Sebigoli, personal communication). This component remained active through the end of the MGP and was embraced by club participants. At the same time the extent of its impact was largely a function of the time, energy, and funding committed to it by project personnel, commitments that varied significantly over the life of the CE project.

PRODUCT

The Mountain Gorilla Project formally ended its operations in 1989: a decision that reflected political difficulties far more than the practical need for continuation. Nevertheless, the MGP produced an unusually comprehensive record over the course of a decade upon which it can be judged. This section will briefly treat its overall accomplishments and provide a more detailed analysis of the conservation education sector.

Tourism, Park Security, and Gorilla Population Growth

Without question, the most dramatic results achieved by the MGP came in the area of tourism development (Weber 1987b, 1989b, 1993; Vedder 1989; Vedder and Weber 1990; Hannah 1992). For this program four free-ranging groups of mountain gorillas (out of thirty-one in the entire reserve) were habituated to the presence of human visitors. Tourist group size was limited, as were the frequency and duration of visits. Still, the virtual guarantee of viewing wild gorillas in their natural habitat created an experience for which thousands of visitors each year were willing to pay almost $200 apiece. As a result, annual park entry revenues surpassed $1,000,000 in 1989 alone. Up to four times that amount was estimated to have been spent elsewhere in the country by tourists seeking to view gorillas (Lindberg 1991). Most important, more than a hundred full-time jobs were created and supported by this MGP component, most of which went to residents of the region. Even more benefits would have accrued locally, however, if the park service had not systematically rejected proposals for more direct revenue sharing with communities around the PNV. Nonetheless, a primary objective of the gorilla tourism program was to generate revenues to offset alternative government development options.

Reinforcing the "carrot" of tourism-related jobs and revenue was the traditional "stick" of the anti-poaching component of the MGP. More than fifty guards were hired, trained, and provided with the necessary equipment to work in the difficult environment of the Virungas. Their efforts brought about a rapid decline in gorilla hunting, with no known cases of gorillas killed in the PNV by poachers after 1984.[4]

---

[4] One gorilla was killed in May 1992 when it apparently surprised rebel soldiers attempting to enter Rwanda through the park.

The bottom line for any wildlife conservation project is the status of the focal area and/or population and, here again, the impact of MGP is clearly positive. From its low point of barely 254 individuals in the 1981 census, the Virunga gorilla population rose steadily to a total of 320 in the most recent census of 1989. Equally encouraging, the percentage of young also increased significantly, from 36 percent to more than 51 percent of the total population. Combined with the cessation of further forest clearing, these findings indicate a more promising outlook for the mountain gorilla than at any time in recent memory.

MGP Education Results

Though an integral part of the MGP, the contribution of the conservation education component to the mountain gorilla's well-being is more difficult to ascertain than that of tourism and park security. There are nonetheless both direct and indirect indicators of its impacts.

The most revealing results come from a 1984 follow-up survey of attitudes and awareness among the rural population living closest to the park (Weber 1987a, 1987b; 1989). Interviews conducted with the same

Rwandan primary schoolgirl looking at the mobile education display (*photo by Vedder and Weber*).

Table 3.2. Changes in Rwandan Perceptions
of Park Conservation Values (1979–1984)

QUESTION RESPONSE	1979 %	1984 %
Forest values[a]		
No value	17	22
Rain/climate	19	29
Erosion control	17	14
Wildlife refuge	19	33
Research	0	2
Tourism	0	8
Don't know	38	11
Animal values[a]		
No value	14	24
Tourism	39	53
Research	1	1
Aesthetic/ethical	1	1
Species preservation	0	1
Don't know	44	16
Other	1	0
Open park for exploitation?		
Yes	51	29
No	49	71

[a] Nonconsumptive values; multiple responses permitted.

farming population found much greater recognition of nonconsumptive values related to forest and wildlife conservation than had been the case five years earlier (table 3.2). In particular, the forest was better recognized for its ecological roles in maintaining a beneficial climate (29 percent), preventing erosion (14 percent), and supporting wildlife (33 percent), as well as for its tourism value (8 percent). Tourism was also more widely cited (53 percent) as a value for conserving wildlife, though almost to the exclusion of other attributes. In fact, almost all the values cited were of a distinctly utilitarian nature. Tourism was important because it generated local employment and national revenues. Even the meaning of "wildlife refuge" was widely understood as a potential food reserve in hard times. Simply put, foreign arguments stressing scientific, aesthetic, moral, and species-preservation values continued to carry little weight with the average Rwandan farmer working in her field.

Even though Rwandans had not been converted into gorilla "huggers" by 1984, their broader recognition of conservation values contributed to a major shift in local attitudes toward the PNV. Whereas more than half the farmers surveyed in 1979 wanted to open the park to exploitation, only 29 percent supported this idea five years later. On closer examination, only one-fourth of that group felt that agriculture was an appropriate form of use. The tide was clearly turning.

Did education play a role in this change? The 1984 survey found that more than half (53 percent) the sample population had attended at least one MGP/CE presentation over the preceding years: an indication of the project's success in reaching its primary target population. When this group's responses to core questions are compared with those of nonattendees, the differences are clear (table 3.3). This is especially true with regard to wildlife values, where attendees at a CE presentation were almost twice as likely to recognize the importance of tourism as

Table 3.3. Relationship Between Attendance at a Conservation Education Program and Perceptions of Park Conservation Values in the Virunga Region

	ATTENDANCE AT MGP/CE PROGRAM		
QUESTION RESPONSE	NO %	YES %	SIGNIFICANCE LEVEL
Forest values[a]			
No value	31	13	
Rain/climate	25	33	
Erosion control	13	15	
Wildlife refuge	27	39	
Research	2	2	
Tourism	6	9	
Don't know	10	11	Not significant
Animal values[a]			
No value	31	17	
Tourism	38	65	
Research	0	0	
Aesthetic/Ethical	0	'0	
Species preservation	0	0	
Don't know	21	11	.02
Open park for exploitation?			
Yes	44	11	
No	56	89	.001

[a] Nonconsumptive values; multiple responses permitted. Questions asked of 102 farmers living in the vicinity of Volcanos National Park in 1984.

The author outside a Rwandan secondary school with a group of students and the mobile education unit or the "gorilla mobile" (*photo by Vedder and Weber*).

those who had never attended (65 percent versus 38 percent). The attendee group also included the very small minority of individuals who cited other wildlife conservation values. Most significant, 89 percent of those who were exposed to a CE program supported continued park protection as opposed to only 56 percent of the nonattendees. The negligible difference between the latter figure and the 51 percent opposed to the park in 1979 indicates the potential importance of the CE effort. In fact, most of the change noted between the two surveys can be accounted for by the attendance variable. It is possible that those who attended presentations may have had a predisposition toward conservation, but this was not evident from the earlier survey. There were also other variables that correlated with changes in attitudes. That the education program of the MGP had a positive impact, however, seems undeniable.

Many indirect indicators of the CE program's influence have also been evident. In dealing with government officials, it was no longer necessary by the early 1980s to explain the importance of gorillas and their mountain forest habitat: most officials had already been exposed to various media presentations. At about the same time, other initiatives reinforced the MGP effort at the level of general public consciousness. First, postage stamps were produced depicting gorillas; then a frequently used Rwandan currency note was issued with a direct copy of the gorilla picture from our first MGP calendar; and, eventually, even a brand of soap was produced with the embossed image of a strutting silverback on each bar. Perhaps the single most impressive occurrence, however, was the appearance on Radio Rwanda of a hauntingly beautiful song entitled, in Kinyarwanda, "Where Can They Go?" Played on the traditional zither, the song told of the mountain gorilla and its plight, between refrains that returned to the central question: If they can't live here, where else can they go? This song, like the soap, the stamps, and the currency note, was not a direct result of the MGP, but came about because of the independent initiative of a concerned Rwandan.

Finally, it must be recognized that Rwandan support for gorilla conservation has come at a cost. Population growth did not come to a halt as a result of the MGP, nor did solutions to the farmland crisis miraculously appear. In the same 1984 survey, farmers who felt they had sufficient land to feed their families had dropped from 80 percent of the population five years earlier to only 28 percent. Barely 6 percent had enough land to subdivide among their children. When asked to name the most pressing problems that confronted them in life, the lack of land, water, and wood, along with soil erosion, health, and poverty, were at the top of the list. Asked to think about the future, overpopulation rose to the number two position, behind land and ahead of food and poverty (table 3.4). Wildlife conservation was never mentioned in any of their open-ended accounts (Weber 1987b, 1989).

Education played an unquestionable role in changing Rwandan attitudes toward conservation, but tourist-related income and employment provided a more tangible justification in the face of constant conflicts. Today, in 1992, Rwanda faces its most severe set of challenges yet, as a two-year-old civil war has added previously unknown burdens to the problems at hand, including a sharp decline in tourism. Thus far the park and gorillas remain secure, but the long-term legacy of the MGP will be in serious jeopardy if the conflict continues much longer.

In conclusion, it is impossible to fully assess the impact of the MGP education program, given the lack of written records and other objective criteria—not to mention the biases of the participant-evaluator. Certainly the project has had its share of problems. These have included a lack of continuity because of personnel changes, inadequate training of

Table 3.4. Perceptions of Priority Problems at Different Levels in Ruhengeri Prefecture

PROBLEM	IMPORTANCE FOR FAMILY	IMPORTANCE FOR REGION	IMPORTANCE FOR FUTURE
Lack of land	1	1	1
Poverty	2	3	4
Soil erosion, degradation	3	4	6
Lack of water	4	2	9
Lack of wood	5	5	8
Lack of food	6	7	3
Lack of pastures	7	9	10
Health	8	11	7
Housing	9	12	12
Education	10	10	5
Overpopulation	11	8	2
Lack of roads	12	6	15
High dowry costs	13	14	11
Wild animal damage to crops	14	15	13
Climate	15	13	14

Survey of 320 households in Ruhengeri Prefecture.
Source: Weber 1987b.

personnel, inconsistent financial support from abroad, shifting institutional linkages within the Rwandan government, and a premature termination of its activities. Nevertheless, a succession of committed individuals, both Rwandan and expatriate, were able to achieve some notable successes as a result of their enthusiasm and perseverance. As such, perhaps the MGP embodies much that is common to conservation education efforts throughout the developing world.

What is somewhat different about the MGP education effort is its interdisciplinary research foundation, especially its use of attitudinal surveys. These surveys first generated baseline information for the design of the educational program; they then provided a means of monitoring that program's effectiveness. If one principal lesson can be drawn from this experience, it is that we need to do more of this kind of work and improve our techniques if we want to produce and assess quality programs in conservation education. In the process we will also contribute to a better understanding of the cultural and socioeconomic complexities that make conservation the challenge that it is.

Endnote: In April 1994 the president of Rwanda was assassinated, triggering a violent escalation of the three-year-old civil war referred to in this chapter. Between 100,000 and 500,000 civilians are reported to have died in the ensuing outbreak of political and ethnic killing. As of July 1994, the opposition Rwandan Patriotic Front (RFP) has taken control of most of the country and a multiparty opposition government has been declared, however fighting continues in some areas.

The northern region of the country around the Volcanos National Park was one of the first areas occupied by the RFP. They have permitted armed park guards to continue their work and, to this date, there is no evidence of any serious harm to the park or the gorillas. All tourism, education, and related activities have been halted, however, and prospects for restarting them are highly uncertain.

The situation in Rwanda is exceptional in many respects, but not unique. It stands as a cautionary example of the need to recognize that conservation takes place within a socioeconomic and political context. When the latter reaches the point of armed conflict, wildlife values and interests may be reduced to insignificance.

PART TWO

Protecting Declining Species

4

Reversing Population Declines in Seabirds on the North Shore of the Gulf of St. Lawrence, Canada

Kathleen A. Blanchard

A seabird management plan that included a strong educational component was developed and tested for more than fifteen years along the North Shore of the Gulf of St. Lawrence, Canada. The program proved successful in helping to reduce human predation of seabirds and eggs and in contributing to improvements in the knowledge, attitudes, and hunting behaviors of residents. Those changes, combined with other factors, resulted in significant increases for populations of nesting seabirds that had declined during previous decades because of illegal harvest and disturbance on the nesting grounds. Evaluation of the program's educational component builds a strong case for the efficacy of education in helping to solve conservation problems.

PLANNING

Breeding populations of nesting seabirds on the North Shore of the Gulf of St. Lawrence have fluctuated dramatically over the past two centuries as a direct result of exploitative and conservation activities. Drastic declines occurred during the middle of the nineteenth century owing in large part to the destructive actions of commercial "eggers" (Fortin 1866; Frazar 1887; Audubon 1897). Gradual increases in breeding populations of seabirds occurred between 1925 and 1955, following regulations and enforcement emanating from the international Migratory Bird Treaty of 1916 and the creation of ten federal migratory bird sanctuaries in 1925 (Lewis 1925, 1931, 1937, 1942; Hewitt 1950; Tener 1951; Lemieux 1956). During a twenty-three-year period, between 1955 and 1978, breeding populations within sanctuaries declined dramatically—including an 84 percent decrease (from about 18,500 to 3,000) for razorbill (*Alca torda*) and a 76 percent decrease (62,000 to 15,000) for Atlantic puffin (*Fratercula arctica*), along with decreases for common eider (*Somateria mollissima*), black guillemot (*Cepphus grylle*), and common murre (*Uria aalge*) (Nettleship and Lock 1973; Chapdelaine 1980). The Canadian Wildlife Service has monitored the populations since 1925 by means of a census every five years within the sanctuaries. The most recent published accounts of the censuses are by Chapdelaine (1980) and Chapdelaine and Brousseau (1984, 1991).

The population declines of 1955 to 1978 were caused by direct exploitation of birds and eggs and disturbance on the sanctuaries by mostly non-native inhabitants of the coast (Nettleship and Lock 1973; Cairns 1978; Chapdelaine 1980; Blanchard 1984). In 1980 we began a research program designed to provide information about the harvest—what species it affected and where it was most acute—and its sociocultural context. We conducted a face-to-face survey of heads-of-households along Quebec's Lower North Shore, where the population decline was most acute. The results found that residents lacked knowledge regarding wildlife regulations, possessed a utilitarian perspective of wildlife, and hunted illegally according to the terms of the Migratory Birds Convention. For example, only 46 percent responded correctly to a question about the legal status of common murre, 59 percent for razorbill, and 69 percent for Atlantic puffin. Ninety-five percent considered it acceptable to harvest seabirds for food. Families along the coast harvested eggs, young, or adults of all nesting gulls, terns, eiders, and members of the Alcidae (murres, razorbills, puffins, and guillemots). An average of forty-four birds were reportedly needed per household per year (Blanchard 1984).

The harvest stemmed from a traditional semisubsistence relationship

Atlantic puffins on St. Mary's Island, Quebec, Canada (*photo by Henry Harding, Atlantic Center for the Environment*).

of people to seabirds. Quebec's Lower North Shore comprises 450 kilometers, where no road links the approximately six thousand residents of fifteen villages to the outside world. For generations, seasonal subsistence activities such as seal fishing, berry picking, and egg gathering supplemented the market economy, whereby approximately 50 percent of the work force was employed in cod fishing. The introduction of electricity in the early 1960s reduced the dependency on spring birds for survival by allowing residents to freeze store-bought meat throughout the year. Yet they perceived seabirds and eggs as sources of fresh food, and they valued the preparation and consumption of a meal of birds as an important tradition. Thus, even though the illegal harvest of seabirds was linked to cultural norms, by the late 1960s it no longer served vital food needs (Blanchard 1983, 1987c). From 1955 to 1978 the situation was exacerbated by a reduction in federal migratory bird enforcement and by a rapidly evolving economy, with its emphasis on unemployment insurance, which gave residents increased free time and spending power to engage in illegal, sometimes wasteful hunting (Blanchard 1983, 1987a, 1987c).

Beginning in 1978 the Quebec-Labrador Foundation (QLF), a not-for-profit U.S. and Canadian organization, responded to the problem by collaborating with the Canadian Wildlife Service in developing a management plan for seabirds that would include an educational program for residents. The goal was to restore depleted seabird populations while preserving the integrity of the local culture. This necessitated addressing the illegal harvest in a manner sensitive to cultural norms and traditions. The three desired outcomes were: (1) increased population levels for seabirds nesting in sanctuaries; (2) sustained improvements in local knowledge, attitudes, and behavior toward seabirds; and (3) greater local involvement in the management process (Blanchard and Nettleship 1992).

Achieving sustained improvements in local knowledge, attitudes, and behavior became our educational goal, from which we derived four objectives that encompassed both short- and long-term strategies: (1) teach practical seabird biology and conservation principles; (2) encourage the development of a conservation ethic; (3) train residents for leadership roles in conservation; and (4) build local support for wildlife policies and regulations. Target audiences included children (who, we hoped, would influence other age groups), influential community leaders, persons causing the most disturbance, conservation organizations that could help, and policymakers of federal and provincial governments.

We developed many educational strategies during the fifteen years and modified each one as a result of public input, further research, yearly evaluation, and funding availability. Certain activities were developed directly from local requests. Because the problems covered a vast geographic area, we concentrated on communities that were situated in close proximity to the most important seabird sanctuaries. We developed timetables for the gradual introduction of concepts and sensitive issues. The project director met regularly with Canadian Wildlife Service (CWS) biologists to ensure that the project's educational objectives met CWS management goals and that strategies coordinated with CWS enforcement efforts (Blanchard and Nettleship 1992).

During the first five years, we secured major funding to develop, implement, and evaluate the educational programs from the private sector: foundations, conservation organizations, and individuals. As the project became better established and local training became a high priority, both federal and provincial agencies provided support. Owing to socioeconomic conditions of the Lower North Shore, we sought in-kind and minor financial support from the local sector, where we discovered support to be generous, consistent, and vital to the program.

It was essential that we obtained permission and cooperation from CWS—given the project's focus on migratory bird sanctuaries—without appearing to represent the government (Blanchard 1989). The QLF's image as a nonprofit organization with a history of providing educational and community services to the people of the coast provided a tremendous boost to achieving local support. The founder of QLF also served as the Anglican Archdeacon for the Quebec North Shore; the project director was an American whose father had come from rural Newfoundland. We emphasized that our focus was neither preservationist nor antihunting.

An important aspect to the project's planning phase was our assumption that the achievement of a long-term solution to the problem of illegal harvest would not come merely from the enforcement of regulations and the provision of information (Blanchard and Monroe 1990). We drew from lessons learned in other projects, such as the conservation of geese on the Yukon-Kuskokwim Delta of Alaska (Blanchard 1987b). These projects, plus the information gained from our own research, suggested the importance of local involvement in all aspects of a project and, ultimately, in the management of seabirds.

IMPLEMENTATION

Four general strategies to the educational program included youth instruction, leadership training, information dissemination, and support building. The cornerstone activity was a four-day experiential program for youth at the St. Mary's Islands Seabird Sanctuary, 15 kilometers from the village of Harrington Harbour. Using a former lightstation as classroom and dormitory, the program gave children (ages eight–fifteen) from eight villages hands-on instruction in seabird biology, sanctuary etiquette, and wildlife law. The curriculum emphasized biological and human factors affecting breeding success in seabirds. Instructors, who were university students and local instructors-in-training, were told not

Local fishing communities were directly involved in various program activities (*photo by Anne Hallowell, Atlantic Center for the Environment*).

to preach conservation, but rather to create learning opportunities that were fun and to encourage group discussions. The crucial activity was a visit to a puffin colony, where participants observed birds at close range.

Children returned to their families with increased knowledge, greater concern, and the motivation to tell their family members and friends about their adventures. The watershed experience occurred when, seated around the kitchen table with their families, only to be served a meal of birds, these children in the absence of instructors, initiated lively discussions about the possible impact of their families' actions on the local bird populations. The provocative dialogue among family members carried into discussions among community members: fishermen gathering on wharves and in the village stores exchanged views on the sudden outspoken opinions of their children, while parents registered more children for the program at St. Mary's (Blanchard 1994).

Other strategies for youth programs targeted communities that were more hostile to conservation agents and their programs. In one such village, a staff member produced a play for children in which the actors, who in real life were the sons and daughters of local "poachers," played the roles of seabirds. By practicing their lines at home, these children taught their parents about seabird biology and conservation. Thus, while youth programs targeted long-term behavioral change among the younger generation, their influence spread among all ages, particularly since these were small communities where family ties and group norms were powerful influences (Blanchard and Monroe 1990).

Other important youth activities included the creation of action-oriented conservation clubs, the presentation of school programs from 1985 to 1989, the development of classroom materials about seabirds, and the promotion of a coastwide children's poster contest. All youth programs received widespread support from parents.

During the fifteen years of the project, more than fifty local volunteer and paid staff were trained in field ornithology and teaching methodology. By 1989 half the staff consisted of teenagers from the coast. Meanwhile, the Canadian Wildlife Service increased its enforcement staff by training persons from the coast. Some, who formerly hunted illegally, became exceedingly effective migratory bird officers with a desire to use education, as well as enforcement, as management tools. The project also worked to build the capacity of local organizations to sustain the conservation programs, by providing technical assistance, study-tour opportunities, and seed grants in areas of wildlife management, tourism development, and the preservation of historic buildings. The effect of this training has been enhanced collaboration among government agencies, private organizations, and local citizens' groups for protecting the seabird colonies. Technical training, leadership development, and building the capacity of local organizations to sustain the

Experiential environmental activities for youth were a cornerstone of the program (*photo by Atlantic Center for the Environment*).

conservation programs are the project's most important objectives for the 1990s.

Information and education materials were developed in a style that was locally relevant and practical, then introduced by person-to-person contact rather than through mass mailings. Materials included a seabird identification poster, a citizen's guide to regulations protecting seabirds, a primary school newsletter, and a calendar produced from the children's poster contest. Although these materials were well received, we considered them less important than person-to-person and group activities. We also made abundant use of Canadian Broadcasting Corporation (CBC) and community-sponsored radio to deliver conservation information and to train young people in communications. With the CBC, we produced a nine-part radio series that aired across the province. We also assisted the CBC with the production of a documentary film about the project, which was introduced by the well-known conservationist David Suzuki and was aired across Canada and the United States in 1987.

Building support for conservation was implemented in part through study tours for leaders from national and provincial conservation organizations. The study tours included homestays in a remote village, visits to the sanctuaries, and participation in community forums on conservation. These activities produced many benefits, including new sources of income for the project. More important, they fostered pride, broadened residents' perceived value of the seabirds, and inspired local action to improve the sanctuaries. They also triggered alliances between local and regional conservation groups and sparked the development of more tourist services.

These activities were run by a project director and staff consisting of students and recent graduates of Canadian and U.S. universities, plus younger students from the coast. The project director's chief responsibilities included fund-raising, planning, reporting, supervising public relations and staffing, as well as evaluation, promotion, and coordination with local, regional, and federal groups. The same individual served in this position for fifteen years. The student staff, who changed an average of about every two and one-half years, were selected as much for their motivation and sensitivity to others as for their knowledge and experience with birds. The orientation period for a typical nine-week position with the project lasted approximately one and one-half weeks, which included three days at a QLF office and several days traveling to the site. Staff members learned a great deal on the job, particularly from the people of the coast. They recorded their observations, lesson plans, and daily activities in logbooks, which served as training manuals in successive years.

While the project's field operations maintained an annual budget of $8,000–$15,000, the costs associated with administration, research, recruitment and hiring of staff, publications, and promotion were two to three times that amount. Costs were particularly high, since the project operated in an outpost region. The project benefited tremendously from QLF's financial security and fund-raising experience as a nonprofit organization with an annual budget of $1.2 million by 1990. Project funding from private sources was relatively stable, while add-on funds from federal and provincial sources were more unpredictable. Three-year anchor grants, first from the Donner Canadian Foundation and second from the Canadian government, served to leverage additional funds and became vital to the project's continuity and long-term success.

PRODUCT

By 1988 each goal of the management plan and of the educational program in particular was achieved: (1) increased population levels of seabirds nesting in sanctuaries; (2) increased knowledge, enhancement of attitudes, and improved hunting behavior of residents; and (3) greater local support for and involvement in the management process (Blanchard and Nettleship 1992; Blanchard 1994). For example, during the period from 1977 to 1988, notable increases were evident among the Alcidae: common murre increased from approximately 10,200 to 26,000 individuals, razorbill from 3,600 to 7,000, Atlantic puffin from approximately 15,200 to 35,100 (Chapdelaine and Brousseau 1991). Probable explanations for increases in populations of these and other seabird species are an augmented and more effective enforcement team, QLF's educational program, and the likelihood of enhanced abundance of prey food for seabirds (Chapdelaine and Brousseau 1984, 1991).

We documented improvements in residents' knowledge, attitudes, and behavior by means of a follow-up survey of heads-of-households, using the same sample size, survey techniques, and much of the same question wording. Table 4.1 shows significant increases in the proportion of heads-of-households that correctly stated the legal status for selected species. For instance, in 1981 the proportion of respondents that correctly stated the legal status for common murre was only 47 percent; it rose to 64 percent in 1988 ($\chi^2 = 26.3$, $P = 0.001$). Significant changes in the proportion of respondents that believed it should be legal to hunt selected species is reported in table 4.2. Another example supporting the program's success is the significant drop in the proportion of respondents that believed it is "okay" to take seabirds and eggs for food—from 95 percent in 1981 to 90 percent in 1988 ($\chi^2 = 6.5$, $P = 0.039$) (Blanchard 1994).

Table 4.1. Changes in Knowledge of Wildlife Laws: Percentages of Heads-of-Households Correctly Stating the Legal Status of Select Seabirds

SPECIES	1981	1988	P	χ^2
Razorbill	62.1	70.3	<0.001	22.9
Common murre	47.1	64.1	<0.001	26.3
Atlantic puffin	70.7	76.5	<0.001	16.0

Source: From Blanchard (1991).

Table 4.2. Changes in Attitudes About Wildlife Laws: Percentages of Heads-of-Households That Believe Hunting Should Be Allowed

SPECIES	1981	1988	p	χ^2
Razorbill	58.5	37.9	0.002	12.53
Common murre	76.4	64.8	0.038	6.58
Atlantic puffin	54.3	26.9	<0.001	22.22

Source: From Blanchard (1991).

Despite the continued belief that birds should be harvested, an individual's perspective of the level of harvest in his or her village changed dramatically. The mean response to the question "What percentage of families in your village harvest seabirds and eggs?" dropped significantly from 77 percent in 1981 to 48 percent in 1988 (t = 7.19, P = .0001). The average number of birds reported as needed per year by families dropped from forty-four in 1981 to twenty-four in 1988 (t = 2.68, P = .00078) (Blanchard 1994).

We measured greater local involvement in wildlife management qualitatively by using several indicators: increased membership in the local wildlife society and youth conservation clubs, more local applicants for conservation jobs, a surge in local demand (i.e., use of a waiting list) for the St. Mary's Island Youth Program, emerging conservation committees and organizations, increased local environmental activism (e.g., clean-ups), and grant requests by local committees to government funding sources for conservation projects. The federal government encouraged and supported these activities by using QLF as a facilitator of local involvement, particularly through leadership training and technical assistance.

One challenge our training programs faced is the lack of new employment opportunities on the coast. This is a particularly important issue in light of the depletion of cod stocks and the potential for a government-imposed moratorium on cod fishing, as is currently the case in Newfoundland. QLF is focusing on finding means to diversify the region's economy by encouraging new activities, such as ecotourism development, in ways that are sustainable and that maximize the potential for local involvement in seabird conservation.

Another challenge for the project was how to spread the effort effectively along the entire coast. Illegal harvest has diminished in villages where enforcement and educational programs are in place; in

Children from isolated Quebec North Shore communities present the play *Dreambird* to their parents. The activity is an integral part of learning seabird biology (*photo by K. Blanchard*).

villages beyond the project's reach, the problem has remained acute. We have focused our efforts in the vicinity of the most important seabird colonies, while allowing persons trained in the program to help spread the conservation message elsewhere. As the problem stabilizes within the priority areas, we are planning strategies for new areas that will be implemented in the coming years.

An overriding challenge was how to accomplish more with limited funds. The project logically expanded to include new target audiences, geographic regions, and year-round programming as a function of available funding in that particular year.

Perhaps the most important ingredient to the conservation education program on the Quebec Lower North Shore has been persistence. The geographic isolation, vagaries of the weather, lack of infrastructure, and strong traditions meant that progress could not be achieved overnight. Likewise, although the project has been successful to date, the conservation gains brought about through the educational programs should not be perceived as providing a quick-fix solution to the overall problem. As this project attempts to demonstrate, it is essential for conservation projects to work within the local culture and with traditions, group norms, and patterns of communication in order for the achievements to endure.

Information from this project has been disseminated through a variety of print, film, and radio media. More than 120 lectures, papers, and workshops were presented at conferences, universities, colleges, conservation organizations, and schools in North America and abroad between 1978 and 1992. The project director maintained an ongoing correspondence with conservation professionals around the world in an effort to share strategies for bird conservation in rural areas. She has since been involved in developing training programs for the U.S. Fish and Wildlife Service on using education as a management tool (Pomerantz and Blanchard 1992).

The future challenge facing the Quebec Lower North Shore is one of stimulating economic development while meeting conservation priorities. The current decline of the cod fishery may render serious consequences to the people of the region. The federal and provincial governments, QLF, and the people of the coast are working on the development of environmentally sensitive and locally run tourism as one of several ways to diversify the local economy. In the meantime, the coast may experience a variety of social changes associated with temporary or long-term unemployment. While the situation for seabirds on the Quebec Lower North Shore was relatively good in 1992, conservation efforts must persist and remain strong. Long-term solutions to economic and conservation needs along this coast will depend, as they have for centuries, on local involvement.

5

Golden Lion Tamarin Conservation Program: A Community Educational Effort for Forest Conservation in Rio de Janeiro State, Brazil

■■

Lou Ann Hollingsworth Dietz and
Elizabeth Yoshimi Nagagata

The major threat to the survival of endangered species worldwide is the destruction of their habitat. The people responsible are either unaware of other options or have no other choice for their own immediate survival, or do not understand the importance of natural ecosystems in maintaining the quality of their own lives over the long term. Saving habitats requires work on all aspects of the problem: conducting biological research to understand more about the species involved and their interrelationships; implementing long-term management and protection of the habitat and key individual species involved; and gaining the support of those causing the destruction. Without public support, no amount of biological research or protective efforts will result in long-term conservation of either the habitat or individual species.

Public support can be gained in two ways: by providing economic alternatives that are compatible with the maintenance of the natural

Adult male golden lion tamarin carrying his two young, Poço das Antas Biological
Reserve, Silva Jardim, Rio de Janeiro, Brazil (*photo by James M. Dietz*).

ecosystem and through educational programs targeting the groups that
determine how the ecosystem is used. Most often, a combination of the
two is necessary for a long-term solution. Effective education programs
for species and habitat conservation cannot be carried out in isolation.
They require the close collaboration of biologists involved in research
and management to set the goals for educational action and to provide
the basic information to be communicated to the public.

Certain species with which people identify can serve as excellent
focal points or "flagships" for programs in order to gain public support
for habitat conservation. Nationwide surveys conducted in the United
States (Kellert and Berry 1980; Kellert and Westervelt 1983; Westervelt
and Llewellyn 1985) and our own work in Brazil have documented
that preferences of both adults and children for animal species varied
consistently and dramatically according to whether the species is considered attractive. Children liked beautiful and lovable animals significantly
more than other animals equally important to the balance of nature.
Factors with a substantial negative influence on adult preferences were
fear of the animal; responsibility for property damage; predatory or
carnivorous behavior; association with the wilderness; and cultural/

Figure 5.1 Model for the development of a conservation education project.

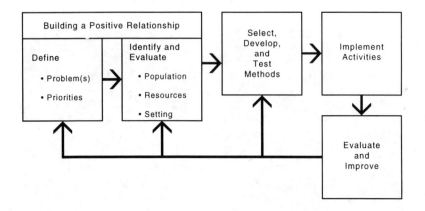

historical antipathies. Factors that positively influenced preferences were large size, advanced intelligence; phylogenetic relatedness to human beings; and complex social organization. Most people relate to animals anthropomorphically. To understand concepts such as ecological interdependence, people need direct experience such as observation of the natural processes in the habitat in order to discover how these animals, and even people themselves, depend on a delicate balance. The cited studies showed that education was one of the most important factors associated with positive attitudes toward animals. Environmental educators can begin with people's natural interest and anthropomorphic understanding of why animals behave as they do in order to broaden people's *understanding* of the environment, heighten their *concern* for the plight of endangered species and ecosystems, and thus lead them to *action* for long-term conservation. The human interest aroused by "attractive" species can be a springboard to educating people about the bigger picture—the interrelationships of wildlife, people, and the environment. It is the system balance that must be conserved, not just the individual species.

Since 1983 we have been involved in a multidisciplinary project to assure the long-term conservation of the golden lion tamarin (*Leontopithecus rosalia*; an endangered, half-kilogram monkey) and what remains of its lowland Atlantic forest habitat in the state of Rio de Janeiro, Brazil, one of the world's most endangered tropical rain forests (Kleiman et al. 1986). We have used a systems model (figure 5.1) to develop and implement a program in order to gain the necessary public support to ensure a future for this ecosystem. Such a model, similar to Jacobson (1991) and described in the first chapter in this volume, helps to prioritize problems, focus efforts on developing appropriate and effective solutions, and conceptualize a complex process that is not necessarily linear in nature.

PLANNING

Step 1—Defining Priority Problems

What are the most important conservation problems? Can they realistically be addressed with education or must some other type of solution, such as an economically viable alternative, be found?

In 1983 biologists studying the ecology of the golden lion tamarin as part of our field project identified the major threats to the forest and to the survival of the golden lion tamarin. In the first year of the program the principal problem identified was habitat destruction, although hunting in the Poço das Antas Biological Reserve and the capture of golden lion tamarins for the pet trade were identified as additional problems. The researchers, the reserve manager, and our educational team then worked together to establish and prioritize conservation objectives to address these problems. As more scientific information on the status of the species and its forest habitat is accumulated and analyzed each year, the team revises its objectives. As we have learned more about the community and the underlying forces causing the problem, it has become clear that education is indeed one of the most important methods to achieve the program's conservation goals.

One of the main objectives of the Golden Lion Tamarin Conservation Program has been to protect enough forest to sustain a genetically viable population of golden lion tamarins. Soon after the project's ecological studies began, it became clear that the 5,000-hectare Poço das Antas Biological Reserve, the only protected area containing the species, was not large enough. The educational program had to not only enlist public support for the protection of the Poço das Antas Reserve, but also enlist the support of landowners to protect forests on private land. Another objective was to reduce the capture of tamarins for pets.

In each instance where public education efforts were needed, we established specific objectives toward which progress could actually be measured:

1. reduce deforestation in the lowland areas surrounding the Poço das Ants Reserve
2. assure the permanent conservation of the remaining privately owned lowland forests in the region
3. reduce fires in the forests and cleared areas in the region
4. reduce the illegal commerce of golden lion tamarins
5. reduce the illegal hunting in the reserve

In addition to the direct conservation objectives, we also set out to document our results in order to contribute to the improvement of our own program and justify the continued expense, as well as to contribute to the general credibility and methodology of environmental education as a conservation tool.

Step 2—Identifying and Evaluating the Target Population, Resources, and Setting

This stage is the equivalent of market research. To sell a product or idea one has to know the market. Who really is the target population? What are the reasons for the current behavior? What resources and support are available to reach the target population? Given the realities of the local setting, what is feasible and what is not? In addition, to determine if any changes take place as a result of the program's efforts, we must know the initial attitudes, behaviors, and level of knowledge of the target population to serve as a baseline for later comparisons.

The golden lion tamarin educational project began with a series of informal interviews with community leaders to gain insight into the local situation and identify partners for the development of the program. Initially, the local mayor, teachers, and students showed the most interest. Teachers and other leaders helped to perfect a basic questionnaire (table 5.1), which the program used in its long form as an interview with adults and in a short, written form with school students. A team of local high school student volunteers conducted initial surveys of local knowledge and attitudes regarding wildlife, forests, and local protected areas. This information served as a baseline for later comparisons with results of surveys conducted after two years of project activities. The information collected in the initial interviews also served as a basis for planning strategies that capitalized on interests the target population had in common with the conservation objectives.

Table 5.1. Survey About Fauna and Flora

Date ___/___/___
School _____ Municipality _____
Grade _____
Age _____   Male ( )   Female ( )

Mark an "x" on the number of the answer you select:

1. Do you know the name of this animal?
   Yes, its name is _____ 1
   No, I don't know.. 2

2. Have you seen the animal...
   in the forest?.. Yes-1   No-2
   captive at someone's house?.. Yes-1   No-2
   in a zoo?.. Yes-1   No-2
   on posters, in photos, or in books?.. Yes-1   No-2
   in presentations at school? Yes-1   No-2
   in another place?.. Yes-1   No-2
       If yes, specify place _____ .

3. Does this animal exist in this municipality? Yes-1   No-2

4. What does this animal eat? _____

5. How does this animal live?
       alone... 1
       in pairs with young... 2
       in large groups 3
       I don't know 4

6. Do you think the numbers of this animal...
       are decreasing?.. 1
       are increasing?... 2
       are staying the same? 3
   Why? _____
   _____

7. Is this animal important for man?
       Yes 1
       No 2
       I don't know... 3

   If yes, what is its importance? _____
   _____

8. Does the forest bring you some benefit?
       Yes... 1
       No... 2
       Don't know... 3

Table 5.1. (*Continued*)

9. Have you done something to help conserve your community's forests?

Yes 1

No 2

If yes, what have you done? _____

_____

Do you agree with these statements?

10. There is a protected area for forest plants and animals near your municipality.

	Yes	No	Don't know

11. In forests, the golden lion tamarin exists only in (name of student's municipality) and nearby municipalities.

	Yes	No	Don't know

12. The majority of forest animals are harmful to man.

	Yes	No	Don't know

13. By law, each landowner must conserve a part of his or her property in forest.

	Yes	No	Don't know

14. Hunting, sale, purchase, and transport of forest animals are prohibited in Brazil by federal law.

	Yes	No	Don't know

How much do you know about these subjects?
(Mark only one answer.)

15. species endangered with extinction

I know a lot 1

I know some 2

I know little 3

I never heard of it 4

16. Poço das Antas Biological Reserve

I know a lot 1

I know some 2

I know little 3

I never heard of it 4

17. the effect of deforestation on man

I know a lot 1

I know some 2

I know little 3

I never heard of it 4

If you found each one of these animals in the forest, what would you do?

18. a baby bird

take it home to raise 1

leave it alone 2

kill it... 3

take it to sell 4

something else (specify _____) 5

19. a snake

take it home to raise.. 1

leave it alone 2

kill it... 3

take it to sell 4

something else (specify _____) 5

20. a little monkey

take it home to raise.. 1

leave it alone 2

kill it... 3

take it to sell 4

something else (specify _____) 5

21. a paca

take it home to raise.. 1

leave it alone 2

kill it... 3

take it to sell 4

something else (specify _____) 5

22. a caiman

take it home to raise.. 1

leave it alone 2

kill it... 3

take it to sell 4

something else (specify _____) 5

23. During the last year, did you raise any animals at home?
(Mark all that you raised.)

dog.....................	1	fish.........................	6
bird......................	2	chicken	7
parrot...................	3	other (which? _____	8
monkey.................	4	none......................	9
cat.........................	5		

Thank you for your answers.

Note: Written questionnaire used in student survey (English translation). A different form of the questionnaire was used for interviews with adults before project activities. Students completed the questionnaire both before and after the two years of project activities.

Initially, 41 percent of the 518 adults interviewed living within the habitat of the golden lion tamarin could not recognize the animal from a photograph. Most of the adults interviewed did not even know the Poço das Antas Reserve existed. Our surveys found no negative attitudes about the golden lion tamarin or the forest. Of those who indicated that

Percilia Machado, an education team member, interviewing a local farmer, Silva Jardim, Rio de Janeiro, Brazil (*photo by Lou Ann Dietz*).

they valued the tamarin or the forest, many indicated aesthetic as well as economic reasons. We thus determined that we could use the golden lion tamarin to increase levels of knowledge concerning the relationships of wildlife, habitat, humans, and the well-being of all. Emphasizing the tamarin's relationship with the forest would help to decrease people's natural desire to keep these fascinating animals as pets. We hoped to increase awareness of the importance of each element of the forest in the proper functioning of the whole. We needed to stress the long-term and global consequences of local human actions on the environment. Most interviewees, for example, who recognized that local wildlife was diminishing did not connect the situation with habitat destruction, the major cause. They attributed it to hunting. We could stimulate local residents' thinking by using arguments, such as: "One forest patch might seem like a little, but cutting many small patches destroys a large total area. Where does the wildlife go? Where does the water go? What happens to the soil? What would happen if we killed *all* the snakes?"

We found that we needed to show those who were already aware of the conservation problems how they could help work toward solutions. Much of the population lacked pride in their local region. As in most forested regions, the area still harboring golden lion tamarins provides few economic and educational options for young people. For example, when asked what they would show to a newcomer, many interviewees said, "Nothing, all we have is forest here." Creating pride in local natural resources became an important part of our strategy.

The interviews also showed that the mass media were a potentially powerful means for reaching the general public with our message. Print media were not appropriate for the 40 percent of the adult population who were illiterate. Moreover, direct contact was difficult in the many areas without regular rural mail delivery or telephones, and where rural roads are often impassable. Eighty percent of those interviewed watched television regularly and 99 percent listened to the radio, even though the rural residents of this area lack electricity. Only the absentee landowners read the newspaper. We decided to target a media effort at the illegal animal purchasers in Rio de Janeiro and Brasilia, as well as to the public at large.

In addition, we initially selected several target populations of three municipalities surrounding the reserve for our more intensive direct action. These target groups included the owners (largely absentee) of forested land and local leaders. We decided to try to reach parents, and thus the wider community, through action with teachers and schoolchildren.

Step 3—Building a Positive Relationship

Because human attitudes and behaviors change slowly, a conservation education effort must be ongoing. To ensure support of educational activities, we encouraged community involvement in their planning and implementation. When a community makes an investment, it takes ownership of the activities and has an interest in seeing that they are effectively carried out. Community involvement also assures that the activities and language are appropriate for the local situation. At the beginning of our project in 1983, we began building a constructive relationship with the local community leaders. We spent many weeks conducting informal conversations with these leaders to learn about the community and ask for their ideas. Before long, our program was perceived as a local resource. These leaders also began to see the reserve and our work as something that could draw positive public attention to their community. As the program has grown, it has continued to include the community in its efforts. All parts of the project seek to train and employ people from the local community.

Although basic funding for salaries for the development of the educational program has been obtained on a yearly basis from grants from conservation organizations, the program has made an intensive effort to obtain as much support (monetary and in-kind) as possible from local sources for other aspects of the project. Although this is a very time-consuming part of the project, it is an investment in developing long-term and continuous local support.

IMPLEMENTATION

Step 4—Selection and Testing Methods

We selected methods that interested local leaders and that seemed most likely to have the widest results for the least cost. Making the golden lion tamarin a symbol for forest conservation was easy. What was difficult was arousing people's interest—especially rural residents—in saving a snake, even though the snake is just as important as any other part of the forest. To save tamarins we must save forests; thus by saving tamarins we can save all the elements of their forest ecosystem. Our educational materials were multipurpose, short, simple, and low-cost. All resulted from requests or local needs that we had identified. Since almost no information existed in Portuguese on the local flora and fauna, our materials included as much up-to-date information as possible—even the as yet unpublished results of the ecological studies underway in the reserve. We employed audiovisual and live presentations for most local adults, 41 percent of whom had no formal education. Prototypes of all materials were tested and revised before final production. It was especially important to test the language. An expression that was perfectly understandable in Rio de Janeiro, 60 kilometers away from the reserve area, was not necessarily understandable near the reserve.

Materials the project has produced to date include:

• press releases to encourage coverage that included the project's main messages
• video copies of news and other programs in Portuguese on Brazilian conservation
• public service messages for radio and television

- educational posters and pamphlets
- school notebooks with an educational story on the cover
- a slide collection for the reserve
- slide-tape programs
- information packages for landowners that explained how to obtain tax benefits by registering private forest reserves
- a logo for the reserve, which serves to identify all materials and activities
- an electronic question-and-answer board for use in classes and exhibits
- a traveling exhibit for local festivals
- T-shirts, stickers, and buttons (for recognition of contributions to conservation, for local fund-raising, and as reminders of our larger conservation message)
- a nature discovery trail in the reserve
- a teacher's training manual to enable teachers to instruct elementary school students in basic ecological concepts

We used these materials in a variety of combinations and activities with the hope that *some* would be effective with each group of our target population.

Step 5—Implementing Activities

Our project began work in one municipality, gaining momentum and experience that carried over to improve the development of the program in two other municipalities. We have concentrated our efforts on working with existing groups and institutions to identify and achieve mutual objectives. Direct contact with the public is accomplished by interns, volunteers, and young graduates of local teacher-training high schools. Activities are continually developed or modified as the need arises in the local communities.

Activities conducted to date include:

- classes about the tamarins and the local forest for schools and farm workers
- training classes for reserve guards, project personnel, and local teachers
- invited lecturers for local groups
- educational field trips to the reserve for farmers, school groups,

and families (habituated tamarins and a guided discovery trail encourage observation of the details of the forest)
- press events
- support for local conservation clubs that we formed
- a children's play performed in the town squares
- parades organized by local teachers
- encouragement, through the agricultural extension service, of planting native trees for watershed protection and fire prevention
- personal visits to landowners encouraging them to register their remaining forest patches as permanent reserves (if they do not already have wild golden lion tamarins on their land, they are qualified to receive captive-born tamarins in their forest as part of the project's reintroduction program)
- recognition awards for landowners conserving their forests
- contests among school students and the larger community
- participation in local festivals, agricultural expositions, and other community events
- regular meetings with local leaders

PRODUCT

Step 6—Evaluation

Evaluation is a crucial step to achieving an effective educational program. By establishing clear objectives from the beginning, we could plan the project systematically to include evaluation. Clearly, our goals will be achieved only over the long term, but it has been possible to collect concrete evidence of short-term progress toward those goals. Evidence includes changes in knowledge, attitudes, and actions of our target public.

The formal evaluation of the first phase of the golden lion tamarin educational project involved the comparison of results of initial surveys (interviews with adults and written questionnaires with school children) conducted in 1984 with the results of surveys conducted in 1986 after two years of activities with our target audience. Results (based on the Chi-square Test) indicated significant changes in knowledge and attitudes of local adults and students. Since no other activities or media

Local children dressed as golden lion tamarins for a parade in Silva Jardim, Rio de Janeiro, Brazil (*photo by Lou Ann Dietz*).

Figure 5.2 Do you recognize this animal (golden lion tamarin)?   Recognition of a tamarin from a photograph, before and after two years of educational activities.

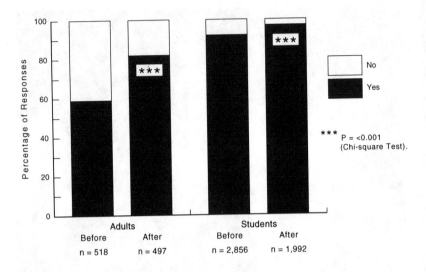

events occurred in the area except those that we had generated, these changes can be attributed to this project's activities.

The following are examples of our findings:

1. To save a species the public must be able to recognize and relate to it. In our survey respondents were shown a photograph of a golden lion tamarin and asked to give its name. In the preinterviews, 41 percent of the adult respondents were unable to identify the animal. Two years after our educational activities, there was a significant increase ($\chi^2 = 25$, $P < 0.001$) in the percentage of adult respondents able to correctly identify the animal (figure 5.2). A much higher percentage of students was able to recognize the tamarin initially, probably because the pre-questionnaires with students were conducted at the beginning of the school year, just after our public service messages were broadcast. Even so, there was a significant increase ($\chi^2 = 109.2$, $P < 0.001$) in the percentage of students who were able to identify the tamarin after two years of activities with the schools.

2. In our educational activities we tried to communicate some of the habits of tamarins, both to interest our public and to

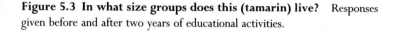

Figure 5.3 In what size groups does this (tamarin) live? Responses given before and after two years of educational activities.

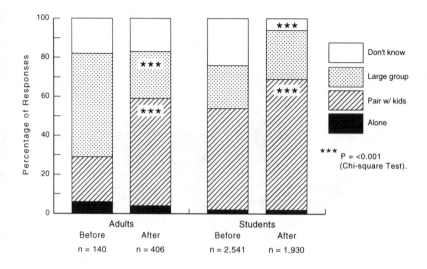

demonstrate the tamarins' relationship with the forest. Figure 5.3 shows another example of a question we used to evaluate changes in knowledge. We asked "How does the tamarin live?" and gave the choices "alone," "in pairs with young" (the correct answer), or "in large groups." After two years of our project's efforts, there was a significant increase in the percentages of both students (χ^2 = 119.4, $P < 0.001$) and adults ($\chi^2 = 78.4, P < 0.001$) who gave the correct answer. There was a significant decrease ($\chi^2 = 70.8, P < 0.001$) in the percentage of adults who thought that the tamarins lived in large groups, as do some other monkeys in the region. There was a significant decrease ($\chi^2 = 278.4, P < 0.001$) in students who answered that they didn't know.

3. To measure values we asked questions such as, "Is the golden lion tamarin important or beneficial?" (figure 5.4). The percentage of adults who answered no did not change significantly two years after their exposure to the project, but there was a significant decrease ($\chi^2 = 243.0, P < 0.001$) in the percentage of adults who responded that they didn't know and a significant increase ($\chi^2 = 238.6, P < 0.001$) in those who responded yes. A much higher percentage of students than adults responded in the pre-questionnaires that the tamarin was beneficial. Again this may

Figure 5.4 Is the golden lion tamarin beneficial?   Responses given before and after two years of educational activities.

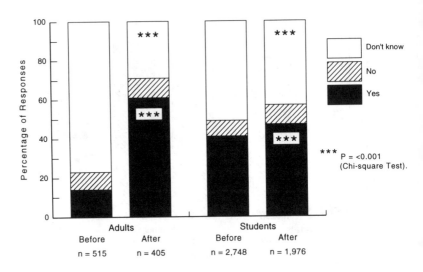

have been because the public service messages were broadcast on television shortly before the questionnaires were distributed to the students. Two years after the program, there was a significant increase ($\chi^2 = 20.3$, $P < 0.001$) in the percentage of students who responded that the tamarin is important, and a significant decrease ($\chi^2 = 38.5$, $P < 0.001$) in the percentage of students who responded that they didn't know. As in the preinterviews, many of the adults who responded yes in the postinterviews gave reasons related to the animal's beauty or pleasure in seeing the animal. However, others gave reasons such as "the tamarin is a part of nature" or "it has a right to live." These answers were not given in the preinterviews. We attribute them to our project efforts.

4. We couldn't ask people directly about many of their behaviors, such as hunting or keeping wild animals as pets, because these behaviors are illegal in Brazil. However, we developed one question that indicates the respondents' intentions regarding certain activities. We chose several representative animals and asked what the respondents would do if they found each in the woods. There were no changes in their proposed behavior after two years of our activities among the adults regarding "a little monkey" (figure 5.5). Most answered that they would take it home or leave

Figure 5.5 What would you do if you found a little monkey in the woods?   Responses given before and after two years of educational activities.

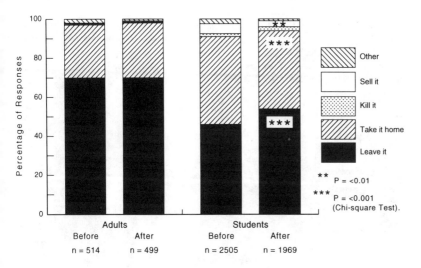

it alone. Among the students, however, there was a significant increase (χ^2 = 31.0, P < 0.001) in the percentage of students who reported that they would leave the little monkey alone, as well a significant decrease (χ^2 = 14.2, P < 0.001) in the percentage of students who responded that they would take the monkey home. Realizing that seeing tamarins might create a desire among students to keep them as pets, our activities with the students heavily emphasized the reasons for leaving tamarins in the forest. This clearly caused a difference in the adult and student responses.

With regard to "a little bird" (figure 5.6) there was a significant decrease (χ^2 = 66.8, P < 0.001) in the percentage of adults who responded that they would raise it at home and a significant increase (χ^2 = 66.2, P < 0.001) in those who responded that they would leave it alone. There were no significant changes in the answers to this question among students. Most students answered in the initial questionnaires that they would leave the bird alone.

The answers concerning a snake were of particular interest (figure 5.7). After two years of our project, fewer adults (χ^2 = 39.0, P < 0.001) and students (χ^2 = 1120.4, P < 0.001) answered that

Elizabeth Nagagata (*on the right*) and another education team member giving a class in a school in Silva Jardim, Rio de Janeiro, Brazil (*photo by Lou Ann Dietz*).

they would kill a snake that they found in the woods and more adults ($\chi^2 = 4.9$, $P < 0.001$) and students ($\chi^2 = 145.7$, $P < 0.001$) answered that they would leave it alone. We had not aimed our program at conservation of snakes. This attitudinal change is an indication that the Golden Lion Tamarin Project activities have played a role in encouraging the emergence of a broader conservation ethic.

To discover which of our methods reached the most adults, we asked those respondents who had correctly identified the tamarin to indicate where they had seen the animal, from a list of places and various media both related and unrelated to the project (figure 5.8). Most often mentioned were television; conversations; T-shirts, stickers, and buttons; and the forest. Our efforts to provide information to television journalists and the public service messages broadcast on television clearly reached more of our target audience than any other method. Unfortunately, in-depth information is not easily communicated through the mass media. These are best used to raise awareness and to remind the public of larger messages communicated in a different way.

Figure 5.6 What would you do if you found a little bird in the woods? Responses given before and after two years of educational activities.

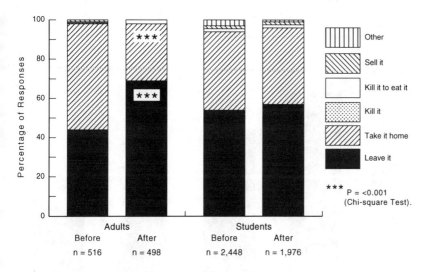

Figure 5.7 What would you do if you found a snake in the woods? Responses given before and after two years of educational activities.

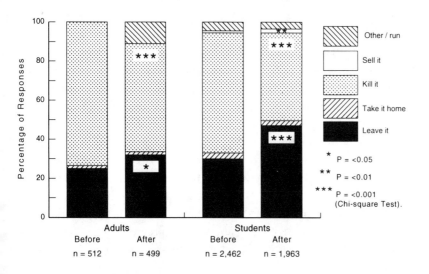

Figure 5.8 Where did you see or hear of the golden lion tamarin?   Responses given by adults of the municipality of Silva Jardim after two years of educational activities.

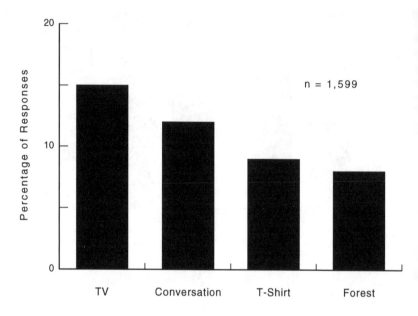

In this rural community, much information is transmitted by word of mouth and personal observation. More recent project activities have taken this into account.

In addition to the surveys, the Golden Lion Tamarin Project has collected other types of data that indicate significant progress toward our objectives. More than twenty illegally held golden lion tamarins (approximately 4 percent of the wild population of the species) and twenty-five maned sloths (*Bradypus torquatus*), another endangered species endemic to the region, have been voluntarily returned to the reserve since our work began. Although tax benefits did not attract landowners to preserve their forests as we had originally hoped, the educational team discovered that the landowners wanted to have tamarins in their forests. Reintroduction has thus become a tool for saving habitat. After agreeing to protect their forest, ten landowners have received tamarins on their land. Others who already had wild tamarins have joined the group. They, their families, and their farm workers are actively involved in monitoring the animals' progress. Other landowners are included on a waiting list, but more are still needed.

The golden lion tamarin has truly become a Brazilian symbol for Atlantic forest conservation. The project today has many more requests for advice, materials, internships, and information than it can fill. The documentation of the results of this educational program has called attention in Brazil to the importance of education as a natural resource management tool. Many conservation activities have been initiated by local communities themselves. This includes Rio de Janeiro where our only contact with the public was through the mass media, as well as in our primary target region immediately surrounding the Poço das Antas Reserve. The Brazilian federal Environment Institute, which previously had barred visitors to the reserve, has constructed the first building dedicated to community and visitor education in any Brazilian national biological reserve. An unseasonal fire that occurred in the reserve in 1990, although devastating to the habitat, demonstrated the level of public support that this project has developed for the conservation of the reserve. Whereas our surveys showed that in 1983 almost no one in the region knew the purpose of the Poço das Antas Reserve, or that it even existed, the outpouring of local, state, and federal support to combat the 1990 fire was unprecedented for any protected area in Brazil. The new educational center in the Poço das Antas Reserve and the reintroduced tamarins in the forest of a nearby farm were part of an ecotourism itinerary for several hundred visitors who were in nearby Rio de Janeiro for the United Nations Conference on the Environment and Development in 1992.

Step 7—Recycling

Our continual informal evaluations have helped us to improve our methods as we developed the program. The results of the formal surveys, as well as concrete evidence of progress toward our goals, have enabled us to determine the cost-effectiveness of many of our individual project activities. With this information, the project team can better decide which activities to continue over the long term and where new activities must be directed.

The project has managed to bring the local and even the national public to the critical point of awareness of the problems of a disap-pearing species and its forest. More widespread behavioral changes require a continued effort over the long term. As a result of the project ecologists' evaluation of efforts and advances in 1992 in determining the status of the wild population of golden lion tamarins and that of all available habitat, the project's educational program has reprioritized actions. The project now knows that to guarantee survival of golden lion tamarins in the wild for the next two hundred years, it must increase the amount of forest habitat under protection from 10,550 hectares to 25,000 hectares by the year 2025. To achieve this goal, educational efforts in the next few years must focus much more intensively on landowners and other adults in the areas of targeted remaining forest islands. The entire project is working hard to organize a stable project structure that can assure sufficient resources for project components to achieve their objectives. We are convinced that it is a continued systematic team effort—including ecological research, habitat and species management, and public support and involvement—that will assure the future of the golden lion tamarins and their Atlantic forest.

Acknowledgments

We would like to acknowledge the contribution of all those organizations and individuals involved over the years in the conception and implementation of the Golden Lion Tamarin Conservation Program, in particular, those who worked with us as a part of the project's education team: Percília Maria Ferreira Machado, Norma Silva Araújo Rodrigues, Maria Sônia de Oliveira, Rita de Cássia Santos Gonçalves, Rosinete Ferreira Pinheiro, Lenimar Christina dos Santos Alcântara, and Denise Marçal Rambaldi. Without their vision, ideas, perseverance, dedication, professionalism, and hard work, there would have been no real experiences from which to draw these conclusions. We wish to thank Ruth Flanagan and Carlos Miller for their assistance in tabulating the survey data. In addition, we acknowledge the commitment of the World Wide Fund for Nature (WWF), the Brazilian Institute for the Environment and Renewable Natural Resources (IBAMA), the Smithsonian Institution—National Zoological Park, the Canadian Embassy in Brazil, the Roberto Marinho Foundation, the O Boticário Foundation, the Frankfurt Zoological Society, and the Friends of the National Zoo, whose financial support has made the educational effort of the Golden Lion Tamarin Project possible. We wish to thank James Dietz for his assistance in the statistical analysis of our evaluation data and his personal support of our involvement in this and other conservation efforts. We dedicate this chapter to Denise Marçal Rambaldi and the current education team of the Golden Lion Tamarin Project who are now using what we learned in the effort's first years to modify and continue the program to achieve its long-term goals.

6

Marketing the Conservation Message: Using Parrots to Promote Protection and Pride in the Caribbean

::

Paul J. Butler

Conservation is a difficult concept to sell, especially in developing countries where it is perceived by many as a barrier to material progress. One person's scenic forest vista is another's vision of land ripe for clearance and cultivation.

The concept of "selling" environmental protection through conservation marketing programs has been very successful in the small islands of the Caribbean. Using endemic, endangered parrots as emotive keys to engender feelings of nationalism and pride, such programs have helped to bring these birds and their habitats back from the brink of extinction.

PLANNING

We are constantly told that conservation is not antidevelopment and that sustainable growth must be built on the husbanding and wise use of the planet's natural resources. Although this might be true in the long term, it is difficult to demonstrate in the short term. When one is eking out a living, only today matters. Leaving the seed tree and taking only those saplings that would otherwise die might make ecological sense. But to the subsistence woodsman, the larger the tree the more timber or charcoal it will yield and thus the more money he can make—money that he needs today. Even if people do not harbor negative environmental attitudes, they are often apathetic. Many people often view the environment as having little to do with their day-to-day lives and see expenditures on its protection as wasted resources better spent on the provision of schools, clinics, and roads, and the generation of employment.

The Institute of Social and Economic Research (1980) conducted a questionnaire survey under the auspices of the Man and Biosphere Program in four Caribbean territories. Respondents were asked about the seriousness of selected environmental hazards. When questioned about deforestation, a scant 26 percent of Saint Vincentians described it as being "very serious." Yet in almost the same year, a study found that agricultural development for banana production had resulted in the loss of almost all forested areas in the Mesopotamia region of Saint Vincent (Lambet 1983).

Ignorance and indifference spill over into resource management. Although legislation and reserves may exist, the former are often unenforced while the latter may exist only on paper. The islands of the eastern Caribbean have "protected" their forest and wildlife resources for decades through the enactment of legislation and the establishment of forest reserves, national parks, and conservation areas. Despite this, deforestation and reserve encroachment has continued, as has the hunting and taking of protected wildlife, including the region's endemic, and now highly endangered, parrots.

Indeed, for almost ninety years no wildlife offenses were recorded in Saint Lucia during a period when it was estimated that more than forty parrots per year were shot illegally for food or trade (Wingate 1969). Even in cases when offenders are taken to court, wildlife offenses are not considered serious. The penalties handed down by local magistrates are often inadequate to serve as an effective deterrent.

If we are to make conservation of the environment a daily reality in the actions of the rural poor, the environment will have to deliver tangible economic benefits in the short term. These benefits must not only be payable to the government but also at the community level. Providing fast-growing fuelwood species as an alternative to using mangroves for charcoal; opening up areas to tourism, and then training

Puppet Show at the RARE Center, St. Lucia (*photo by P. J. Butler*).

and employing local guides; and developing markets for less ecologically damaging crops are all examples of needed action in the region.

Hand in hand with making the environment pay must come initiatives in environmental education. In our case it may be more truthful to say that our hopes are not so much to "educate" the masses, but rather to manipulate their thoughts and actions to conform to what we consider is in their best interest. Where this is being attempted, environmental education would be more accurately termed *environmental marketing*. Parallels can be drawn between selling a difficult product and "selling" a difficult concept, that of conservation. For example, in theory it should be impossible to sell cigarettes; not only are they harmful to the smoker's health, but warnings are even written on the packet. Yet millions are sold daily. The marketplace is filled with synthetic foods and products that make fanciful claims—yet these products sell as well.

Conservation marketing programs being carried out in the Caribbean suggest that approaches using nationalism and pride as emotive keys can have dramatic results. This can translate into attitudinal changes followed by environmental action. These island nations have proved to be a good testing ground for this concept. Few places face a more serious conservation dilemma than these micro-states. Faced with the triple effects of rapidly rising populations, high unemployment, and increasing material expectations, tremendous pressure is being placed on their physical environment.

The following factors aid in the dissemination of conservation messages in the Caribbean:

1. These societies have youthful populations with a high percentage attending some type of school. In the eastern Caribbean, between 23 percent and 28 percent of island populations attend school. This includes both primary and secondary schools in Dominica and Saint Vincent, respectively. Materials targeting this sector will reach a considerable proportion of the populace.

2. Family size is large. In Saint Vincent, families average five members; thus information disseminated at the household level can be especially effective.

3. The communication media often guarantee government access to radio or television broadcasts and to press releases, affording an ideal opportunity to direct environmental messages to a captive audience.

4. There is a paucity of locally produced educational materials, yet teachers wish to use information relating to their own country. Materials produced that fulfill this need are readily accepted and used.

5. A strong sense of national pride permeates these West Indian societies, many of which have only recently gained their independence. Pride can be a powerful emotion and serves as a vital key to the campaigns outlined below.

RARE Center for Tropical Conservation

RARE Center for Tropical Conservation is a nonprofit organization based in Philadelphia. Its goal is to develop innovative programs that protect endangered tropical wildlife and ecosystems. These programs are developed by RARE Center staff and a volunteer board of trustees, which includes conservationists, scientists, and business people with broad experience in tropical America. Programs are always implemented in partnership with government agencies and conservation groups in host countries—because conservation is only sustainable when it is locally supported and maintained.

RARE Center's Conservation Education Campaign (CEC). For the past five years RARE Center has been actively involved in promoting protection and wildlife conservation through pride. Its CEC programs are now being successfully implemented by local counterparts in ten Caribbean nations. RARE Center provides these counterparts with a "recipe book" (the CEC manual), basic ingredients (posters, badges, and vehicles), and a lot of advice and encouragement. The result is a year-long educational program full of local flavor that reaches out to every segment of a country's population.

Using a target animal, such as an endemic or endangered bird, the program focuses attention on the species and its habitat. Outreach techniques include posters, badges, songs, billboards, bumper stickers, music videos, puppet shows, school presentations, and church sermons.

The result is a dramatic increase in public support for government measures to protect the environment. In the Caribbean, CEC programs have sparked the establishment of forest reserves as well as changes in legislation.

The goal of the marketing campaign described in this chapter is to rally grassroots support around a living symbol in order to promote its own conservation, and to subsequently use it as a "spokesperson" for the wider environment. The selection of a suitable target species on which to focus the campaign is thus a critical step. Ideally the species should be endemic, symbolizing the uniqueness of the host country; reside in a critical habitat that provides a focus for the project; and be "sexy" and "marketable." The use of a national symbol facilitates the campaign, since a linkage to nationalism is direct and can be used to foster pride. Furthermore, the target species should carry "no baggage," such as being a pest species, as it is far easier to change apathetic attitudes than negative ones.

Birds make ideal target species. They are a good indicator species of a healthy environment, and many eastern Caribbean islands already have designated national birds. Flagship species, such as the parrots of the eastern Caribbean, carry few, if any, negative attributes, and national pride is nonpolitical and a natural rallying point for newly independent peoples. The campaign's goal is not simply to reach out to a single segment of the nation but rather to reach out to the entire population, striving to build massive support over a relatively short period of time, usually a year.

A number of Caribbean nations (e.g., Saint Lucia, Saint Vincent,

Dominica, and Montserrat) are currently undertaking conservation marketing programs to promote environmental pride. In most cases these projects focus attention on existing national birds. In other Caribbean nations, like Grenada, the government has declared a new national bird to facilitate the program. The Bahama parrot was declared a quincentennial symbol of that island in recognition of the five hundredth anniversary of Columbus's first landing there. This provided a focal point for the island's conservation program. Under the direction of the islands' forestry departments and/or national trusts, and with financing and technical assistance from RARE, these Caribbean islands are achieving spectacular results.

The following notions reflect the philosophy behind RARE Center's Caribbean Education Campaign:

1. Any conservation program that relies exclusively on foreign aid is doomed to failure. Too often work ceases when the funds are exhausted. To prevent this, local businesses must be encouraged to support environmental initiatives through the financing of conservation materials and activities that link local sponsors to a popular cause.

2. Reliance on external technical assistance does not provide local conservationists with lasting tools to enact or continue their projects. Involving and training forestry or National Trust personnel in every aspect of the work promotes greater local commitment long after foreign agency involvement has departed.

3. The use of proven marketing techniques with the islands' colorful national birds as flagship species and national pride as the emotive key can generate widespread grassroots support. This support translates into advocacy for wildlife conservation and can be used to promote a more general environmental ethic.

RARE Center provides materials, such as posters, badges and technical assistance; the local counterparts do the rest.

IMPLEMENTATION

As in any marketing scheme the program commences with a "consumer" research study, with 1 percent of the island's population being surveyed by questionnaire. The questionnaire enumerators are told to go back into their communities and to randomly survey the inhabitants.

Billboard on St. Lucia using the "target animal" theme (*photo by P. J. Butler*).

They are told that good sites for interviewing include shops, post offices, banks, schools, churches, and buses.

Since the enumerators are all volunteers and receive only minimal training some bias is likely to occur, although our analysis has consistently shown that returns *broadly* reflect real life. Questionnaires are analyzed by age category and by sector. Because the population of the islands varies greatly, there is a large variation in the number of individuals surveyed. In the Bahamas more than 2,000 questionnaires were distributed, while in the Caymans the figure was 254.

Distribution is by district, parish, or political constituency and is based on 1 percent of that area's population as determined by the 1980 census. Surveys take about three weeks to complete. Each volunteer enumerator—usually from the local Forestry Department or a conservation NGO (nongovernment organization)—is given between thirty and fifty questionnaires and is responsible for their return. These volunteers are not penalized if some questionnaires are returned uncompleted, since it is obviously better to have ten correctly completed forms than thirty that have been faked.

To cope with low literacy levels, the questionnaire is simple in format

Table 6.1. Forestry and Wildlife Division Questionnaire

Sector: _____
(To be completed by enumerator)

Dear Friend,

As Dominicans we should cherish our natural environment and protect it.

Symbolic of our island's natural beauty is its national bird, and by answering the following questions you will help us to protect it and ensure that we never lose our national pride.

Thank you for your assistance.

(1) What is the national bird of Dominica?
    1. _____ 2. Don't know ( )

(2) Is it only to be found in Dominica?
    1. Yes ( )   2. No ( )   3. Don't know ( )

(2a) If "No," where else does it live? _____

(3) How scarce is our national bird?

    1. Less than 100 remain   ( )
    2. 101–250 remain   ( )
    3. 251–500 remain   ( )
    4. 501–1,000 remain   ( )
    5. More than 1,000 remain ( )
    6. Don't know   ( )

(4) What is one of the main reasons for our national bird becoming rare?
    1. _____ 2. Don't know ( )

(5) Do you think that our national bird is a good choice?
    1. Yes ( )   2. No ( )   3. Don't know ( )

(6) What is the fine or penalty for hunting / shooting our national bird?
    1. $48 ( )   2. $250 ( )   3. $2,500 ( )   4. $5,000 ( )   5. Don't know ( )

(7) What is the fine / penalty for illegally clearing lands in the forest reserve?
    1. $48 ( )   2. $240 ( )   3. $720 ( )   4. Don't know ( )

(8) Protecting our national bird is going to cost money that could be used for other things. Do you think it is important that the government spend time and money on our national bird?
    1. Not important ( )   2. Important ( )   3. Very important ( )   4. Don't know ( )

(9) Why? _____

Biographical Data

(10) What is your age?
    1. 1–11 years ( )   2. 12–16 ( )   3. 17–25 ( )   4. 26–35 ( )
    5. 36–45 ( )   6. 46–55 ( )   7. 56–65 ( )   8. 65+ ( )

(11) What is your job?
    1. Government employee ( ) 2. Farmer/Laborer ( ) 3. Private sector ( ) 4. Unemployed ( )
    5. Housewife ( )   6. Student ( )   7. Other: _____

(12) Do you listen to the radio?
    1. Every day ( )   2. Occasionally ( )   3. No ( )

(13) What is your favorite radio program? _____

(14) Do you read the local paper?
    1. Yes ( )   2. No ( )

You do not need to write your name on this form.

Return to: Forestry Division
           Ministry of Agriculture, Trade, Industry, and Tourism
           Botanical Gardens
           Roseau
           Commonwealth of Dominica

Thank you.

(table 6.1). While one of its functions is to gather data, it plays an equally important role in initiating the program's educational component. The survey is used to determine existing levels of knowledge about the target species and its habitat, and attitudes toward its conservation.

The questionnaire also assists in determining the percentage of the population that listens to the radio and/or reads newspapers. This information aids in ascertaining the type and format of educational materials to be developed. Information concerning favorite programs is also solicited in order that these can be targeted during the project.

Perhaps most important, the survey involves all local resource managers, such as forest officers, who act as the enumerators or agents for its distribution, and whose responsibility it is to distribute them in the communities where they live and work. The number of enumerators depends on the number of questionnaires distributed; in the Caymans eight volunteers were used, while in the Bahamas more than seventy were needed!

After respondents have completed the questionnaire they are informed of the correct responses relating to the target species and conservation legislation. In addition, they are informed of the plight of the target species and the multiple benefits of its habitat. This serves to begin the process of stimulating awareness and knowledge of the bird and its environment. As a token for their assistance, respondents are given a colorful badge depicting the target species.

The questionnaires' results suggest that the island's population is subdivided into a number of target groups, and materials are produced for each. The first audience to be addressed is the nation's children. Forestry staff have visited all the schools in Saint Lucia, Saint Vincent, and Dominica, and have made presentations to more than 90 percent of the islands' children. In Saint Lucia and Dominica the project team dressed up as parrots as part of the presentation. Conservation songs were taught and badges distributed at each school.

For younger children the school component has been supplemented with the development of puppet shows, and in all three of these islands the program is complemented by the monthly production of an environmental newspaper which uses the target species to teach the paper's readers about other environmental problems facing their island home. Written, funded, and produced locally, these handouts also appear as supplements in local newspapers.

School dropouts and teenagers are targeted through the use of music, dance, and theater. Local musicians and artists are encouraged to write lyrics and tunes promoting conservation and national pride. Local musicians are invited to a meeting where they are given an overview of the target species, its status and plight. They are invited to listen to conservation songs from neighboring territories and challenged to do better. Musicians are each given posters, badges, and fact sheets which serve as a modest incentive and provide factual details that can be included in any song that they may write.

School programs all follow the same kind of format with the objective to visit all primary and secondary schools and to speak to as many children as possible. These school visitations serve to introduce students to the wildlife and forest habitat of their surrounding area. Emphasis is placed on how wildlife help us in many different ways and on the laws protecting wildlife. Participation of primary school students is encouraged through interactive questions, as well as singing and dancing to a conservation theme song appropriate for the program. Secondary school programs offer a more formal slide presentation given by a local counterpart.

Colorful posters depict the target species and link its survival to national self-esteem. This is achieved through the use of a flag or by slogans such as, "To protect your national bird is to love your country." These are distributed throughout the participating country, and are displayed in store windows, bars, health centers, post offices, and police stations.

Recording studios and television stations are urged to support the cause by providing assistance in producing audio and video tapes for public broadcast. Television and radio stations in the Caribbean have strong links to the government; indeed many receive financial assistance from the government. As such, it is not difficult to persuade them to air public service broadcasts and conservation songs. The conservation program also appeals to their sense of national pride. They are asked to give maximum air time to any songs produced or music videos released. In Dominica six songs were recorded, including reggae, cadence, and gospel styles. In addition, a ten-song, forty-five-minute children's musical depicting the plight of the island's national bird also was produced by a local music school.

Meetings are held with religious leaders of all denominations. They are told of the plight of one of God's creatures and of the interdependence between man and the environment. Sample sermons, prayer readings, and other information is supplied, and participating priests and pastors are invited to support the program by addressing their respective congregations on an environmental theme. The methodology employed with churches varies. In the Bahamas, church leaders were invited to a meeting and given a package of materials that included such items as sample environmental sermons, fact sheets and posters. In Dominica the Catholic bishop prepared a sermon and sent it out to all churches under his "jurisdiction."

All farmers and youth and community groups are also visited to further spread the conservation message. Meetings with farmers are held through their cooperative groups; for example, in Dominica we visited all the banana cooperatives at their monthly meetings. Community groups, such as Rotary and Lions clubs, are visited at their regular luncheon meetings.

Businesses are encouraged to link their products to the conservation

Parrot key ring on St. Lucia, a product that reinforces the conservation message (*photo by P. J. Butler*).

of the target species and to sponsor booklets, bags, bumper stickers, and other educational materials. In St. Vincent the local brewery included a painting of a St. Vincent parrot (*Amazona guildingii*) on the label of their Bitter Lemon, along with the motto "*Save our National Bird.*" These efforts are supplemented in turn by the production of large colorful billboards erected at prominent roadside intersections and in urban parks.

PRODUCT

After the first year, the questionnaire survey is repeated using the same questions and the same approximate 1 percent sample size (a thousand people in Saint Vincent, twenty-five hundred in the Bahamas, and so forth). Response return rates varied from 64 percent in Saint Lucia to 100 percent in the Cayman Islands. In all cases the results have been dramatic. In Grenada post-project results recorded 86 percent (up from 11 percent in the pre-project survey) of respondents knowing the Grenada dove (*Leptotila wellsi*) to be their national bird, and in St.

Vincent more than 60 percent (up from 35 percent in the pre-project survey) knew the population status of the St. Vincent parrot. Seventy-two percent (up from 55 percent in the pre-project survey) realized this species to be endemic, and 24 percent (up from 1 percent in the pre-project survey) knew the legislative protection afforded this species. Most important, 93 percent of the surveyed population on St. Vincent believed it to be "important" or "very important" for the government to spend time and money protecting the parrot and its forest home (Butler 1988).

In response to this overwhelming support, the government of Saint Vincent and the Grenadines revised its wildlife legislation, ratified CITES (Convention on International Trade in Endangered Species), designated preserves, and constructed a captive breeding complex for their endemic parrot, the focus of our program.

Today, the national bird also has become a voice for a variety of other environmental issues. As a caricature on billboards and in "Vincie's Nature Notes," the parrot continues to advocate water quality, a litter-free environment, and even the protection of marine resources.

Similar changes in awareness have been noted in Dominica, where as a result of a plea for assistance to secure critical parrot habitat, more than 40 percent of the nation's school children contributed cash, and an additional 40 percent signed a petition saying that they would have contributed if they had had any money (Butler 1989).

These educational programs are beginning to pay dividends for the targeted species. In Saint Lucia the hunting and illegal trapping of the Saint Lucia parrot (*Amazona versicolor*) has ceased. Today its population is increasing and its range is expanding. The government has allocated increased resources toward forest protection and sustainable use. In less than a decade, expenditure on forest management has increased almost tenfold and harvesting has been reduced to minimal levels. This has enabled the Forestry Department to better train its officers, to establish community woodlot projects, and to develop income- and employment-generating nature trails.

The success of these programs has led the RARE Center to publish a manual outlining the conservation-marketing concept. This is now being provided to Caribbean nations, and programs are in various stages of implementation on eight islands. The manual is directed at mid-level technical officers and educators who are actively involved in initiating and implementing species-related conservation programs. It serves to guide its user through a step-by-step process of setting up a national campaign to protect a target species.

The core of the manual comprises a series of twelve monthly chapters that cover a total of fifty-eight tasks. These include activities such as conducting a questionnaire survey and producing bumper stickers, puppet shows, and music videos. The pages of the manual are printed in different colors. Sample letters, press releases, and work sheets are yellow, and designs for costumes and puppet shows are blue. As project coordinators progress through the manual, these samples will be replaced with copies of their group's own work. Also included is information on census techniques, sample wildlife legislation, and copies of slides, tapes, and videos to illustrate similar efforts in the region.

It is difficult to assess which program techniques are the most effective because the scope of the project is so broad and the individual counterparts vary in their skills. Nonetheless, let us look at the achievements of our Bahamian counterpart as an example:

- Bahama parrot (*Amazona leucocephala bahamensis*) declared national Quincentennial symbol by the Bahamian government
- almost 2 percent of the population, on the four target islands of New Providence, Grand Bahama, Abaco, and Inagua, sampled in the pre- and post-project questionnaires
- 5,000 fact sheets on the Bahama parrot printed and distributed
- school song produced and taught to more than 20,000 children
- 8,000 Bahama parrot posters distributed across the four target islands
- 870 tennis-ball puppets produced for use in primary schools
- 2 costumes designed and constructed for use in school visitation and community outreach programs
- some 27,750 schoolchildren addressed in more than 75 schools across the four target islands
- 700 entries from 39 schools on three islands returned in a nationwide Bahama parrot art competition
- minister of agriculture received more than 800 letters from schoolchildren requesting the establishment of a national park on Abaco (as a percentage of the total population, this equals the U.S. president receiving 1.5 million letters)

- 26,500 Bahama parrot bumper stickers donated by a local corporate sponsor
- Bahama parrot rap song hit Bahamian radio stations and discotheques and was made into a music video
- community groups and media targeted
- parrot costume wins Junkanoo Parade competition watched by tens of thousands of spectators
- 6,000 Bahamians wore Bahama parrot T-shirts on national T-shirt day pledging allegiance to the conservation campaign
- churches preached conservation messages on nationwide sermon day
- 29 local businesses pledged support and provided more than $30,000 in sponsorship to program components
- local grocery store printed 2.5 million grocery bags advertising the Bahama parrot and its conservation needs
- 16 billboards produced and erected on the four target islands
- 8-page newspaper supplement on the Bahama parrot included in *The Tribune,* a Bahamian newspaper with nationwide readership
- an A-to-Z environmental booklet for local schoolchildren produced and distributed
- 2,000 legislation booklets printed and distributed to members of the police, customs, and defense forces, as well as to members of the public
- 10 million letters franked with parrot cancellation stamp
- government of the Bahamas introduced a new dollar bill portraying the Bahama parrot; 5 million now in circulation

Can this type of program be replicated outside of small island nations? Probably not, as its success relies on the close-knit makeup of small societies, the accessibility of local politicians, and the acceptance of low levels of technology.

The programs' achievements also have much to do with linking preservation to pride—an emotion common in small, newly independent nations—as well as using a colorful, easily recognizable animal. It would be far more difficult, perhaps impossible, to achieve results using a deadly spider.

RARE Center is planning to test and adapt the concept in mainland South America and to work with target species other than birds. Only when the results of these programs are known will we understand the wider potential of using marketing methods to sell the conservation ethic.

Ten years after implementing the program in Saint Lucia a questionnaire survey was carried out to monitor environmental knowledge and perceptions. Forty-eight percent of the respondents knew the penalties protecting the island's wildlife, and 46 percent knew those for reserve protection. Overwhelming support remained for the protection of the target species; 83 percent of the respondents believed that it was "important" that the government spend time and money protecting the parrot and its rain forest home (Butler 1991a, 1991b).

Acknowledgments

The campaigns described here are the work of many dedicated individuals; most important were the officers of the forestry departments of Saint Lucia, Saint Vincent and the Grenadines, and Dominica, without whom nothing would have been achieved.

I should also like to thank Gabriel Charles, Brian James, Anita James, Alleyne Regis, Felix Gregoire, Arlington James, Brian Johnson, Nigel Weekes, Ruth Reddock, Pat Scharr, Keith Campbell, Maurice Isaacs, Francis Garraway, Gary Larson, Susan Larson, Monique Clarke, and Lynn Gape. All have proved invaluable in working with conservation marketing campaigns.

7

Comprehensive Approaches for Saving Bats

■■
■■

Patricia A. Morton and
Mari J. Murphy

Few animals are as poorly understood as bats. After centuries of myth and superstition, people nearly everywhere fear and persecute them, hunting some species to extinction and threatening the survival of many more. Yet the nearly one thousand species of bats are among our most diverse and beneficial animals. Insectivorous bats are the most important predators of night-flying insects; other bats pollinate flowers and disperse seeds in ecosystems from rain forests to deserts. As bats decline, entire systems are threatened, placing the survival of numerous other animals and plants at risk.

Bat Conservation International (BCI) was founded in 1982 to address the alarming decline of bats worldwide. Today thousands of educators, organizations, agencies, and conservationists depend on BCI as a primary source of information about bats. BCI audiovisual programs, printed material, and activity books are the basis for educational outreach from the classroom to the community and for many state, federal, and international education efforts about bats.

PLANNING

Most of the world's bat species are not well known nor are their needs understood. Additional scientific knowledge is essential for saving both bats and the habitats that rely on them. What we do know is that bats are among nature's most important animals, increasingly recognized by biologists as "keystone" species. This is especially true in rain forests, where bat diversity is at its highest.

Rain forest conservation is one of today's most urgent environmental issues. Bats constitute a majority of all mammals in tropical forests, yet they are frequently ignored in management plans and preservation efforts. Throughout the world's tropics, plants that depend on bats for pollination or seed dispersal are also often of great economic importance. Bat-dependent fruits and products, such as durian fruit, hardwood timbers, and medicinals, add millions of dollars to local and national economies, especially in developing countries. Documentation of the vital role of bats to economically important crops and to rain forest regeneration is often the key to convincing governments and others to protect them.

In Latin America, countless thousands of bats essential to rain forest maintenance are destroyed each year in misdirected vampire bat control campaigns. Finding solutions to legitimate problems that have major impacts on bat survival, such as vampire control, will be an important focus in the decade ahead.

In the United States nearly 40 percent of our bat species are on the federal endangered list or are candidates for it (Anonymous 1989). The single most significant cause is repeated disturbance and vandalism at bat roosts. Formerly vast populations at some sites have declined by as much as 99 percent (Cockrum 1970), leaving countless millions of insects without their major predators to keep them in check. Protection of important bat-roosting sites is critical, and education is equally vital.

Education is perhaps the most essential component to lasting success in any conservation initiative. Nowhere is this more true than in bat conservation, since bats are destroyed largely because of ignorance and misunderstanding. As long as people hold false beliefs about bats, they will continue to fear and persecute them. A major thrust of BCI's efforts is therefore directed toward education.

Replacing myths with facts and teaching people at all levels about the importance of bats is critical to saving these animals. Thus it is

BCI bat study workshops provide professional biologists and others with the techniques needed to study bats. Here, participants receive instructions from Dr. Brock Fenton on using light-tagging to observe bat foraging behavior (*photo by P. A. Morton*).

important to provide accurate information and a broad range of expertise about bats to health, agricultural, and government agencies, to conservation planners, educators, the news media, and the public. To disseminate such information and to help resolve common bat-human conflicts, such as bats entering buildings, BCI makes use of its international scientific advisory board and network of colleagues and active members.

Educational resources include publications and audiovisual programs addressing both international and domestic issues, as well as general information about bats. A strong emphasis is on providing innovative and entertaining classroom materials for environmental and science educators. Learning the truth about bats before stereotypes become established is key to breaking the cycle of misinformation in future generations.

A comprehensive bibliographic database of scientific literature about bats and the world's largest collection of bat photographs aids in educational efforts. Including some ninety thousand transparencies, the photo collection of bat biologist Dr. Merlin Tuttle documents bat behavior on all continents where bats occur. Scientists, educators, and publishers rely on this unique collection for a wide variety of needs.

IMPLEMENTATION

Bat Conservation International is a nonprofit organization supported by membership contributions and grants used for public education, research, and conservation of bats. Membership dues support base operations, conservation, research, and many educational efforts; specific projects are funded through grants and restricted donations.

With its multitude of resources, BCI is in a strong position to effect change. BCI's most important educational resource is its photographic slide collection. Bats are difficult to understand and appreciate because they are active only at night when most people cannot observe or become familiar with them. Without handsome and descriptive photographs, it would be almost impossible to convince people that bats are harmless and as attractive as other more popular animals. Providing strong visual images of bats in their natural environment, such as pollinating flowers or catching insects, also helps persuade people that bats are beneficial.

The photo collection is used extensively by the communication media in newspapers, magazines, textbooks, encyclopedias, and wildlife books, including many for youth. Major educational articles using these photographs have introduced people to bats in more than fifty countries. These images have contributed more than any single resource to bat conservation progress over the past decade.

Among BCI's primary objectives are educating the public and expanding its network of conservation professionals. Creating ways for these groups to participate and become active is central to achieving BCI's educational goals. BCI receives frequent requests for technical assistance with conservation planning from state and federal natural resource agencies where the need is high, yet few staff members have had any experience working with bats. To facilitate training of this important group, BCI contracted with Canadian bat biologist Dr. Brock Fenton to organize bat study workshops for professional biologists. This collaboration resulted in a ten-day field workshop to provide training in

Educating the next generation is key to breaking the cycle of misinformation about bats. Author Patricia Morton introduces children to a live bat as part of her educational campaign to raise awareness about the importance of bats in Costa Rica (*photo by S. Poisson*).

the technical skills needed to census and study bats. The workshops have filled to capacity each year.

Graduates are now making major conservation contributions throughout the United States, Canada, and Mexico by functioning as bat experts who can assist with local initiatives and problems. For example, Terri Marceron, assistant district ranger for the Lewis and Clark National Forest in Montana, took the workshop to learn more about bats for her conservation education work. Today she travels nationally and internationally to teach Forest Service workers how to implement regional forest plans that include emphasizing the importance of forest habitat to bat survival.

The success of the ten-day workshop led to the creation of one-day workshops designed specifically for active members and the lay public. Held twice a year at various sites in North America, these workshops provide participants with the basics of bat biology and the techniques for conducting educational programs for the public. Small-group activities include hands-on experience with live bats.

Sponsored trips offer another opportunity to become involved and more knowledgeable about bats. International ecotours are organized each year, allowing participants to become acquainted firsthand with tropical bat faunas and the ecosystems that depend on bats for survival.

Workshops and ecotours greatly expand BCI's information network and help raise public awareness about bats. The rapid growth and success in changing attitudes about bats is due, in no small part, to a strong advocacy network. Members purchase audiovisual programs which they then show in their communities. Some go on to become local celebrities and often gain attention from local news media, allowing them to reach an even greater audience. Becoming a community bat advocate can be rewarding, benefiting both bats and people. Bats are exceptionally interesting animals, and watching a friend or neighbor make the transition from fear to fascination is both fun and satisfying. It is this "multiplier effect," one person educating others, that has led to wide dispersal of the truth about bats. The results are significant positive attitude changes about bats, especially in North America. This has in turn led to a large increase in the number of positive articles in magazines and newspapers. Negative press about bats now draws numerous angry letters from the public, which frequently leads to a retraction, sometimes accompanied by a factual, pro-bat article.

The moniker "born again" aptly describes some avid bat conservationists. Many adults grew up disliking bats due to myths and superstitions they learned as children. Feeling guilty for behavior that may have hurt bats, and wanting to make up for past misdeeds, they become assertive conservationists who actively campaign for bats. Their tools are factual information and well-designed educational materials.

The educational efforts of BCI and its members have changed the climate for bat conservation, resulting in projects that would otherwise not have been possible. To facilitate conservation initiatives, BCI frequently works with other organizations. In Texas, partnerships with the Texas Parks and Wildlife Department and Texas Nature Conservancy served to assist with critical site protection. Providing management plans, designing interpretive exhibits at sites open to the public, and training stewards to give public presentations about the bats at protected sites are other valuable conservation and educational efforts.

Sharing resources to protect bats has also been successful in establishing international partnerships. A recent collaboration with Mexican bat biologists led to a series of cave surveys in northern Mexico to deter-

Beneficial bats, necessary for the regeneration of tropical forests, are often the victims in misdirected vampire bat control efforts in Latin America. This long-tongued bat (*Glossophaga soricina*) is an important pollinator of many rain-forest plants (*photo by M. D. Tuttle, Bat Conservation International*).

mine the status of bat populations and site conditions for the migratory Mexican free-tailed bat (*Tadarida brasiliensis*). The survey revealed that most sites had been vandalized, indicating severe population declines, from 95 to 100 percent at half the sites (Moreno and Robertson 1992). Follow-up public education campaigns for the communities around these Mexican caves are now being implemented.

PRODUCT

As a resource center for bats, BCI is often the catalyst for action, eliciting the assistance of others to achieve organizational objectives. Educational campaigns, protection of critical bat habitat, and advancement of scientific knowledge about this group of mammals all benefit from collaboration. Nowhere has this been more apparent than with educational initiatives. Requests for help from around the world have led to several significant efforts.

In 1989 a hurricane struck American Samoa, stripping island forests of foliage and fruit, and driving thousands of starving flying fox bats to feed in home gardens. Teenagers with slingshots began killing them for sport. Le Vaomatua, a local conservation organization, alerted BCI, which then sent immediate financial help. As a result, Le Vaomatua was able to institute a mass media campaign to stop the killing of bats. At particular risk was a threatened species. Le Vaomatua produced newspaper advertisements and radio spots, and the public responded quickly to the plight of the bats. Many set out food for the hungry animals, and some even rescued and cared for the wounded. Local officials collected the slingshots, turning them in to fish and wildlife authorities. Within a few months after the hurricane, the forests began to recover and the bats returned to their natural habitat (Daschbach 1990).

In the mid-1980s BCI also responded to the need for help in stopping the poisoning of bat caves in Israel. Over many years the practice had decimated nearly 90 percent of the country's insectivorous bats, leading to a population explosion of noctuid moths, which in turn caused extensive crop damage (Makin and Mendelssohn 1985). Through the efforts of bat conservationists, the practice has since been stopped. In addition, BCI provided Israel's Mammal Information Center with photographs and information for a major traveling exhibit and audiovisual and other educational materials, which were translated into Hebrew. The materials are still in use and reach a broad group from youngsters and their parents to nature reserve rangers and government officials. As is true nearly everywhere, the problem for bats in Israel is one of education.

Few parts of the world are more ridden with myth and superstition about bats than Latin America. Bat diversity is high with about a third of the world's species found there. Included is *Desmodus rotundus,* the single species of bat that feeds on the blood of mammals. Found only in Latin America, vampires have proliferated with the expansion of human settlements and growth of the cattle industry. In some areas they have become significant agricultural pests. Because of misinformation about vampires, countless thousands of other bats are needlessly exterminated each year. Ranchers, mistaking all bats for vampires, indiscriminately eradicate hundreds of thousands of beneficial bats annually, sometimes completely destroying cave ecosystems as well.

In 1986 Morton launched an educational campaign in Costa Rica about the importance of tropical American bats (Morton 1991). Using BCI's photographic and advisory resources, she conducted an eighteen-

Bat conservation efforts in Thailand have resulted not only in benefits for bats but also for the local economy. These Thai students reap many benefits from the sale of guano fertilizer collected in a nearby bat cave (*photo by M. D. Tuttle, Bat Conservation International*).

month campaign in association with the Fundación de Educatión Ambiental of Costa Rica and World Wildlife Fund. She and Costa Rican colleagues traveled around the country giving programs to local communities. While Costa Rica has recorded 107 species of bats, Morton found in surveys conducted during her campaign that most people believed there were only a few kinds of bats and that most fed on blood. Through grassroots educational efforts and by using photos, displays of bat-dependent products, and live bat exhibits, she was able to dispel myths and provide the facts about Latin America's bats.

She also worked with the communication media to produce newspaper articles and television and radio interviews. Local veterinarians heard about her work and put her in contact with Ministry of Agriculture personnel in charge of vampire control. Today ministry veterinarians are some of the strongest proponents of bat conservation in Costa Rica and are now working with BCI to develop their own program to train technicians in the vampire control techniques that don't harm other species. Morton's campaign also resulted in the production of a book, poster, and audiovisual program about the importance of bats to Latin American ecosystems, resources that were distributed to many of Costa Rica's conservation agencies. Morton still hears from Costa Rican conservationists who continue to use the materials she developed.

A commitment has now been made to a long-term educational campaign of vampire bat management assistance in collaboration with Latin American colleagues. Legitimate vampire problems must be solved before people can be expected to participate in bat conservation initiatives. Educational materials about the identification and appropriate control of vampires are being developed. These will be distributed to agricultural schools and ministries, as well as to cattlemen's agencies, public and private academic institutions, and conservation organizations.

In Thailand educational efforts are needed to solve different problems. Collaboration with public and private agencies in Thailand has led to successful bat conservation efforts and improved conditions for people. In the early 1980s Tuttle visited several important bat caves in southwestern Thailand where extraction of guano (bat excrement) for fertilizer is a primary source of village revenue. Locals informed him that in the previous five years sales had dropped by 50 percent because of decreasing guano production. Tuttle determined that decline of the bats was the result of heavy poaching. Hunters provided restaurants with fruit and nectar bats, considered a delicacy in many parts of Asia. Thousands of insectivorous guano bats also became ensnared in poachers' nets each month. Unwanted, these bats were simply killed and discarded, decimating local guano bat populations.

Tuttle recommended to local officials that they hire a game warden to protect bats near the cave, reasoning that the cost of a warden's salary would more than be covered by the increased sale of guano. He also provided the mayor and local Buddhist monks, who owned the cave, with educational resources to help produce materials for the community and schools.

Eight years later Tuttle returned and was overwhelmed with the changes. Protection had been successful; the colony had greatly increased, and annual guano sales had risen from $12,000 to more than $88,600. The nightly emergence of bats was drawing busloads of tourists, and local vendors were profiting from the sale of refreshments and souvenirs. Local students now use educational materials developed from the original materials provided by BCI, and bat T-shirts are part of at least one school's uniform. Thanks to successful educational efforts, the

BCI, local caving groups, and several state and federal agencies joined forces in Tennessee to construct the 120-ton gate that now protects one of the world's largest bat hibernation sites (*photo by M. D. Tuttle, Bat Conservation International*).

Thai government designated the cave region as a nonhunting area, and the Royal Forest Department is creating broader protective legislation (Tuttle 1990).

The actions of bat conservationists have been the catalyst in saving other bat populations around the world. In 1989 intensive efforts by conservationists led to the protection of nine species of flying fox bats under the CITES treaty (Convention on International Trade in Endangered Species), which regulates international commercial trade (Graham 1989). Pacific island flying foxes, essential to the maintenance and regeneration of forests, had been decimated by unregulated hunting. Such hunting led to the extinction of several species and the endangerment of others, seriously jeopardizing fragile island ecosystems throughout the Pacific. An international conference organized by BCI followed, enabling wildlife managers from fourteen island nations and countries to meet with an international group of bat biologists to learn about the importance of their bats and to discuss solutions, many of which centered around educational initiatives.

To preserve the habitat of threatened and endangered flying foxes in Samoa, bat conservationists successfully led efforts by Samoan and U.S. government officials to create a 198-square-kilometer national park in American Samoa. This landmark legislation set aside land to establish the first park in the U.S. National Park Service to protect tropical rain forest as well as bat habitat. Many bat enthusiasts wrote letters of support, visited with congressional leaders, and assisted in helping to educate the Samoan and U.S. politicians about the importance of bats in maintaining the forests in the new national park. Bats and thousands of other animal and plant species are now protected there.

Education about bat conservation is vital to protecting essential habitat in many areas. Hubbards Cave in Tennessee provides shelter for six species of hibernating bats from much of the southeastern United States, including two endangered species. In 1984 an enormous gate was built across the entrance of the cave to protect bats from human disturbance and vandalism. The project was made possible through cooperative efforts of BCI, the Nature Conservancy, the National Guard, the U.S. Fish and Wildlife Service, and National Speleological Society caving groups from five states. It would not have been possible without substantial efforts by bat conservationists to educate the parties involved about the importance of the site.

As habitat is altered or destroyed, some bats have adapted to living in human-built structures. In Austin, Texas, more than a million Mexican free-tailed bats moved into spaces under a downtown bridge, today's largest urban bat colony in North America. City officials and residents were initially alarmed and planned to exterminate the bats. BCI convinced the city that not only were the bats harmless but that they also had great potential for drawing tourists to view the spectacular nightly flights. Thanks to positive national publicity, Austin is now famous for its bats. A large interpretive exhibit was constructed at the bridge to provide additional information about the bats. The bat colony also inspired the Austin school district to work with BCI on organizing bat clubs for elementary students. Along with their classmates, teachers, and parents, "Bat Awareness Teams" arrive at the bridge during bat flights to answer tourists' questions. The Austin experience has demonstrated that people and bats can live together in harmony and both benefit from the experience. Collaboration is now under way with the state highway commission to design additional bridges that provide roosting space for bats and to create space under existing bridges.

Biologist Marty Fujita visits an Asian market to collect data on the economic importance of bat-dependent products to cash-poor developing countries. In the BCI-sponsored project, her research revealed that more than three hundred plant species rely on bats for propagation in the Old World tropics (*photo source unknown*).

Activities by BCI, its colleagues, and members have dramatically increased public awareness about the importance of bats. Interest has also been heightened in the scientific community, and funding for bat-related research is becoming more readily available. In 1989 a multiyear study began on the importance of nectarivorous long-nosed bats to the pollination biology of three species of Sonoran Desert columnar cacti. Long-nosed bat populations have declined, and two species (*Leptonycteris curasoae* and *L. nivalis*) were declared endangered by the U.S. Fish and Wildlife Service in 1988. Funded by grants from the National Geographic Society and the Fish and Wildlife Foundation, the study is evaluating the role of these bats as pollinators of saguaro, cardon, and organ pipe cacti (Tuttle 1991). Understanding the relationship between the bats and cacti is essential to conservation planning for the Sonoran Desert ecosystem. Scientific discovery, such as the bat-cactus relationship, plays a major role in educational efforts to demonstrate to people the ecological values of bats and therefore the need to save them.

Studies on the regeneration of tropical forests are beginning to look at the important roles played by bats. Approximately half the mammal species in most tropical countries are bats, and ecologists are only beginning to realize their importance to a variety of ecosystems. The pollination and seed dispersal activities of tropical bats are essential to the survival of many economically important plant species. A study by Fujita and Tuttle (1991) identified 289 plant species that rely in varying degrees on large populations of flying foxes for propagation. More than 448 economically valuable products are known to have been developed from these plants, many of which are important to local economies in developing countries. Products include food items, drinks, dyes, fiber, animal fodder, fuel wood, medicines, ornamental plants, timber, and other wood products.

In a separate study, Thomas (1982) found that 90–98 percent of the seeds of woody "pioneer" plants that drop on clear-cut land in tropical Africa are dispersed by bats. Similar studies are being conducted in French Guiana and Costa Rica. Few people are aware of the vital roles bats play in sustaining ecosystems and economies. The value of such research activities to subsequent educational efforts should not be underestimated. For example, information from these studies was included in the recently published *Educator's Activity Book about Bats.* Based on research on the importance of bats to rain forests, a new activity book and two audiovisual programs, one for adults and another for youth, are now in preparation.

Because of the many economic and ecological roles played by tropical bats, their conservation and management must be considered essential elements in sustainable development programs. However, much more research needs to be done to further document the roles of bats. This information is also vital to building appreciation through educational programs for bats in areas where their populations are in serious decline.

The long-term effects of bat-focused educational and research efforts mean a better future for bat populations everywhere, thereby benefiting countless plants and animals living in the ecosystems that bats help sustain through pollination or seed dispersal of plants. Many new initiatives are beginning each year. The work of the network of bat conservationists has influenced millions of people around the world. Many of them are applying what they have learned to help their own communities and to resolve local bat-human conflicts.

Over the past ten years in the United States alone, conservation decision makers, natural resource agency personnel, and educators of all kinds have become more aware of bats. Students all across North America now have opportunities for learning about bats that few adults have had. Growing up with factual information instead of erroneous myths, today's youth can break the chain of misinformation that traditionally has painted bats as pests and dangerous animals. The ability of tomorrow's decision makers to make sound judgments based on facts will enhance the continued success of conservation programs being initiated today.

The future for many bat species depends on the success of habitat protection efforts currently being made. No greater conservation challenge exists than to preserve ecosystems in their entirety and to maintain adequate populations of the animals that service them. The rate of changing land-use patterns increases each year, decreasing the amount of habitat available for bats. Migratory species are especially at risk as they travel seasonally between habitat types. Today's efforts to protect critical habitat around the world in forests, caves, mines, and bridges will be essential factors in the survival of many bat species.

Although greatly improved, bat research today still lags far behind what is needed to plan for the conservation needs of bats. Efforts to protect bats are severely impeded by lack of information. Both scientists and conservationists have long neglected bats; a recent survey showed that bats are only one-fifteenth as well studied as other mammals (May 1988). Major emphasis must be placed on training the next generation of bat-conservation biologists, including teaching them how to apply their knowledge to solve global environmental problems for bats. To address this, BCI has recently entered into a landmark partnership with Texas A & M University to develop the International Center for Bat Research and Conservation. Working together, BCI, university scientists, and students will be able to design applied research projects to solve serious bat conservation, management, and educational problems. The center will be the first of its kind, filling an essential niche and utilizing the resources and talents of both organizations.

Future conservation efforts on behalf of bats must also focus on helping to solve specific bat-human problems and on working with the key groups that have a major impact on the survival of bat populations. Reaching health and pest control personnel, cave explorers, Latin American cattle ranchers, and others through educational initiatives will be a significant factor in the success of many bat conservation projects. Addressing problems will help ensure the survival of countless beneficial bats that are destroyed each year in indiscriminate campaigns. This, in turn, will benefit ecosystems such as rain forests and deserts, which rely on these seed-dispersers and pollinators for regeneration and maintenance. Such conflicts must be resolved before bats can be afforded long-term protection.

Today's bat conservation issues are no less urgent than when Bat Conservation International was founded. Nonetheless, after a decade of progress, the future is considerably more promising.

Acknowledgments

The success of the projects covered in this chapter would not have been possible without the many bat conservationists around the world who have collaborated with BCI to help protect and raise awareness about bats and the habitats that depend on them. We thank M. D. Tuttle for his critical review of the manuscript and use of the photographs.

PART THREE

Targeting Resource Users

8

Integrated Crane Conservation Activities in Pakistan: Education, Research, and Public Relations

■■
■■

Steven E. Landfried, Muhammad Mumtaz Malik,
Ashiq Ahmad, and A. Aleem Chaudhry

The precipitous decline of the western population of Siberian cranes along the Indo-Russian flyway has been well documented since 1965. Beginning fifteen years later, efforts integrating education, research, and publicity activities were initiated to save the birds from extinction. A wide variety of challenges were encountered as conservationists sought to develop strategies to protect this critically endangered migratory species in a vast subcontinent known historically for great cultural differences, intense political conflicts, and difficult terrain. The situation was further complicated by minimal awareness among government officials and conservationists of the plight of the Siberian crane—especially the impacts of the custom of live-crane catching and keeping in Pakistan or the effects on migratory wildlife of the Afghanistan war. This chapter documents a diverse mix of conservation education strategies employed over a fourteen-year period.

PLANNING

Siberian cranes (*Grus leucogeranus*) have migrated from breeding areas in remote northern latitudes to southern wintering grounds for thousands of years. However, little research was done on their migration routes, and the ornithological literature contained only incidental reports (Hume and Marshall 1881; Meinertzhagen 1955; Ali and Ripley 1969). It was not until the mid-1970s that systematic research was started on Siberian crane behavior at wintering grounds in India (Sauey 1976). As the 1980s dawned, virtually nothing was known about these birds except that they bred in Siberia and wintered in three distinct groups in China, India, and Iran. The Chinese population of two thousand birds was the largest of the three wintering groups. The Iranian group of fifteen birds wintering near the southeastern shore of the Caspian Sea was the smallest flock, and its numbers had remained relatively stable for some time (Ashtiani 1987).

In contrast, steady declines had occurred over a ten-year period in the number of Siberian cranes found at wintering grounds at the Keoladeo Ghana Bird Sanctuary in Bharatpur, India (subsequently known as Keoladeo National Park [KNP]). Whereas two hundred birds had been seen at the former private hunting ground in 1964 (Walk-inshaw 1973), only sixty-three were found in 1977–78. This decrease accelerated to a dramatic 43 percent plunge in their numbers as the Bharatpur population dropped from sixty-three to thirty-six birds during the three winters from 1977–78 to 1979–80. For concerned conservationists, the speed of this decline dramatically raised the specter of the imminent extirpation of the Indo-Soviet flock—and provided the impetus for an educational, publicity, and research campaign on behalf of these magnificent, large, white birds from the north.

Recognizing the minimal governmental and public awareness of the Siberian crane's apparent slide toward extinction in India, the International Affairs Office of the U.S. Fish and Wildlife Service (USFWS) asked Landfried, then serving as Public Affairs Officer for the International Crane Foundation, to attend an international environmental education conference in India during the summer of 1980 and to publicize the plight of the Siberian crane. The goal was to raise awareness among different audiences in India concerning the following problems: (1) the threats to the Keoladeo Ghana Bird Sanctuary in Bharatpur, the Siberian crane's only known wintering ground in India; and (2) the urgent need to mobilize national and international cooperation for migration research and conservation strategies to protect the bird along its undocumented 5,000-kilometer migration to unidentified breeding areas in northern Siberia. The initiative was funded by the USFWS with U.S.-owned Indian rupees acquired through the Indo-U.S. Special Foreign Currency Program (PL83–480) and authorized under the Endangered Species Act of 1973.

Through consultations with individuals and groups knowledgeable about the Indian situation, particularly the International Crane Foundation, potential strategies and target audiences were identified. Ultimately five primary target audiences were selected, based on their potential impact on our goals:

- high-level government officials—to inform decision-makers in the central government in New Delhi and the state government in Jaipur (which administered Keoladeo Ghana Sanctuary), as well as Prime Minister Indira Gandhi (known to be a student of birds and a friend of wildlife)
- the mass media—to identify and develop ongoing contacts with key members of the print media capable of bringing high visibility to the project by publishing feature articles, photographs, and news stories about the Siberian crane
- conservation groups—to lobby government agencies and to implement educational campaigns of their own (e.g., World Wildlife Fund-India, the Tourism and Wildlife Society of India, the Ghana Keoladeo Natural History Society, and the Ecological Society of India)
- scientific organizations—to lead research activities (e.g., the Bombay Natural History Society and the Forest Institute of India)
- environmental educators—to develop curricular materials and teacher-training activities for primary, secondary, and college students

In June 1980 Landfried participated in an international environmental education conference in Bangalore, India. Afterward he traveled to Delhi, Bharatpur, and Jaipur to seek input from representatives of all target audiences about strategies for publicizing the Siberian crane's plight. In addition, meetings were held with leaders of the Bombay Natural History Society (BNHS) to discuss likely Siberian crane migra-

Figure 8.1 Siberian crane-migration route through northern Pakistan (Roberts 1977).

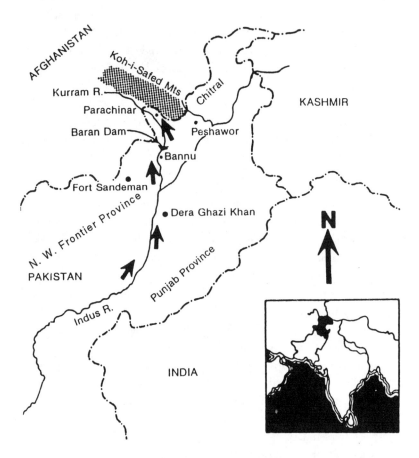

tion routes from Bharatpur to Lake Abi-Estada in Afghanistan—their only known staging area on the northward migration (Sauey 1985). BNHS had conducted extensive bird-banding studies for many years, and its president, Dr. Salim Ali, was an expert widely respected by both the scientific community and the government.

At first glance it seemed clear that Siberian cranes could not make the 975-mile flight migration from India to Afghanistan without stopping at least once in Pakistan to feed and roost (figure 8.1). This view was buttressed by North American research, which documented that the longest distance known to be traversed by whooping cranes in a single day's migration was 515 miles. This observation suggested the

Under his father's watchful eye, Azam Khan, seven, learns the art of throwing a
soiia (a thirty-meter-long, lead-weighted nylon cord) at slowly descending cranes
(*photo by S. Landfried*).

importance of including Pakistan in our research and conservation
strategies. BNHS facilitated contact in late 1980 with T. J. Roberts, a
long-time resident of Pakistan and the leading authority on birds in that
country. Roberts (1977) had documented the live catching of cranes in
the Kurram Valley of the North-West Frontier Province (NWFP). He
recognized that crane catching may have contributed to Siberian crane
decline and expressed interest in collaborating in our project.

Meanwhile, the public information campaign in India during 1980–
81 had succeeded in attracting attention from all of our five target
audiences. Interviews with key reporters had netted widespread publication of photographs and prominently placed stories about the Siberian
cranes in most major Hindustani and English newspapers in northern
India. Good exposure had been achieved through presentations to
prominent Indian conservationists and government officials. These individuals could have a major impact on decisions about the Siberian
crane's last-known wintering area in their country. In addition, slide
programs and educational activities were provided to leaders and membership of Indian science, environment, and tourism organizations.

These efforts produced a sympathetic response and heightened concern about the Siberian crane. In turn, the Tourism and Wildlife Society
of India and the World Wildlife Fund-India (Landfried 1980a; Sawhney
1981) created effective media and educational activities to publicize the
importance of maintaining and upgrading the Keoladeo Ghana Bird
Sanctuary as a safe haven for the Siberian crane. This activity attracted
the attention of Prime Minister Gandhi—who had a longstanding interest in the Siberian crane and actively supported the upgrading of
Keoladeo to national park status.

In December 1981 meetings with officials in Pakistan and a crane
hunter from Bannu underscored the importance of expanding the project to Pakistan in more than a superficial way. The hunter's identification of a Siberian crane gave credence to his report of having shot and
eaten three Siberian cranes along the Kurram River in 1961 (Landfried
1982a).

Popular articles about crane hunting in Pakistan were soon published
in the Indian press, which stimulated great international interest in the
Siberian crane and the establishment of a national bird-sanctuary park
in Bharatpur, India. With financial support from the USFWS, the
International Crane Foundation stepped up its research into former
Siberian crane wintering grounds in India and joined with the World
Wildlife Fund-India in organizing, funding, and publishing the proceedings of an international crane conference in Bharatpur in February 1983.
This activity spawned more interest in the situation in Pakistan and
spurred more publicity in the media and organs of international conservation organizations (Landfried 1980b, 1980/81).

At the end of the crane-hunting season in October 1982, a five-day
study of Pakistani crane-hunting camps along the Kurram River was
conducted. Roberts and Landfried were shocked to find hundreds of
captive cranes in the Bannu area—and to hear reports that those birds
represented only a portion of the cranes in captivity. The journey
demonstrated that crane hunting in the NWFP operated on a larger
scale than anyone had imagined and was expanding to the adjacent
province of Baluchistan. The magnitude of the uncontrolled crane
hunting was potentially bad news for the Siberian crane and its more
numerous cousins—the demoiselle crane (*Anthropoides virgo*) and the
common crane (*Grus grus*). The movement of crane hunters into Baluchistan was ominous, too, because it meant that Siberian cranes would

almost certainly encounter crane hunters on any migration route they might fly between Bharatpur, India, and Lake Abi-Estada, Afghanistan.

Refocusing the Project

Duplication of the Indian research, education, and outreach program in Pakistan would not be possible because of the many differences between the two countries. Although both countries shared a similar legal and bureaucratic system inherited from the British colonial period, recent history illustrated contrasting sociopolitical situations. India had an open government structure whereas Pakistan was governed by martial law. Moreover, India had a longstanding interest in wildlife research and active support of conservation activities both within the government and among a diversity of nongovernment organizations (NGOs). In Pakistan, relatively little infrastructure or human resources were directed toward wildlife issues. Resource agencies in Pakistan were often led by individuals with little formal training in wildlife research or management, and NGOs were small and received little support.

International politics also placed limitations on planning a cooperative program involving Pakistan and India. Relations between the two countries were still strained by the Indo-Pakistan War of 1977—making joint conferences or meetings extremely difficult. Furthermore, U.S.-Pakistani relations also were cool because of the U.S. antinuclear proliferation policies. These situations hampered communication and cooperation and restricted the use of U.S. PL-480 funds in Pakistan.

Despite the complexities involved, consultation with potential collaborators in the Asian subcontinent, Europe, and the United States revealed a general appreciation that publicity alone would not be sufficient to save the Siberian crane. The lack of migration data or information about hunting threats in Pakistan and Afghanistan severely impeded the project. Finding ways to address them were felt to be central to any conservation initiatives. Given the progress made with the public awareness campaign and the mobilization of international interest in the migration of the Siberian crane, we decided that the publicity component of the project should be upscaled in Pakistan at the earliest opportunity and that research should be conducted into crane migrations and hunting pressures in that country. This decision required a major shift in the content, direction, and complexity of the project.

With time, the main focus of project activities shifted from India to Pakistan. Necessarily, this required the development of indigenous and foreign funding sources to facilitate the change. Educational activities and publicity tied to crane research initiatives in India continue to the present day and interface with activities in Pakistan. We focus here primarily on project activities in Pakistan as they occurred against the backdrop of the precipitous decline in the number of Siberian cranes wintering at Bharatpur, India.

IMPLEMENTATION

The Bharatpur Crane Conference

The expansion of the project in 1983 was timed to coincide with the International Crane Conference at Bharatpur in February of that year. This event was attended by hundreds of representatives of Indian scientific, governmental, and NGO groups, and representatives from more than twenty countries—including delegates from every country within the range of Siberian cranes. The conference showcased the Keoladeo National Park and underscored its importance in the survival of the Siberian crane and other migratory birds. It also allowed us to introduce all primary target audiences to the threats posed by crane hunting in Pakistan's North-West Frontier Province and to emphasize the need for international cooperation in Siberian crane migration studies (Roberts and Landfried 1987).

The release of a Siberian crane stamp in India commemorated the event and brought additional media exposure. This provided a successful demonstration of the potential value of stamps as publicity and educational tools (Landfried 1982b). The success in India also encouraged Landfried to share this idea with postal authorities in all Siberian crane range states. Within the next four years, all four countries represented at the conference (Pakistan, China, Mongolia, and Russia) released Siberian crane stamps.

In a fundamental sense, the Bharatpur crane conference was a transitional event for the project. It culminated the initial stage of publicity and public education efforts in India and set the stage for the next phase of the project in both India and Pakistan. Seeking to build on the interest in crane migrations created at the conference, Landfried left with Ronald Sauey (cofounder of the International Crane Foundation) for a survey of common and demoiselle crane wintering grounds in the Indian state of Gujarat—which borders on Pakistan. Meetings in Bombay with Dr. Salim Ali and BNHS staff and membership brought additional publicity to the cause and further underscored how little was known about crane migrations northward from Gujarat. With that momentum, the next phase of the project began in Pakistan in March 1983. The basic strategy initially was fourfold: (1) to publicize the impending migration of Siberian cranes through the country, particularly with top government officials, the media, and crane hunters; (2) to train Wildlife Department staff on survey administration techniques; (3) to conduct field research on crane hunting in Pakistan, on crane-migration patterns, and on factors motivating the crane hunters; and (4) to develop an infrastructure of individuals and organizations committed to crane conservation.

Crane hunter field survey. The first step was to assess the magnitude of crane hunting in the Kurram Valley. To accomplish this goal a comprehensive questionnaire (representative questions are given in table 8.1) was directed toward crane hunters at various sites around Bannu and in the Kurram Valley. With the NWFP Wildlife Department and local officers, the questionnaire was designed to generate information on which to base future government policies and project activities. The questionnaire was translated into three dialects of Pashtu to assure that subtle nuances of language and cultural propriety did not cause problems with the major Pathan tribes in the crane-hunting area. Students at the nearby Pakistan Forest Institute were apprised of the unfolding research project in hopes of encouraging their eventual participation in the crane research.

Once the final draft was completed, two days of extensive staff training followed in Bannu for twenty-five participating wildlife staff. Training included background information on cranes, orientation to the purpose of the research, and rationales for specific questionnaire items. Because all cranes are known as *koonj* in Pashtu, special attention was given to assuring that field staff could help hunters distinguish between demoiselle, common, and Siberian cranes. The importance of using the proper dialect of Pashtu during interviews was also stressed. A list of effective interview techniques was given to all participants and discussed at length before a series of role-playing exercises were enacted. Simu-

Table 8.1. Representative Questions from 1983 Crane Hunter Questionnaire, Kurram Valley, North-West Frontier Province, Pakistan.

1. What is your name and village?

2. How many Zanrain (common cranes) and Karkara (demoiselle cranes) do you own?

3. How were your cranes obtained?
   a. caught
   b. borrowed
   c. purchased
   d. inherited
   e. received as a gift
   f. bred in captivity
   g. other

4. What is the main reason you keep cranes?
   a. decoys for hunting
   b. ornamental pets
   c. for future sale
   d. for food to eat
   e. protection ("watchdogs" for the family compound)
   f. to give to others
   g. other

5. Did your father hunt cranes?

6. On average, how many cranes do you catch each year?

7. Since you began hunting cranes, what has been the trend of the number of these birds seen migrating through the area?
   a. considerable increases
   b. slight increases
   c. no change
   d. slight decreases
   e. considerable decreases

8. Have you ever seen a white crane? If yes, describe the appearance of the bird.

9. What is the main reason why you hunt cranes?

10. If you are alive ten years from now, do you still expect to be hunting cranes?

11. Will there be as many cranes to hunt ten years from now?

lated interviews were video-taped and thoroughly critiqued by workshop leaders and participants alike.

With the spring crane hunting in full swing, Malik and Ashiq took NWFP Wildlife Department and Pakistan Zoological Survey staff into

NWFP Wildlife Department staff with no experience in migration research receive training in techniques for releasing leg-banded cranes back into the wild (*photo by S. Landfried*).

the field to demonstrate interview techniques and to give slide shows (with projectors powered by portable generators) to teach hunters about the plight of the Siberian crane. A review session followed before the newly trained wildlife staff was released to interview crane hunters throughout the area. By the time the crane-hunting season ended in early April, a total of 921 questionnaires had been administered. The next step was to undertake the tedious process of tallying the responses.

Several sources supported the field research. The NWFP Wildlife Department provided staff, vehicles, and organizational backing for the survey. World Wildlife Fund (WWF)-Pakistan funded data analysis, photocopying, gasoline, and printing, and the USFWS paid for Landfried's international travel and expenses.

Publicity/infrastructure building. Other crane-project activities were initiated concurrently with the surveys in the Kurram Valley. Slide shows were frequently presented to hunters in camps and in villages. Contacts were made with middle- and high-level government officials to alert them to the Siberian crane situation and to apprise them of the survey research. Such government contacts were essential to gain approval for project work done in semiautonomous regions of the NWFP and Baluchistan controlled by tribal chiefs. In addition to facilitating travel in the region, these meetings served an educational purpose—thereby enhancing the likelihood of official support for conservation activities.

Meanwhile, plans were being laid back in India for the first count of Sarus cranes (*Grus antigone*) at Keoladeo National Park. At the end of March 1983 Landfried returned to Bharatpur for planning sessions organized by the Keoladeo Ghana Natural History Society (KGNHS) in conjunction with park staff, field staff of the Bombay Natural History Society, and the local Maharini Shri University. Designed to draw attention to problems facing local and migratory cranes alike, the Sarus count brought sixty young children, students, faculty, scientists, and wildlife watchers into the park for four to five hours of birdwatching and data gathering. A film about the ecological cycle at Keoladeo National Park funded by the USFWS—"Birds of the Indian Monsoon"—was shown, along with slides about the work of the International Crane Foundation, to villages bordering the park, a local elementary school, and members of the KGNHS. Highly successful, the Sarus crane count was widely covered in newspapers throughout India and garnered a congratulatory letter from Prime Minister Gandhi.

By early June 1983 field site visits, meetings, and presentations throughout Pakistan had been completed—as were the final tallies of the crane questionnaire. Wildlife Department officials in Peshawar were surprised by the level of crane hunting reflected in questionnaire data. While suspecting that hunters had underreported their crane holdings, officials were impressed that hunters acknowledged having as many cranes as they did.

Hunters reported owning 5,701 cranes (3,223 common cranes and 2,478 demoiselle cranes). Of that figure, 51 percent had been caught by the hunter and 42 percent had been purchased. Most of the hunters kept their cranes as decoys (85 percent) or for gifts for friends (10 percent). Very few hunters (5 percent) reported eating the cranes that they caught. A relatively small number of the hunters (15 percent) said their captive cranes had produced eggs—and, of those, fewer than half the hatched chicks survived more than a year. Hunters apparently took great pride in the survivors because all of the home-produced chicks were kept as pets.

Virtually all the crane hunters (92 percent) said that they practiced their sport in both the spring and the fall at more than seventy-five sites in north-central Pakistan. A majority of the hunters (66 percent) said that their main reason for hunting cranes was "for the sport of it"; other motivating factors included enjoyment of the outdoors (11 percent) and sale of the birds (11 percent). The growing popularity of the sport was intimated when only 35 percent of the hunters said that their fathers had hunted cranes.

A majority of the hunters (56 percent) felt that the trend of the number of cranes migrating through the area was one of "considerable decrease"; nearly a third of them (30 percent) felt that the decrease had been "slight." Hunters overwhelmingly (90 percent) felt that the number of cranes actually caught had declined. Nevertheless, the vast majority of hunters (88 percent) indicated that they expected that cranes would be as numerous in ten years.

In general, wildlife staff believed that the findings accurately reflected hunting practices and the attitudes of the crane hunters. The data were seen as reliable, and the results of the crane questionnaire were taken seriously. As a result, the data had considerable impact on government policies and the evolution of the crane project in Pakistan. The following salient conclusions resulted from the survey:

- crane hunting was more extensive than previously believed and was rapidly increasing in popularity
- heavy hunting pressure in the Kurram Valley was causing hunters to consider other provinces as potential crane areas
- few hunters had seen or caught Siberian cranes
- widespread hunting in the spring posed immediate threats to the survival of the Siberian crane and had serious long-term implications for common and demoiselle cranes
- hunters knew little about crane reproductive biology or why cranes were breeding very poorly in captivity
- hunters did not acknowledge the negative consequences of growing hunting pressure for declining crane populations

Although the location of hunting camps in Baluchistan and Punjab provided evidence of crane-migration routes through those provinces, the data allowed no firm conclusions about crane-migration routes through Pakistan.

Lengthy discussions about how to respond to the questionnaire results ensued within the Wildlife Department, the conservation community, and among high-level provincial and federal officials. Special efforts were made to involve the martial law governor of the NWFP in the debate. An avid hunter with a particular interest in wildlife, he was the only person in the province powerful enough to stand up to the pressure hunters might place on government officials if hunting restrictions were imposed as a result of the research.

Clearly something had to be done to harness a growing sport that was sure to mushroom in popularity once the children produced by the growing population in the Kurram Valley reached adolescence. Everyone knew this would not be easy because the Pathans had historically and repeatedly demonstrated their independence from outside intervention. For this reason it was agreed that educational components should be integral to any future project activities.

The survey results pointed to four general areas for the crane project to address: (1) restrictions on crane hunting; (2) educational programs for virtually everyone impacted by crane hunting in the short and long term—crane hunters, Wildlife Department staff, government officials at all levels, magistrates, teachers, and youth; (3) educational research; and (4) the establishment of crane reserves and an educational center.

Restrictions on crane hunting. Alarmed by the growth of crane hunting, new crane-protection laws were pushed through the NWFP Provincial Assembly by the martial law governor. Basically the laws had three goals: (1) to reduce specific problems that contributed to an unsustainable level of crane hunting; (2) to create specific discussion points around which to educate hunters about crane biology, wildlife conservation, environmental preservation, and repercussions of skyrocketing human population growth; and (3) to create incentives for crane hunters to learn about conservation through active involvement in migration and captive-breeding research (Landfried 1984a).

The new laws required hunters in the NWFP to obtain hunting licenses to pursue their sport, doubled camping fees in the spring as a means to decrease hunting in order to allow more cranes to reach breeding grounds, banned the shooting of cranes, increased incentives for captive crane breeding, provided incentives for hunter cooperation in migration research, and included other prohibitions.

The governor announced the laws to the public in February 1984, and they were later published in local languages in a small booklet funded by WWF-Pakistan. It included an attractive full-color cover of a family of Siberian cranes in flight and an educational message explaining reasons for the laws. The Pashtu-language booklet concluded with the message: "Please remember that we have a special responsibility to protect the extremely threatened white Siberian crane."

Careful planning went into the timing of publicity about the new crane laws in the spring of 1984. The new crane-hunting restrictions were announced at the last minute to prevent hunters from organizing before the spring hunt. By the time it was clear to the hunters that the laws would be enforced, the hunting season was half over and many camps did not go out. As a result, Malik estimated that hunting was reduced that spring by at least half.

The legalistic, martial law approach reduced hunting in the spring of 1984, but not for long. Indeed, the "end run" led hunters in the NWFP to feel that they had been tricked—that their participation in the 1983 crane survey had been used against them. Realizing that the provincial assembly had capitulated under pressure from the NWFP Wildlife Department and the governor, the hunters began to organize against the new crane laws. Strong stances by the governor and the conservator of wildlife withstood the pressure as long as martial law was in effect. However, hunters would not be deterred and met strength with visibly greater numbers of supporters and firearms. Thus the strategy of changing laws rather than minds essentially backfired.

Crane hunters organized and pressured officials for changes in the regulations. The hunters further demonstrated their resolve by displaying an increased number of arms, including Kalashnakov submachine guns, in their camps and firing on wildlife staff on several occasions. Martial law ended in 1985, changing the political landscape. The continued pressure of the hunters resulted in the reduction of the camp licensing fees in 1989.

Conservation education programs. From the beginning it was clear that educational activities should have a high priority in Pakistan. That new crane-hunting laws were drafted with educational functions in mind bears witness to the importance of education to the whole project. Indeed, we recognized that the general lack of attention paid to wildlife migration and the minimal conservation infrastructure within the country meant that virtually every initiative would have informational value for someone. The need for tactically specific educational activities left us with the question of where to start teaching: with the hunters? with the wildlife staff? with the top of the martial-law bureaucracy? with mid-level bureaucrats? with magistrates who would be asked to render decisions on infractions of the new laws? or with school teachers whose students might educate their parents about the importance of conservation?

At the time the problems were so complex that the best strategy seemed to be to focus on wildlife staff—for they would repeatedly be asked to function as educators as they monitored, and sought to restrict, hunting practices with hunters and children in the crane camps. Additionally, they could make presentations to government officials, magistrates, and the general public. Forest Department staff also needed to learn about wildlife field research, cranes, wetlands, and environmental concepts. With time and resources at a premium, we felt it was important to try, whenever possible, to educate staff at the same time that information was being targeted at other audiences.

For instance, we always invited Wildlife Department field staff to participate whenever we made presentations to hunters, to those in crane camps, or to magistrates. Their opinions were also actively sought whenever policy or strategy decisions were made. Similarly, mid-level managers (e.g., provincial or federal wildlife officials) were always included in meetings with the NWFP governor or agriculture secretaries. Through this process, research and educational functions merged in symbiotic ways that set the tone for future project activities.

The last-minute imposition of the new crane-hunting laws created a relative lull in crane hunting during the spring of 1984. We seized this opportunity to take several educational initiatives, including:

- presentations about captive crane breeding to several groups of crane owners in Bannu and Lakki by an expert from the National Zoo in Washington, D.C.
- a training and strategy session for wildlife and forestry officers
- planning meetings to improve the wildlife curriculum for foresters

The Siberian Crane Working Group, meeting in December 1991, brought representatives from India, Iran, Russia, and the United States to Karachi, Pakistan, to discuss education, research, and conservation strategies (*photo by S. Landfried*).

- sessions with government and NGO officials to seek their input into strategies for responding to crane hunters' resistance to the new laws; official interest was reinforced with copies of national and international news stories about the project (Landfried 1983, 1984b)

The visibility and importance of the project at provincial and national levels was underscored by the release of a Siberian crane stamp with artwork done by world famous naturalist Sir Peter Scott. Active efforts were also made to maintain exposure in the media by cultivating personal relationships with key newspaper writers and top executives at Pakistan Television headquarters in Islamabad. The governor of the NWFP assisted us in this endeavor by repeatedly inviting television crews to cover periodic meetings at his mansion—four to five of which appeared on prime-time provincial and national news broadcasts.

By the winter of 1984–85 the number of Siberian cranes wintering at Bharatpur had risen to forty-one birds. That increase may have been independent of the project, but it did help to draw attention to our work throughout the subcontinent and elsewhere. This coverage made high-level officials more aware of the international scrutiny the project was drawing and further reinforced their commitment to the project. Predictably, some crane hunters cited the increase as another reason to relax hunting restrictions. This reaction highlighted the limited impact of our intermittent educational programs on hunters in the Kurram Valley. Indeed, the hunters' strong and growing resistance to crane conservation measures emphasized the importance of developing educational audiovisual materials that could be provided to them, as well as to teachers or wildlife staff, for self-education purposes.

The need for educational materials was addressed in a variety of ways in the mid-1980s. For example, a twelve-minute radio feature—"Koonj Ki-Judai"—was made for an illiterate audience in remote areas of Pakistan beyond the reach of stories in the print media or on television. Included in the popular World of Science series (produced by United States Information Service [USIS]-Islamabad), the program also aired on nineteen local-dialect radio stations around the country. Other radio features produced by the British Broadcasting Company and the Voice of America were broadcast in the subcontinent through their English-, Urdu-, and Hindi-language services.

Audiovisual programs were created for multiple uses in hunter education, staff training, public presentations, and schools. A forty-slide English-language filmstrip—*Cranes of the Subcontinent: Great Birds in Peril*—was produced in 1985 with financial support from outside sources, including the International Council for Bird Preservation in England. An Urdu narration of the script was completed the next year with extensive input from all key project collaborators. Ultimately, transcripts of the script were distributed with audio tapes and filmstrips to a limited number of wildlife and conservation officials in Pakistan and India. Unfortunately, few of them made their way into the hands of hunters or teachers.

In the spring of 1985 a three-person U.S. television crew traveled to Pakistan with funding from a number of sources to document the project. The goal of the film was to record crane hunting and spotlight the challenges of implementing education and conservation programs in a region with a long tradition of unrestricted hunting.

In November 1985 crane hunting in the Kurram Valley was seen outside Pakistan for the first time when a fourteen-minute video feature aired on Wisconsin public television. In the spring of 1986 a thirty-minute English-language film, *Crane Hunters of Pakistan,* was completed. The film was shown throughout Pakistan in the spring of 1987 and earned state, national, and international awards. A valuable educational resource, the film helped to clarify the diverse cultural factors that make it difficult to limit crane hunting in Pakistan. However, its utility among the hunters was limited since it was not in their native language.

Recognizing that crane conservation could only be achieved if crane hunters understood and supported conservation goals, hunter education programs were implemented by the wildlife departments in the NWFP and the Punjab—and, to a lesser degree, by the Zoological Survey of Pakistan. These sessions utilized the new slide program and the film—with translations provided by project leaders or local field staff. The presentations usually occurred in Bannu, Lakki, and hunting camps, and often coincided with the spring and fall crane-hunting seasons. Leaflets and brochures about cranes, in local languages, were also circulated among the hunters. Yearly visits by Landfried to the Kurram Valley emphasized continued international interest in the status of cranes in Pakistan and added credibility to conservation messages from local officials. Special efforts were made to hold meetings in family compounds of prominent crane hunters so wildlife officials from Peshawar could explain the rationale for crane conservation face-to-face and engage in thoughtful debate with influential hunters.

Other educational initiatives targeted different audiences in Pakistan. For example, information about cranes was incorporated into the curriculum of the wildlife course at the Pakistan Forest Institute. Beginning in 1987 Ahmad worked with the USFWS, the University of Maine, and the National Council for the Conservation of Wildlife to organize a series of workshops to train teachers and Forest Department staff in Baluchistan, the Punjab, and the NWFP in ecological concepts and in the organization of youth conservation clubs. The NWFP Wildlife Department started wildlife clubs at twelve leading schools in the Peshawar in 1990. Eventually the WWF-Pakistan hired a national coordinator for the Pakistan Youth Conservation Clubs Project to provide support to youth club leaders. Crane and wetland topics are included in the club education programs and the teacher-training activities of these groups.

The Zoological Survey of Pakistan developed an educational pamphlet entitled *The Cranes of Pakistan* (Ahmad et al. 1993). The staff of the

Punjab Wildlife Department received training in crane-migration research techniques in 1987. Information was provided to the general public about underlying reasons for crane research, and efforts were undertaken to discourage NWFP crane hunters from crossing into Punjab Province. In addition, a public awareness campaign was initiated in 1992 in the Punjab that placed greater emphasis on the value of conservation measures for people, cranes, and other wildlife.

Throughout the project, collaborators have made presentations to a wide range of international conferences on themes such as environmental education; conservation in rural areas; crane biology, conservation, and management; wetland and waterfowl management; and national parks and protected areas. Such forums serve many useful functions, including allowing project collaborators to share the project with others, to solicit suggestions for improvement, and to garner international visibility that reinforces support from provincial and national officials.

Research with educational purposes. As described earlier, biological research activities also served an educational function since they were first incorporated into bird migration studies in 1982 and the crane hunter survey of 1983. Crane-migration studies by Pakistani researchers not only broke new ground but also provided a vehicle for exposing Wildlife Department staff and college students to a new model for conducting biological research. In addition, the visibility of the field research impressed both Wildlife Department staff and hunters with the importance that the investigators placed on crane conservation.

Ashiq's travels around the country as the wildlife specialist of the Pakistan Forest Institute allowed him to discover the magnitude and breadth of crane migrations through the country and to define areas where crane conservation education initiatives should be focused (Ashiq and Najam 1991). From a practical standpoint, his work provided insights into how to conduct research with rural people unfamiliar with conservation. Teaching colleagues and local people as he did his research, Ashiq's curiosity and commitment to protecting the cranes became contagious, and others consequently offered to assist his efforts. This was particularly significant in Baluchistan where some local *maliks* (tribal chiefs) were eventually inspired to deny traditional hospitality to Pathan cousins from the NWFP who had come there to hunt cranes illegally. Instead, they insisted that hospitality (in the form of unfettered resting sites) should be accorded to cranes during their twice-a-year migrations.

The head of the Punjab Wildlife Research Center in Faisalabad, Dr. Aleem Chaudhry, also made cranes a research priority. Starting in 1987 he directed district wildlife officers and assistant game wardens to check likely crane-roosting areas during migration seasons and to collect information about crane migrations from local residents. In addition, he directed them to engage in educational activities with local people whenever possible.

These research cum education activities established their leaders as role models for students, staff, and hunters unaccustomed to seeing teachers or government officials doing research in the field. In the process, they sent an important message: research and educational activities can be conducted outside a library or classroom. As such, it put them in an excellent position to recruit and train others in crane research and conservation—and thus to perpetuate the work. Ashiq and Najam (1991) document the results of these field studies and the symbiotic effects of this recruitment process.

The fruit of educational seeds are also seen in a master's degree crane research project at the Pakistan Forest Institute (Farooq 1992). Inspired by the crane hunter survey of 1983, Farooq revised the questionnaire and administered a new version in local languages to fifty hunters near the Indus River border of the NWFP and the Punjab. The questionnaire served as both a research and an educational tool. Aside from gathering new insights into the practice of crane hunting at the southern end of the Kurram Valley, it clarified hunters' attitudes about the problems facing conservationists and solicited their ideas about measures that might prove useful in conserving cranes.

The study proved significant because it indicated that some crane hunters had come to accept that unabated expansion of crane hunting posed real long-term threats to their sport. By asking the questions it did, the research also served as a way to solicit conservation ideas from the hunters—while getting them to think about ways to assure that the pastime would be passed down to their children. Finally, it reaffirmed an emerging interest among some crane hunters in crane migrations and captive breeding—as well as their readiness to become more actively involved in conservation activities. As a result, activities were proposed that would augment hunter training in 1993 and 1994. We would embrace the hunters as colleagues and recruit three or four leaders to come to the United States to learn about aviculture, satellite tracking, and conservation education. By continuing to blend education with research, we hope to add to the ranks of conservation allies without having to increase the payroll of already beleaguered wildlife departments.

Incorporating education was not particularly difficult as efforts to interest crane hunters in migration studies had already begun in 1985 when some crane banding was done in the Kurram Valley. Although another attempt was made in late 1988, that initiative eventually floundered. During this period, Landfried first urged the international conservation community to utilize satellite-tracking technology to study and devise measures to protect the Siberian crane. He shared this idea with crane hunters in December 1988 during the first of a series of year-end visits to the Kurram Valley and discovered that the hunters were very interested in avian satellite tracking. As a result, he kept key crane hunters apprised of pioneering efforts to adapt satellite tracking to cranes. We anticipate that the hunters' curiosity about technology will soon involve them in catching cranes for a new initiative—the first avian satellite-tracking research in Pakistan.

Establishment of crane reserves/education centers. The most recent aspect of the crane conservation project in Pakistan that integrates education with research and conservation activities is the establishment of crane refuges and reserves by the government of the NWFP. Launched under a project entitled "Protection, Conservation, and Management of Migratory Bird Species in the NWFP," the first refuge was conceived as a secure area where cranes might find respite from extensive hunting along the Kurram, Gambeela, and Indus rivers and their tributaries. The refuge was approved in 1990—at which time the government also declared an area of 81,000 hectares along the Indus River in the D. I. Khan District as a crane reserve. Hunting in the Indus Reserve is only allowed for hunters who pay a daily fee of 200 rupees (U.S. $6.00) each. This fee has proved sufficiently high to discourage some hunters, and the number of hunting camps in the area has subsequently declined.

Realizing that wild cranes had few other suitable habitats for safe migration stops, the government of the NWFP approved the nearby Lakki Refuge—an area of 20 square kilometers of prime crane habitat

Siberian crane stamps issued by India and Pakistan publicized the bird's plight. First-day covers and information sheets provided additional background for stamp collectors (*photo by S. Landfried*).

at the confluence of the Kurram and Gambeela rivers in the Bannu District. A budget of 5.7 million rupees (U.S. $178,125) allocates substantial funds for establishing an education and research center, buying additional land, and obtaining long-term leases for adjoining properties. The land has been secured and efforts have turned to developing the site as an attractive place for cranes and for people who want to learn about them. A model project is envisioned to teach hunters about crane biology, management of captive cranes, and habitat requirements. Research at the Lakki and D. I. Khan refuges will provide training opportunities for students from the Pakistan Forest Institute, Peshawar University, and other institutions, as well as wildlife staff and crane hunters from the surrounding four provinces.

Finally, great hope exists for creating opportunities for public education at the two sites. As facilities expand, an educational building will provide a resource for showing audiovisual programs about cranes and other wildlife—and, eventually, a facility will be created for teaching about the importance of wetlands for migratory birds and man. The Lakki Refuge and the Indus Reserve will also offer a place where youth conservation clubs, schoolchildren, and government officials can see tangible proof of conservation in action. This aspect of the project has received considerable local and international interest (Waak and Strom 1992), particularly since growing numbers of wild cranes have stopped at the Lakki site since it opened in 1992.

PRODUCT

The success of the project must be judged on the basis of its original goals rather than on uncontrollable circumstances that reduced the Indo-Russian flock of Siberian cranes to a scant five birds. As discouraging as the apparent extirpation of that remnant population may be (no Siberian cranes were found at Bharatpur during the winter of 1993–94), efforts on their behalf have yielded clear benefits for crane research, education, and conservation in Pakistan and India. Indeed, the project has set things in motion which may reduce the likelihood that common and demoiselle cranes will share a similar fate.

Considerable progress has been made in Pakistan and India in educating the five target audiences about the plight of the Siberian crane—and in mobilizing international efforts on their behalf. Numerous clippings from domestic and international newspapers and journals attest to the considerable publicity, spawned directly and indirectly by the project, about cranes, wetlands, and the importance of nature conservation. Other evidence of educational "products" is seen in the booklets, filmstrips, a documentary film, and video tapes developed in local languages and English. Hard data, too, are found in 921 questionnaires given to crane hunters in 1983 and in the 50 questionnaires administered to hunters at the Pakistan Forest Institute in 1991. Lack of staff and resources has not permitted us to do more than speculate on the impacts of the research itself on the attitudes and behaviors of the five target audiences. As a result, this remains a pregnant area for research.

Direct Outcomes

The most obvious direct outcome of this project is that hundreds of thousands of people have been exposed to stories or features about the plight of the Siberian crane in major newspapers, magazines, and on radio and television stations in the subcontinent. Many feel that our education and publicity efforts of the last twelve years have made a difference. For example, T. J. Roberts observed: "Nobody even thought about the 'koonj' (cranes) until a year ago. But now there is a widespread awareness of them in this country" (1983, personal communication). Another manifestation of the project's impact is found in changes in the behavior of prominent individuals. The late governor of the NWFP was so impressed that he eventually gave up hunting entirely. As he reflected after leaving office: "I never permitted more than seven birds to be taken in my hunting groups. Our people think that to flout the law is democracy. But I am finished; I will not shoot again" (Fazle Haq 1987, personal communication).

Progress has been made with rural crane hunters, too. By the end of the 1980s it became clear that conservation messages had started to carry more weight as the decline of demoiselle and common cranes became increasingly obvious. As one hunter noted: "Older parents are starting to say, 'Stop crane hunting. Shooting is cutting down on cranes.' " Another expressed this view: "Baluchistan hunting should be banned entirely and the people selling the cranes should be stopped." Indeed, over the last three to four years, conversations with crane hunters have seen them display much higher interest in crane migration. No longer does one regularly hear the explanation that the decreased number of cranes is the result of changes in their migration routes. A growing number of crane hunters seem to be willing to accept that hunting pressure may be impacting the birds and are ready to participate in research activities. In fact, one group of hunters wrote to request Pashtu versions of the crane film and filmstrip so that they could teach other hunters about cranes and conservation concepts.

While precise causal relationships are difficult to ascertain, it is clear that various project activities have directly and indirectly helped raise the awareness of local, provincial, federal, and international agencies in Pakistan, India, and elsewhere to problems posed by the crane hunting along the Indo-Russian flyway. In turn, the heightened awareness of issues associated with hunting pressures for the endangered Siberian crane has contributed in various ways to these outcomes:

- improved ability of Pakistani crane hunters to differentiate Siberian cranes from common and demoiselle cranes
- passage of restrictive crane-hunting and possession legislation in the NWFP, the Punjab, and Baluchistan, and modest enforcement of such legislation
- domestic and international financial support for the development of audiovisual materials about cranes

- expansion of training programs about cranes, wetlands, and migratory birds for wildlife and forestry officials in all provinces of Pakistan
- development of teacher training and youth nature clubs in Pakistan
- opening of WWF-Pakistan regional offices for conservation education and research in Peshawar and Zhob
- hiring of a full-time director of conservation by WWF-Pakistan
- inclusion of cranes in the wildlife course syllabus of the Pakistan Forest Institute and annual migration research of wildlife departments in Pakistan and India
- recruitment of graduate students for crane-migration studies
- creation of a crane refuge and reserves in the NWFP to provide safe havens for cranes and educational opportunities for people
- an international meeting of the Indo-Russian flyway Crane Working Group in Karachi in December 1991
- offers of satellite-tracking equipment by the Wild Bird Society of Japan for staff training and research on crane migrations
- release of Siberian crane stamps by Pakistan and India
- draft of a Bonn Convention Migratory Bird Treaty for protection of the Siberian crane by the International Crane Foundation and other international groups at the June 1993 Ramsar meeting in Japan

Many seeds sown during the last twelve years are expected to bear fruit in the future. Among others, these will likely include completion of a Bonn Convention migratory bird treaty by the countries along the Indo-Russian flyway; initiation of satellite-tracking studies of crane migrations along the flyway; release of Dari translations of crane and other conservation audiovisual materials; educational outreach and captive breeding training of crane hunters in the United States and their active involvement in ongoing educational activities; and satellite-tracking workshops for field practitioners in India and Pakistan in 1994 or 1995.

The longevity and visibility of the project has also proved helpful at critical junctures when additional publicity was needed for new project initiatives. In particular, long-established relationships with the media paid dividends when the time came to mobilize interest among scientists, government agencies, and NGOs in possible applications of satellite-tracking technology with cranes (Eggleston 1989; Vardhan 1989).

Finally, another direct benefit of the project's notoriety was in drawing considerable attention to Pakistan at a time when international organizations had only limited awareness of the environmental problems there. Indeed, one can argue that the publicity surrounding the project's initial success served to persuade outside skeptics that objectives could be accomplished in Pakistan and may have helped to facilitate the ascendancy of three influential Pakistanis to prominent roles in international affairs of IUCN and WWF. The high international visibility of the project from 1982 to 1988 may have also had a hand in encouraging those organizations to sustain or increase their role in developing wide-ranging research and educational programs for Pakistan (Ferguson 1982, 1986).

Secondary or Indirect Outcomes

The high visibility of the project has produced a number of important secondary benefits. In particular, it has created numerous opportunities for project leaders to make presentations abroad about various aspects of our work. This has fostered academic interest in the project's intriguing marriage of research, education, and publicity activities. New contacts have helped lead us to individuals and organizations whose insights, resources, and skills have benefited the project, both directly and indirectly, in a variety of ways.

In the United States, for instance, the National Audubon Society's awareness of Malik's initiatives in the NWFP led that organization to draw parallels between Pakistan's problems and those faced along the Indus and Platte rivers (Malik 1992). Exchange visits between Audubon and NWFP Wildlife staff ensued, and a chapter entitled "Rivers under Siege: Nebraska's Platte and Pakistan's Indus" was included in Audubon's book about the impacts of population pressure on the environment (Waak and Strom 1992). Audubon also supported Malik's travel to international conferences to spotlight his work and to broaden his awareness of conservation and educational programs that might be effective in the NWFP. In the spring of 1994 Audubon will bring Malik to Nebraska again for an international conference to make presentations with Landfried about the challenges of crane education and conservation in the face of mounting population pressures. We are hopeful that a proposed visit in 1994 by two crane hunter leaders to successful crane projects in North America will motivate them to become active proponents of crane conservation in Pakistan—just as travels have repeatedly stimulated Malik's imagination and redoubled his commitment to implement ideas back in Pakistan.

International recognition of the project and its participants was beneficial in other ways. It gave the project credibility and impressed top government officials in Pakistan of the validity of crane work. The project helped to create educational and training opportunities abroad for Pakistani collaborators, and, conversely, it provided wildlife research opportunities for other individuals when they returned from abroad. The international attention also served notice that the crane situation along the Indo-Soviet flyway was being monitored abroad. In addition, the widespread awareness of the project facilitated the entertainment of proposals by funding agencies and led to presentations at a variety of international conferences. The interest stimulated by these efforts—and the urgency associated with the precipitous decline of Siberian cranes at Bharatpur—directly contributed to the development of new satellite-tracking designs more conducive to crane anatomy.

A secondary benefit of the project has been to instill greater self-confidence in key participants. Success has clearly encouraged individuals to tackle other problems more boldly. The increased self-confidence stemmed in part from the involvement of the international news media. We now know—as do Pakistani government officials—that the media are readily available to scrutinize developments. In fairness, however, we must note that access to the media has not been without cost. Indeed, the attention drawn to project leaders has periodically caused professional jealousy to rear its head and has occasionally made it difficult for some individuals to obtain travel permissions and project approvals.

In many ways the project's direct and indirect benefits are what we expected. Unfortunately, the sobering reality is that the Indo-Russian flock of Siberian cranes is likely extirpated and crane hunting is on the rise. Although inadequate funding and insufficient staff have continually hampered the project, the work accomplished certainly provides an imposing base from which to proceed. Indeed, a major value of a long-duration project is the opportunity it provides for gaining insights that could not be gained from a short-term undertaking.

Lessons Learned and Modifications Made

This project has primarily sought to foster conservation of the Siberian crane. Focusing attention on one endangered species in the region has made its possible extinction more real for many people. Indeed, the quantification of the Siberian crane's demise has dramatized the finality of extinction and has served as an ominous warning regarding the decline of demoiselle and common cranes. Conversations with hunters and government officials indicate that terms like *environmental degradation, severe hunting pressure,* and *overharvesting* have also taken on more meaning for them as the number of wintering Siberian cranes in Bharatpur has plummeted. The ability of the Siberian crane situation to command attention has also facilitated our ability to raise general awareness about the realities of global ecological interdependence for international migratory birds. The challenge for the future is to find ways to actively involve crane hunters and others in the process of educating their peers.

These insights underscore the importance of focusing one's efforts. If this project has taught us anything—it is the disadvantage of spreading ourselves and available people-power too thin. We say this realizing why the enormity of factors originally recommended a broad-brush approach. Educational activities, migration research, development of satellite-tracking possibilities, and efforts to cultivate interest on the part of highly placed government officials have all merited attention. However, the reality of the situation is that these tasks have had to compete with pressing daily responsibilities (e.g., budgetary constraints, administrative duties, shifting bureaucratic personnel, and organizational priorities), which often mean that project tasks are shunted off to another day.

In retrospect, it is clear that the magnitude of the problems involved in crane conservation tempted the project leaders to add more to overburdened work loads rather than to delegate important tasks to others. This was less of a problem for individuals who could incorporate migration research and educational work into their field research in Pakistan, but there can be no doubt that problems of rare birds from Siberia increasingly took a back seat to other immediate and pressing matters.

Some of the diffusion of the project has been self-induced, and we now see that the project's goals would have been better served if full-

The growing interest in crane hunting in the North-West Frontier Province and Baluchistan has greatly increased hunting pressures on cranes. Educational initiatives in recent years by NWFP Wildlife staff and Dr. Steven Landfried (*kneeling*) have sought to win hunters over to the side of conservation (*photo by S. Landfried*).

time staff had been hired to focus on one to two key target audiences. The wisdom of hindsight also suggests that one target audience—the crane hunters of Pakistan—should have received the bulk of our initial attention after the 1983 surveys. Instead, we elected to work with provincial authorities on legislation and enforcement strategies to reduce crane hunting—thereby inadvertently sparking an adversarial relationship with the crane hunters. In retrospect, our awareness of the population explosion in the Kurram Valley should have served notice to us that the ranks of crane hunters and their supporters would increase. Moreover, well-documented aspects of the Pathan character (Spain 1973; Singer 1982) should have told us that the authoritative approach would backfire. The fact was that the crane hunters were not convinced for many years that crane populations in general were declining. Some might have felt a tinge of sympathy for the Siberian crane, but few saw crane conservation as acting in the best interests of the hunters or their descendants. As a result, our early interventions served to reinforce—

rather than diminish—their commitment to crane hunting, since to have acquiesced would have meant a surrender to an outside authority. Thus crane hunting escalated in the ensuing decade—to the point where, now, even veteran crane hunters are alarmed about steadily decreasing crane catches.

This experience should illustrate why infrastructure building is vitally important to the long-term success of conservation projects whose goals run counter to prevailing traditions and social values. It is never easy to change attitudes and traditions in remote areas with little history of government regulation or where a legacy of colonialism, tribal animosities, and frequent military rule are factored into the equation. In this case, martial law was in effect throughout Pakistan—a reality that reinforced a need to receive support and approval from the military in control of provincial and central governments. These factors contributed to the top-down approach that characterized the first six years of this project. Initially we thought that government agencies could do the required job of protecting cranes; but we slowly realized that it is the communities and the people who are directly involved with the sport who need to be motivated about nature conservation. Consequently, we are now determined to actively involve leading crane hunters in the development and implementation of future educational, research, and crane conservation strategies.

We also have learned how vestiges of the colonial period permeate the educational system and create subtle obstacles for the project. One problem in schools is that teachers and professors are seen as repositories of knowledge and almost universally teach in a pedantic and classroom-bound manner. Linked to this, most research is done in libraries rather than in the field. As a result, it is not surprising that others have stressed the importance of expanding "training in wildlife techniques . . . to include more biologists throughout the country" (O'Gara et al. 1985).

We agree and feel that academics and school teachers should be actively included in future training activities for crane hunters and wildlife staff. However, field work *is* difficult and it is not surprising that poor roads and high petroleum costs discourage professors or students from doing it. Fortunately, roads have improved in the NWFP and Baluchistan in recent years and we are hopeful that efforts can be redoubled to encourage more professors and students to participate in crane-related field activities.

This project has also taught us that great care should be taken when preparing educational materials for grassroots audiences. We have learned that audiovisual materials have great appeal and utility where illiteracy is high and televisions are few. However, the technological age has raised the expectations of audiences to higher levels—even in rural areas—and it is important that audiovisual programs be of high quality with evocative visual images and local dialect narration. In addition, producers should realize that educational materials may not necessarily be perceived or interpreted by people from different cultures as the environmentalists who originally designed them may have intended.

In short, the problems associated with assuming too readily that audiovisual programs have communicated effectively cannot be underestimated. These problems affect interpersonal communication, too, and we have become increasingly alert to linguistic sensitivities that can ruffle feathers and impact project implementation at any time (e.g., in interviews, questionnaire construction, written correspondence, and collaboration on professional articles). Thus we feel it is essential to locate effective translators, to identify field staff attuned to nuances of local dialects, to provide adequate time for translations, and to assure that foreign guests understand local variations of British English.

Local advice should also be sought when deciding how educational materials should be delivered to various audiences. Indeed, we discovered too late that in contrast to India, technology in rural Pakistan had skipped the filmstrip and 16-mm film projector and had made the transition directly to video. Our initial audiovisual materials were done in English for film and sound filmstrip projectors—resources seldom found in the NWFP and Baluchistan. Although Wildlife Department and Pakistan Forestry Institute staff had access to projectors, they encountered so many problems carrying them around the bumpy roads of rural areas that the programs were seldom used. Eventually the material was transferred to video tape in the United States, but even it had to be redubbed because initially the fact was overlooked that videos produced in the U.S. format do not work on the video format used on most VCRs in Pakistan and India.

Educational materials must be made more accessible to crane hunters, teachers, and schoolchildren. We are hopeful that recently completed local-language versions of *Crane Hunters of Pakistan* and the filmstrip *Cranes of the Subcontinent: Great Birds in Peril* will be widely distributed to hunters, schools, and government officials. In turn, these target audiences will be encouraged to circulate the videos to colleagues, friends, and relatives.

Looking to the Future

The need to find adequate financial resources for implementing activities presents the greatest immediate challenge for the project. Education, enforcement, and research activities all require money for staff, vehicles, fuel, food, travel, and other expenses. In the past, staff and vehicles were generally diverted from other tasks to the crane project by wildlife departments or organizations already short on resources. From the beginning, available staff, vehicles, and weapons for self-defense have been inadequate. Cameras, extra lenses, and funds for film, processing, and printing have also been minimal. As a result, it has not been uncommon for Wildlife Department staff in the NWFP to walk from camp to camp in remote areas to check crane possession and crane-hunting licenses. Needless to say, this is hardly an efficient way to accomplish project goals or to impress hunters with the seriousness of our intent.

Recognizing inherent limitations to government support, project leaders have been persistent over the years in finding creative ways to build crane conservation activities directly into department budgets. In many cases, crane project tasks have also been piggybacked with other wildlife-related duties. The WWF-Pakistan has periodically provided support to provincial governments for temporary allocation of staff and vehicles specifically for crane work during migration periods. It has recently expanded support for a wider range of wildlife conservation; thus crane education and conservation projects face greater competition for funds. The newly hired education officers for Zhob (Baluchistan) and Peshawar (NWFP) will undoubtedly include cranes in their training activities, but how much time they can devote to cranes remains to be seen. For that reason it is imperative that one to two individuals be hired to work exclusively on crane-hunter education and training, as well as the development of educational and publicity materials.

The most faithful project supporter from abroad—the USFWS—has seen its financial backing of project activities and other wildlife work in Pakistan halted by a freeze on the use of PL-480 funds because of U.S. congressional sanctions. Until that ban is lifted, plans to use PL-480 to help implement new conservation education, satellite-training, and hunter-education programs must be indefinitely postponed. Project leaders are now forced to devote additional time to finding new sources of domestic and international support for crane conservation activities. Cooperation between government and nongovernment agencies has been a hallmark of the project in the past. Present circumstances will force us to redouble efforts to forge new coalitions, particularly with successful hunter organizations with a history of support for wildlife conservation. Greater austerity may also provide the motivation to focus on a main task—winning crane hunters over to the side of conservation. Once training of selected crane hunters has been accomplished, it may be necessary to turn educational activities in the Kurram Valley—and ultimately Afghanistan—largely over to them. Perhaps raising funds will be easier if we try to connect Pakistan with international organizations interested in working in Afghanistan and try to take advantage of the growing cooperation between Russia and India.

In conclusion, it is clear that the crane project in Pakistan has reached an important juncture—one filled with opportunities to build on the spadework of the last thirteen years. Ironically, it comes at the time when wildlife watchers wonder whether *any* Siberian cranes will arrive at Keoladeo National Park for the winter of 1994–95. Whatever the case, there is little doubt that the remnant flock of Siberian cranes on the Indo-Russian flyway is doomed. Therefore attention must be focused on the fate of the common and demoiselle cranes. In so doing, we can take consolation in knowing that a foundation has been laid along the flyway for a mix of education, publicity, and research activities that may at least give them a reasonable chance for long-term survival.

Acknowledgments

This project owes a debt of gratitude to individuals, organizations, and agencies far too numerous to mention. We are particularly indebted to those individuals whose support was essential to getting the project off the ground: David Ferguson and Larry Mason (International Affairs Office of the U.S. Fish and Wildlife Service); Tom Roberts and Syed Babar Ali (WWF-Pakistan); J. C. Daniel (Bombay Natural History Society); Dr. George Archibald (International Crane Foundation, U.S.A.); and the late Dr. Ron Sauey. Olin Harried and the Stoughton public schools were particularly gracious in allowing Landfried to take leave from high school teaching duties on three occasions to play an active role in the project.

In addition, we want to thank those who added so much to crane conservation and educational activities in the early years of the project in India: the late Dr. Salim Ali, V. S. and Lalitha Vijayan, S. A. Hussain, and Dilavaz Variava, (Bombay Natural History Society); Harsh Vardhan (Tourism and Wildlife Society of India); Anne and Belinda Wright, Col. Jack Sawhney and Gen. E. d'Souza, (WWF-India); Bholu Khan and various wildlife wardens of Keoladeo National Park; Prakash Gole (The Environmental Society of India); Krishna Kumar (Ghana Keoladeo Natural History Society); V. D. Sharma (Wildlife Department of Rajasthan); Vickki Nanda, Alice Pandya, and other Science Office staff of the U.S. embassy in New Delhi; and Desh Bandhu (Indian Environmental Society). Special thanks go to the late Mrs. Indira Gandhi and the former Joint Secretary for Wildlife, Samar Singh (now Secretary General of WWF-India).

In Pakistan, we wish to extend appreciation to the following: Khalid Sheikh and Dawood Gaznavi (WWF-Pakistan); Muhammad Arif and K. S. Hasan (United States Information Service-Islamabad); Farooq Ahmad (Zoological Survey of Pakistan); the late General Fazle Haq (former military Governor of the NWFP); W. A. Kermani (former Inspector General of Forests); Abeedullah Jan (Inspector General of Forests); Khan Muhammad Khan (formerly Sindh Wildlife Management Board); Iqmail Shah and staff of the NWFP Wildlife Department; A. L. Rao and the National Committee for the Conservation of Wildlife; the U.S. embassy in Islamabad and U.S. consulates in Peshawar, Lahore, and Karachi; Faqir Abdul Khaliq and the crane hunters of Pakistan; Muhammad Shafique and staff of the Baluchistan Forest Department in Zhob; and staff of the Punjab Wildlife Research Center (Faisalabad).

Individuals in various international organizations have been especially helpful to our crane education and conservation work in India and Pakistan. They include Joan Fordham and Jim Harris (International Crane Foundation, U.S.A.); Mark Boultan (International Center for Conservation Education, U.K.); Paul Goriup (Nature Conservation Bureau, U.K.); Elizabeth Kemf (Worldwide Fund for Nature, Switzerland), and the late Sir Peter Scott (WWF-U.K.).

Throughout the project, journalists and writers have played an important role in relaying information to the public about the plight of the Siberian crane. Special thanks go to these writers: Azmat Ansari (Pakistan), Richard Eggleston and Ellen Porath (Associated Press, Madison, Wis.), Khushwant Singh and Nirmal Ghosh (India), Man Mohan Singh, poet (India), Rick Rockwell and Dave Iverson (WHA-TV) and Bayard Webster (*New York Times*).

9

Education to Promote Male-Selective Harvest of Grizzly Bears in the Yukon

■■
■■

Bernard L. Smith

Conservation of bear (*Ursus* spp.) populations depends on preventing conflicts between bears and people, as well as carefully managing losses to bear populations, particularly females (Miller 1990). Education has long played an important role in bear conservation in reducing conflicts between bears and people (Herrero 1985). However, virtually no educational programs have been developed to teach hunters how to detect, from a distance, the subtle morphological differences between solitary male and female bears, and to assist them to develop hunting methods that would increase their likelihood of encountering male bears. Between 1989 and 1992, in the Yukon Territory of northwestern Canada, an educational component was added to the grizzly bear (*Ursus arctos*) management program to promote the harvest of male rather than female bears by clients of commercial big-game outfitters.

This conservation education program should be of interest to a wide international audience because it (1) deals with commercial uses of wildlife; (2) complements incentives; (3) illustrates an important educational value for habituated wildlife in sanctuaries; (4) describes an educational approach to reduce the risk of unintentional and virtually undetectable overharvest; (5) uses video as an educational medium; and (6) illustrates some limitations of educational approaches to conservation.

PLANNING

Grizzly Bear Hunting and Harvest Management in the Yukon

Each August and September approximately 450 international hunters come to the wilderness of Canada's Yukon in search of up to six species of large mammals. These animals include Dall sheep (*Ovis dalli*), moose (*Alces alces*), caribou (*Rangifer tarandus*), black bears (*Ursus americanus*), wolves (*Canis lupus*), and grizzly bears. Each hunter is accompanied by a guide from one of twenty concessions in which a big-game outfitter has the monopoly to offer commercial, nonresident hunts. Typically this hunter flies into a remote lake and hunts from horseback in parties of two hunters in subalpine settings for ten to fourteen days. Grizzly bears are highly prized trophies by these hunters. Additionally, thirty hunters come to the Yukon in May and early June each year specifically to hunt bears.

Big-game outfitters are expected to harvest large mammals in a sustainable fashion within concessions averaging 14,000 square kilometers. However, grizzly bears can be unintentionally overharvested. Their reproductive rate is one of the lowest in terrestrial mammals (Bunnel and Tait 1981), their abundance is limited to fourteen to twenty-five per 1,000 square kilometers (Smith and Osmond-Jones 1991), and their harvest cannot easily be directed away from those females with high reproductive values. Furthermore, the bears are attracted to the remains of ungulates (e.g., gut and tissue from previously shot moose and caribou) where they are vulnerable to hunters. Localized and regional overharvest of females has been the primary management concern for this species in the Yukon Territory since the mid-1970s (Pearson 1975; Lortie and McDonald 1976; Sidorowicz and Gilbert 1981). Traditionally wildlife-management agencies regulate grizzly bear harvests by restricting the number of hunting opportunities through quotas or limited entry hunts, or by restricting the hunting season to later in the fall and earlier in the spring when males are more vulnerable. Education is not part of this tradition.

The Yukon government proposed concession-specific quotas in 1978 and implemented them in 1980 (Mycasiw 1981). These quotas severely restricted harvests and generated much controversy. Acrimonious debate over bear abundance was almost continuous. In 1985 a number of interventions were made by the Yukon Fish and Wildlife Branch in collaboration with the Yukon Outfitters Association to replace this quota with a point system designed to reduce and distribute the harvest of female grizzly bears, increase male grizzly bear hunting opportunities, and provide between-year flexibility and multiyear certainty to assist outfitters' market hunts (Smith 1990). These interventions included:

- 3:1 incentive scheme to harvest male versus female grizzly bears [1]
- meetings with individual outfitters to review population management, hunt management, and hunting methods
- visits by a biologist to concessions where female overharvest was occurring or other management concerns had arisen in order to assist outfitters in developing alternate approaches to hunting

These interventions marked a significant shift in strategy. If hunting behavior could be changed to reduce and disperse female harvests, then the risk of overharvest could be reduced. This risk was significant because population data were so limited and expensive to obtain, harvest trends imprecisely reflected population trends, and funding for the studies needed to resolve the disagreements over bear abundance was unlikely.

An evaluation of these interventions after four years suggested that significant shifts in hunting behaviors had occurred and that the composition of the harvest had shifted to older bears as hunting parties more frequently passed up smaller bears. However, the proportion of females in the harvest was unchanged (Smith 1990). In the evaluation, outfitters

---

[1] Under this management approach, allowable male and female harvests in each outfitting concession were estimated, and allowance was made for anticipated human-caused deaths from other hunters and kills made in defense of property. The remainder was allocated to the outfitter, calculated using a 3-point value for females and a 1-point value for males, and extended over three years. This point total was often 20 to 25. The incentive to harvest males arose when 1 point was deducted from this point total for each male taken, yet 3 points were deducted for each female taken. Obviously, more bears could be taken by the outfitter if a higher proportion of males were taken. To qualify as a "male" bear, the hide submitted to the government for inspection had to have an attached penis bone which was then separated from the hide. No member of a female-offspring group could be hunted. Government royalties from hunters was $500 for each male harvested and $750 for each female harvested.

unanimously requested tools to train their guides in how to distinguish male from female bears, and how to selectively hunt male bears.

Overall Strategic Design

In programs designed to change human systems, it is common to assume that people behave rationally and that they would not knowingly behave in a manner contrary to their self-interest (Chin and Benne 1985). In this case the assumption would be made that outfitters and guides would not knowingly overharvest bears, and if they did, they were irresponsible and needed to be strictly regulated and monitored. This assumption would favor the planning of an educational program to make outfitters and guides aware of the consequences of female over-harvest, with the expectation that they would change their behaviors once they knew that the damage to bear populations would impact their future hunting opportunities. Concomitantly harsh penalties would be imposed for those who chose to overharvest.

If wildlife conservationists instead view many nonconserving behaviors as an unintentional consequence of the "normal way of doing things," then the focus shifts to the design of various complementary interventions to shift the norms to be more conservation-oriented, within the basic value systems of the people involved (Chin and Benne 1985; Blanchard 1994; Dimock 1992). Hines et al. (1986/87) partitioned this process into several stages. When applied to this case, most outfitters valued the conservation of female bears in that they were aware of the problems of female overharvest, and opposed this practice. However, no outfitters could be convinced that their own harvest of female bears was damaging regional populations, although they would privately concede that local areas might be impacted.[2] Outfitters could not personally detect changes in bear abundance as the result of hunting pressure. They also thought that studies conducted elsewhere of sustain-

---

[2] This process of "convincing" was crucial for it implied acceptance of personal responsibility to redress a real problem. With one exception, this process only occurred when the author was in the field with outfitters and guides in the local areas where harvest statistics suggested female overharvest. There the distribution of guide sightings of family groups could be compared to the distribution of previous female and male kills. Only in these discussions did the author feel confident that outfitters and guides were convinced that local problems existed and that alternative, male-selective hunt strategies that were identified through these discussions should be tested.

able harvest levels of female bears were irrelevant to their situation. Through the 3:1 point-system incentive, outfitters were given an economic incentive to conserve. To try to take advantage of this incentive, most outfitters provided financial incentives for guides and hunters to avoid females. However, they lacked information which they considered to be useful and relevant to their problem of how to identify female bears and how best to locate and harvest male grizzly bears. They *valued* bear conservation, were *aware* of the conservation concern, and were *motivated* to be more conserving, but they lacked *knowledge* on how to conserve. This is not unusual. Smith (1992) found that 114 wildlife conservationists working in thirty-nine countries often perceived that lack of knowledge of how to conserve was a more significant barrier to conservation than awareness of the conservation concern.

Goals and Objectives

The educational program for outfitters and guides had four objectives:

1. to promote awareness among hunting guides of an observation-based, chronological sequence of decisions, which, if followed, would result in hunting parties passing up bears likely to be female
2. to reduce the proportion of female bears taken from 38 percent to less than or equal to 25 percent
3. to provide guides and outfitters with information to enable them to increase their likelihood of encountering male bears
4. to develop a tool for outfitters to evaluate guide competence in judging the sex of distant, solitary bears

Resources

Resources initially available for the program included (1) well-developed sex-identification skills in a few guides, outfitters, and biologists; (2) the McNeil River State Game Sanctuary in Alaska with biologists who knew the sex and age of more than a hundred different habituated bears; and (3) reliable data on the sex, age, and kill locations of harvested bears. Finally, a reasonable potential existed to raise funds owing to public interest in conserving female grizzly bears, the novelty of sex identification in these animals, and the promotion of local sustainable development through the Yukon Conservation Strategy (Government of the Yukon 1990).

Constraints

A number of constraints were associated with the educational program (table 9.1), skepticism being the most significant of these. Agency personnel were doubtful that an educational approach would work but were willing to experiment. They were unwilling to commit funds, however, until they were sure that video footage clearly illustrating sex differences could be obtained. Outfitters were dubious that most guides could ever reliably judge the sex of a bear, but the potential for increasing hunt revenues was sufficiently great to support the program. Many guides doubted that they could dissuade a hunter from taking a bear, even if they could determine that it was a female. Most guides and outfitters saw grizzly bear hunting as a matter of luck rather than design. Fellow bear specialists detected subtle differences between male and female bears but doubted whether sufficient numbers of guides and hunters could acquire these skills. However, once convincing video footage from the sanctuary was obtained (figure 9.1), the skepticism dissolved and funds became easier to obtain.

Participation

It is tempting to stress how "participatory" the design process is in a project. Outfitters, the stakeholders in this program, were pragmatic, busy, and dispersed. They expected the author to retain a high degree of control and to secure information and reviews as needed. Yet three participatory processes were critical. These involved development of the knowledge base, design of the program, and editing the video.

The development of the knowledge base involved bridging fundamentally different ways of knowing about bears. The knowledge system needed for this project merged the understanding of bear morphology gained by (1) the Alaskan Sanctuary biologist who had watched more than a hundred bears grow, over a fourteen-year period; (2) several guides who had watched and hunted bears for twenty years and had incorporated patterns in their hunting behaviors that resulted in particular types of bears being taken; and (3) biologists who had learned about bears from observing radio-collared bears from aircraft. Through

Table 9.1. Constraints Associated with an Educational Program to Promote Male-Selective Hunting of Grizzly Bears

CONSTRAINTS	HOW THESE WERE OVERCOME
Outfitter skepticism over whether bear sex could be determined from a distance.	A workshop was held for outfitters with an Alaskan Master Bear Guide whose clients had taken the largest bears in the world over the previous five years. This individual could reliably judge bear sex, age, weight, and skull size from a distance. A video of this workshop was prepared and distributed.
Agency skepticism over whether guides could judge bear sex and reduce female kills.	Key individuals were shown convincing video footage. Clear outfitter support for the program was demonstrated. Adaptive management strategies were promoted.
Outfitter-guide-client knowledge systems were vertically integrated and horizontally restricted by outfitters.	Programs were designed to fit within this vertical integration and did not attempt between-concession linkages, such as guide workshops. These were resisted by outfitters because they feared the sharing of business-related secrets with competitors.
Sociopolitical systems, particularly impending settlements of outstanding land claims with aboriginal people, did not promote outfitters to invest in bear hunting in new areas using different methods that might favor male harvest.	This constraint could not be overcome, and remains a significant impediment to change.
"Learning by doing" opportunities for guides were not available because guides saw few bears each season.	A train-and-drill component was appended to the video to assist guides in practicing skills learned in the video.
Confusion arising from the simultaneous roles of the biologist as "expert," "educator," "allocator," and "enforcer."	The "regulator" role was transferred to conservation officers, the "expert" role to the master guide and the sanctuary biologist, and the "educator" role to the outfitter using the video as a training tool.

CONSTRAINTS	HOW THESE WERE OVERCOME
Absence of quantitative data on sex- and age-related differences in relative body proportions.	The program was based on rules of thumb used by experts, and tested against body-proportion measures taken from video photographs (figures 9.1a and 9.1b).
Outfitters Association's philosophical reluctance to accept government grants.	Proposals and video credits were carefully worded.
Differences between large, molting coastal bears at the sanctuary and small, well-furred interior bears in the Yukon.	The program stressed that although sex differences were more subtle in the Yukon bears, the coastal bears served as better training guides since the differences were more pronounced.
Sensationalized accounts in popular magazines of the aggressiveness of wounded bears led hunting parties to shoot from a distance, thereby resulting in less selective hunting.	An article in a popular magazine is planned.

personal participation in these activities and long discussions over a twelve-year period, an understanding arose which was an inductive and intuitive synthesis of these ways of knowing.

Participation in the design of the educational program with a small planning team led to a focus on five products (table 9.2). The most extensive participation was in reviews of three drafts of the video script by outfitters, guides, and taxidermists.

The final critical participatory process lay in the selection of twelve minutes of clips from the more than thirty hours of video footage and in the unscripted narration by the Alaskan Sanctuary biologist, which described the sex, age, and distinguishing characteristics of sixty bears.

Alternative Methods

Possible alternatives that were considered and rejected included a booklet with sketches and tips based on interviews with selected guides, a poster for outfitter camps, a guide workshop before the hunting season,

Figure 9.1a Side views of adult female (*upper left*), adult male (*upper right*), sub-adult female (*lower left*), and subadult male (*lower right*) grizzly bears. Images taken from a training video for hunting guides entitled *Take a Closer Look,* a film designed to develop hunters' skills in differentiating, from a distance, male and female grizzly bears based on body shape and proportion (photos by B. Smith).

a semitechnical report on the results of investigations into the morphological differences between the sexes, articles in popular hunting magazines, and information targeted at hunters rather than guides and outfitters. Reasons for selecting video as the educational medium included (1) the need to show animal movement, behavior, and body form in different postures; (2) outfitters' needs to have control over the training of their guides (partly to prevent exchange of secrets between businesses); and (3) outfitters' desires to market their guides to clients as professionals. Materials that might have been effective at training but conveyed a sense that guides were not competent would not have been used. Moreover, it was logistically difficult for outfitters to transport guides to a central training workshop before the hunting season.

Figure 9.1b Front views of adult female (*upper left*), adult male (*upper right*), subadult female (*lower left*), and subadult male (*lower right*) grizzly bears (photos by B. Smith).

IMPLEMENTATION

The various educational materials were made available to outfitters in a sequence over a three-year period shortly before their bear hunts (table 9.2). A workshop with the Alaskan master guide was held in the spring of 1989. The video that followed provided his tips and suggestions, and

Table 9.2. Details of Educational Interventions in the Grizzly Bear Harvest Management Program, 1989–1992

DESCRIPTION	INTENT	COMMENT
Outfitter workshop with Alaskan Master Bear Guide, summarized in a real-time, home video (April 1989).	To convince outfitters that guides could judge age, sex, weight, and skull size and direct clients to take only male bears.	The Master Bear Guide showed other guides that they could apply the same methods that they unknowingly used with dogs (based on head shape). He provided proof of his ability through data and bear slides. His message was credible and convincing.
Twelve-minute training video that stressed observational criteria based on body proportions, for guides to use to decide which bears to stalk and take (April 1990).	To provide outfitters with a tool to train guides in how to direct clients to avoid taking females and small bears and to take adult males.	The decision to stalk a bear inevitably leads to the bear being taken; thus it was important to train guides to pass up bears from a distance, without stalking them.
A sixty-minute video quiz containing sixty pairs of identical clips showing individual bears—the first silent so the guide had to judge sex and age group, the second narrated by the sanctuary biologist describing the sex and age of the bear (April 1990).	To provide a train-and-drill sequence to reinforce the decision sequence and identification skills. To provide outfitters with a tool to evaluate a guide's ability to judge bear sex.	The biologist also commented on behavior and body features that assisted in judging the age and sex of the bear.
A self-adhesive silhouette of an adult male bear listing the identification characteristics of adult males (figure 9.2) (July 1990).	For guides to adhere to spotting scopes to remind them of key points to look for when judging a bear.	Served as a checklist.
A twenty-four-page booklet entitled "Hunt Wisely: A Guide to Male-Selective Grizzly Bear Hunting" (figure 9.3) (July 1991).	To promote strategies and designs that would increase the probability of hunting parties encountering adult males.	Investigated twelve factors such as habitat use, wariness, seasonal and daily activity patterns, and movement rates. These were derived from technical studies and were quite speculative.

Figure 9.2 Adhesive sticker distributed to hunting guides to provide a checklist of identifying characteristics of adult male grizzly bears that had been presented in the video.

persuaded guides that they could judge the sex and size of bears they encountered. This was widely shown within the outfitting and guiding community, but video images of the projected slides were not clear. In 1990 the video on sex identification was presented to outfitters at a spring meeting. They viewed it with much concentration and murmured their guesses of bear sex during the quiz (most of them judged correctly), and they were enthusiastic about the product. That season, outfitters used the video to train their guides. Some flew portable video tape players into remote camps to train guides (and, in a few cases, hunters) to judge which bears to pass up and which to stalk and shoot. Outfitters also were given adhesive decals to distribute to guides to remind them of the identifying characteristics of trophy male grizzly bears that had been emphasized in the video (figure 9.2). At this point in the implementation of the program, the author left the Yukon, and responsibility for parts of the grizzly bear management program was shared by several biologists with responsibilities for other species. At a November 1990 meeting the director of the Fish and Wildlife Branch

168   Bernard L. Smith

Figure 9.3 Example of text from the booklet *Hunt Wisely: A Guide to Male-Selective Grizzly Bear Hunting,* which explained the possible influence of twelve factors on the likelihood of a hunter encountering a male versus a female grizzly bear. This page illustrates the implications of differences in pelage coloration.

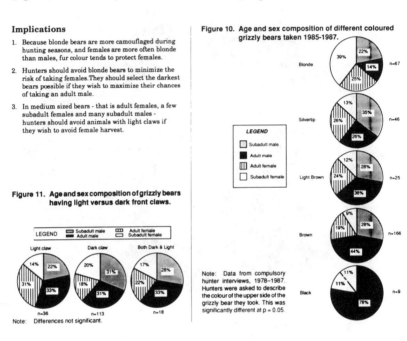

Implications

1. Because blonde bears are more camouflaged during hunting seasons, and females are more often blonde than males, fur colour tends to protect females.

2. Hunters should avoid blonde bears to minimize the risk of taking females.They should select the darkest bears possible if they wish to maximize their chances of taking an adult male.

3. In medium sized bears - that is adult females, a few subadult females and many subadult males - hunters should avoid animals with light claws if they wish to avoid female harvest.

Figure 11. Age and sex composition of grizzly bears having light versus dark front claws.

LEGEND   Subadult male   Adult female
          Adult male   Subadult female

Light claw   Dark claw   Both Dark & Light

n=36   n=113   n=18
Note: Differences not significant.

Figure 10. Age and sex composition of different coloured grizzly bears taken 1985-1987.

Blonde   39%   22%   14%   25%   n=67

LEGEND
    Subadult male
    Adult male
    Adult female
    Subadult female

Silvertip   13%   35%   26%   26%   n=46

Light Brown   12%   28%   24%   36%   n=25

Brown   0%   28%   19%   44%   n=166

Note: Data from compulsory hunter interviews, 1978–1987. Hunters were asked to describe the colour of the upper side of the grizzly bear they took. This was significantly different at p = 0.05.

Black   11%   11%   78%   n=9

complimented outfitters on their more male-selective hunting. In July 1991 the booklet *Hunt Wisely: A Guide to Male-Selective Grizzly Bear Hunting* (Smith 1991) was distributed to outfitters by mail, for distribution to guides to assist them in selecting alternate hunting strategies that might increase their likelihood of encountering adult male grizzly bears (figure 9.3). In 1992 the decals and booklets were available in all offices, and the video was available from a local fish and game association.

The essential process of encouragement to reinforce more sex-selective hunting practices by outfitters and guides was, in retrospect, inadequate. Experience has shown that merely providing information does not lead to enduring behavioral change (Kotler 1982) and that interventions are essential to reinforce an individual's new behaviors and to incorporate these behaviors into the norms of the group (Dimock 1992). Guides and outfitters who had demonstrated improvement should have received strong prestige incentives. A new guide status of "Master

Grizzly Guide" should have been created. It would have had prestige value and economic value in hunt marketing. Personal encouragement to outfitters each year and direct contact with guides should have been stressed.

PRODUCT

Insufficient time has passed to allow a rigorous evaluation; however, some preliminary observations can be made about the degree to which the objectives of the training program were met based on the sex of harvested bears (until 1992), the ages of harvested bears (until 1991), and from interviews with outfitters.

1. *Were guides aware of an observation-based sequence of decisions, which, if followed, would result in hunting parties passing up bears likely to be female?* Yes. Outfitters ensured that guides had wide exposure to the video and decals.

2. *Did the proportion of females in the total kill decline from approximately 35 percent to less than 25 percent?* No, although there have been encouraging statistics. It would be expected that programs to encourage hunting parties to pass up bears that could be female would decrease female harvests and, until male-selective hunting strategies were developed, total harvests as well. This was seen. On average, 18.7 females were taken in 1990, 1991, and 1992 compared to 24.2 taken annually between 1974 and 1989. On average, 56.3 grizzly bears were taken in 1990, 1991, and 1992 compared to 61.2 taken annually between 1974 and 1989. The proportion of females in the kill declined from a sixteen-year average of 38.2 (a range of 31.1 to 49.2) to 25.8 percent in 1990 when enthusiasm for the male-selective hunting was highest. However, it increased to 34.7 percent in 1991 and to 40.4 percent in 1992, partly because male and total harvests also declined.

Forces favoring a reduction in the proportion of females in the kill during the program's first year included outfitters' expectations of greater revenues and flexibility, and their enthusiasm for the project generated by the video. Forces favoring a return to previous hunting strategies during subsequent years may have included (1) a realization among outfitters that the development of successful spring and fall hunting strategies would require significant economic investment; (2) a feeling among outfitters that it was not prudent to invest in new camps, equipment, and experimental hunts, given the concern created by the declining North American economy and the uncertainty with the imminent settlement of outstanding aboriginal land claims; (3) a decline in the government's advocacy and encouragement of grizzly bear conservation following the author's departure; and (4) a concern about bear predation on moose calves (Larsen et al. 1989; Miller and Ballard 1992), which may have contributed to a widespread sense that bears were now abundant, thus rendering their conservation less of an issue.

The age and sex composition of the harvest also changed. In 1990 and 1991, when enthusiasm for selective hunting was highest, the proportion of the total kill that was adult female was 13.6 percent, much less than the 24.4 percent during the point-system incentive period, 1985–1988, and the 18.6 percent during the quota period, 1981–1984 (Smith 1990). This shift is significant to the conservation of grizzly populations because it turned the harvest away from females with high reproductive value.

3. *Did the educational materials provide guides and outfitters with information to enable them to develop hunting strategies that would increase their likelihood of encountering male rather than female bears?* Yes, but it is not clear how widely the information was used. The pretest version of this booklet was enthusiastically reviewed by two outfitters, both of whom were interested in developing male-selective hunting strategies. They indicated that relatively few of their guides shared this desire. Most guides are only interested in happy clients, not long-term business viability or conservation concerns. Hence this information will likely be applied only by individual guides and outfitters who are keenly involved in the subject. The remark by outfitters, "You can take a horse to water, but you can't make it drink," applies to passive information exchange.

4. *Did the video quiz provide outfitters with a tool to measure the bear judging-skills of hunting guides?* Yes, but it is not widely used. Outfitters restrict the hunting of grizzly bears to a few trusted guides. Few outfitters risk the point penalties that could result from allowing a new guide to take out a hunter in search of a bear if the guide had not been able to correctly judge the sex of the bears on the video quiz.

Five secondary results, or coincidences, have occurred. First, low agency expenditures for grizzly bear management has continued, which has not allowed funding of population studies. Smith and Osmond-Jones (1991) identified several mountainous ecoregions where baseline research was needed. Educational and collaborative approaches such as these demonstrate stewardship action for a species. Unfortunately, this may reduce public interest in research for the species, particularly when public and agency research interests are higher for other species. Second, there has been a proliferation in the use of video as an educational medium for fish and wildlife management. Slide-tape audiovisuals are not being produced, although a heavy reliance on print continues. Third, educational efforts to promote male-selective hunting are emerging in other jurisdictions, for example, with polar bears in the Northwest Territories (M. Taylor, Polar Bear Management biologist, Government of Northwest Territory, personal communication). Fourth, the author's exposure to Alaska's McNeil River Sanctuary, the biologists there, and the habituated bears, and agency exposure to the footage, has increased interest in habituating bears in selected areas to allow guided viewing. Finally, the role of extension, education, communication, and collaboration enjoys an increased emphasis in fish and wildlife management within this agency, although much of this emphasis has been related to the shift to much more cooperative management of fish and wildlife with aboriginal peoples, as well as interest and user groups.

Key Elements of Success

Six critical elements were included in this educational program:

1. prior acceptance by outfitters and guides of the conservation concern
2. client demand for the educational program
3. access to the one place in the world with habituated bears and resident biologists who knew the sex and age of the bears
4. early and thorough understanding of the norms in the hunting system, including such factors as how bear hunts were marketed, how bears were hunted, how bears were distributed, and how hunters, guides, and outfitters felt about bear hunting
5. early involvement of a respected peer of the target group to counter skepticism
6. practice and drill component in the video

Product Dissemination

Dissemination of information on the program was widespread. This educational program has been described at three technical workshops, at two sportsmen's group meetings, and in hunter's magazines. Copies of the video were mailed to every jurisdiction managing grizzly or brown bears. Informal dissemination of information on the program has likely been extensive throughout commercial and local hunting organizations in northwestern North America. Additionally, home copying of the video has probably been extensive.

Closing Thoughts

Three points and their concomitant lessons may be unique to this case:

1. *Conservation education for commercial interests differs from that for communities.* Businesses face competitive forces that lead them to resist sharing their innovations. Innovative peers from outside the competitive circle should be used in these situations to minimize tension and maximize learning. Limited interest and investment in experimentation should be anticipated when businesses face uncertainty or feel threatened. In these situations, passively providing information will not lead to change. It may be necessary to minimize experimentation risks and costs as much as possible or delay education and communication efforts until the business climate is more stable. Government emphasis on regulating commercial uses of wildlife creates structures and attitudes that resist educational approaches. People chosen to deliver education and communication programs should be those who are not tainted by past involvement in regulatory roles.

2. *Conservation education efforts need to stress symbolic values relevant to the client group.* Symbolism can be very powerful in social marketing (Kotler 1982), and images symbolizing motherhood, vulnerability, and cuteness are often used to evoke conservation concern. To outfitters, hunters, and guides, grizzly bears symbolize wilderness as well as power, aggression, and danger (Eaton 1978). Imagery in this program's video was selected to be consistent with these symbolic values, and included (a) circles with cross hairs; (b) luxuriantly furred, healthy adult males in wilderness settings; and

(c) smaller bears exhibiting subordinate behaviors to adult males. Audiences who have been observed watching the video have been silent and tense and have enjoyed the imagery. It is important to know your audience, trust your instincts, and pretest, pretest, pretest.

3. *Conservation educators need to carefully design transitions for enduring local conservation action.* The presence of strong, determined conservation educators driving the process of change over a long period is a consistent facet of case studies related to building support for conservation in rural areas (Quebec Labrador Foundation/Atlantic Center for the Environment 1986), protecting endangered habitats in Canada (Hummel 1988), and creating environmental and conservation action in international settings (Pomerantz and Blanchard 1992). In this example, although many factors were involved, the initiative faltered following the diffusion of responsibility for the program. Conservation educators need to carefully design transitions in leadership, control, and economic support, as has been described in agricultural extension projects by Bunch (1982), in community-based resource management programs by Korten (1986), in common-property resource management systems by Berkes (1989), in cooperative management of local fisheries by Pinkerton (1989), and in wildlife extension projects by Berger (1991).

Acknowledgments

Thanks are extended to outfitters D. Dickson, C. Martin, and J. Want; to biologists L. Aumiller, J. Carey, and C. Matt; and to video producer J. Booth. C. Gentry, S. Jacobson, R. Rodden, B. Slough, C. Smits, D. Toews, and E. Vaughan provided useful editorial comments. Financial assistance to this program was provided by the Yukon Conservation Strategy Demonstration Project Program, the North American Foundation for Big Game, and the Government of Yukon's Department of Renewable Resources.

PART FOUR

Programming for Schools

10

The Global Rivers Environmental
Education Network

■■
■■

William B. Stapp, Mare M. Cromwell,
and Arjen Wals

Through the University of Michigan's innovative GREEN (Global Rivers Environmental Education Network) project, teachers all over the world are taking students to their local river and teaching them to monitor water quality, analyze watershed usage, identify the socioeconomic determinants of river degradation, and present their findings and recommendations to local officials. These students are also exchanging their data and insights with other students in other cultures throughout the world. GREEN is designed to empower students, not only to learn in depth about their local environmental problems but also to act on their discoveries, and to share their knowledge in a global, cross-cultural context.

PLANNING

What is GREEN?

Globalization is a word one commonly hears in educational circles these days. It refers to the widely acknowledged need of schools to equip their students for an interdependent world, linked by a closely coupled world economy. This shrinking world is brought closer together by massive environmental problems and issues that transcend national and even continental boundaries—issues we can address only through an unprecedented degree of global cooperation. One major challenge that will increasingly confront environmental educators is to develop curricula and instructional strategies that present local environmental issues in a global perspective—but without overwhelming the students or making them feel hopeless. How can we educate and empower students to take action on local issues while simultaneously developing within them a global, cross-cultural perspective on these issues? How can we best educate this first generation of truly planetary citizens to assume responsibility for their shared, imperiled home?

One promising new approach to meeting this challenge is the Global Rivers Environmental Education Network, recently initiated by Professor William Stapp and graduate students of the University of Michigan School of Natural Resources. Still in its early stages of development, GREEN is an international network that seeks to bring secondary school students, teachers, and communities around the world closer together through the bond of studying and improving our common river systems. The network is an expanding global communication system that invites participants to reflect on ways that land and water usage and cultural perceptions influence river systems, and vice versa. It encourages them to learn about and become involved in complex, real-world concerns that extend across all boundaries. In this way GREEN works to achieve three interrelated goals:

- it acquaints students with the environmental problems and characteristics of their local watershed, giving them "hands-on" experience in the theory and practice of chemical, biological, and sociological research
- it empowers students through community problem-solving strategies, thereby enabling them to see the relevance of subjects they learn in school to the "real world"
- it promotes intercultural communication and understanding, and thereby fosters awareness of the global context of local environmental issues and of the significance of cultural differences in choosing effective problem-solving strategies

Teacher and students gathering water-quality data to determine the "health" of the river for recreation (*photo by W. B. Stapp*).

Why Rivers? Rivers were chosen as the central focus of the project primarily because they are a reliable and informative index of the environmental quality of their watersheds. Additionally, rivers form a nexus for relating chemistry to biology, and for relating the physical sciences to the social sciences and humanities, since rivers bind together the natural and human environment from the mountains to the sea, and from farmland to the inner city. In fact, 85 percent of the world's human population lives on or near a river. For these reasons, the study of rivers forms a coherent curricular framework for the study of a wide range of environmental issues and problems. Rivers also contain a historical perspective on cultures and history, forming an ideal basis for learning about cultural diversity, and for engaging in cross-cultural dialogue.

Through involvement in a network on local rivers, students share information, techniques, and different approaches to problem solving. They also can learn that their investigations have a purpose and are valued by their peers elsewhere in the world. The intention of this process is to motivate students to further their understanding and to work to resolve some of the water-quality problems they have discovered. GREEN is therefore a program designed to bring individuals closer together and encourage them to develop simultaneously a sense of responsibility both for their communities and their planet.

Origin and Development of GREEN

The roots of the Interactive Water-Quality Monitoring Program, adapted throughout GREEN, are from a biology class at Huron High School on the banks of the Huron River, Ann Arbor, Michigan, in 1984.

In 1984 a concessionaire was permitted to operate a wind surfing program at a local park on the Huron River. Subsequently in 1985, the local Public Health Department noted that several persons, including a student from Huron High School who had been active in this park, had contracted Hepatitis A.

Student concern about the river water quality spurred a biology class to want to learn more. Working with Prof. William Stapp and Mark Mitchell of the University of Michigan's School of Natural Resources, Dale Greiner, their teacher, acted on the students' interest in testing the river water. William Stapp had been active in designing pro-active environmental education programs with teachers in the area for more than twenty years. The challenge of student-oriented water monitoring was a natural evolution for him in his work with students and community problem solving. Working collaboratively with graduate students from the University of Michigan and Huron High School, Dr. Stapp designed a two-week model water-quality monitoring program that was appropriate for secondary school students based on the National Sanitation Foundation Water-Quality Index (figure 10.1). This was the seed of GREEN.

The two-week model program involved a packet of instructional materials consisting of maps of the watershed; a manual containing information on how to run the nine water-quality tests accurately and safely; material on how to monitor river water for macroinvertebrates as indicators of water quality; a slide-tape presentation on the characteristics of the watershed and changing land patterns; and a set of water-quality testing kits that are accurate at the 2 percent level for most of the nine water-quality tests. These field test kits are available for purchase on most continents.

Figure 10.1. The National Sanitation Foundation Water-Quality Index

In 1982 the National Sanitation Foundation had requested a group of aquatic specialists to rank thirty-five water-quality tests for inclusion in a water-quality index (WQI). Through a "Delphi Process," information collected was sent back to the respondents for ranking, and, finally, *nine water-quality tests* were selected for the WQI. Weighted curves and values were then created by asking the specialists to graph the level of water quality of each of the selected nine parameters from 0 to 100. The eventual graph for each of the tests was the result of averaging the data collected from the 142 participants. The nine tests are:

> Dissolved Oxygen
> Fecal Coliform
> pH
> Biochemical Oxygen Demand
> Temperature
> Total Phosphate
> Nitrates
> Turbidity
> Total Solids

The following is a chronology of the two-week program:

Day 1:   Discuss river concerns; view watershed slide show

Days 2–3:   Learn the nine parameters

Day 4:   Monitor the river's water quality

Day 5:   Calculate data; interpret results; derive Water-Quality Index; relate data to human and animal use of river

Days 6–10: Develop an action plan and take action

During the second week students focused on the results of their monitoring and the consequent steps they could take based on the data. The bacteria levels in the river were far above healthy levels for swimming or even sailing, with fecal coliform counts over 2,000 colonies per 100 milliliters of water (counts should not exceed 200 fecal coliform colonies for total human body contact activities, such as swimming). The students had monitored exactly where city residents were wind surfing, thereby pointing out a public-health concern.

Although students could not determine the source of the high bacteria levels, they decided to notify the County Health Department, City Council members, and Ann Arbor Parks and Recreation Department. They also submitted articles to local newspapers informing read-

Students entering water-quality data into their international EcoNet computer program (*photo by W. B. Stapp*).

ers that they should take caution in using the river because of the high bacteria levels. The students explained that although fecal coliform were not damaging to human health, high levels of this bacteria had implications for human health because of the pathogens that possibly coexist with it (e.g., hepatitis A, gastroenteritis, dysentery, and cholera, among others). The source of these high levels of bacteria is generally poorly treated or untreated sewage or animal waste, a common phenomena in developing nations—and also an occurrence in the United States.

The class lobbied for a sign to be posted at the wind surfing area, warning windsurfers and others that the area should not be used for swimming or board sailing (total body contact with the water). The wind surfing concession was eventually closed down. The City of Ann Arbor also undertook an evaluation of its underground storm drains and discovered many incorrect connections of sanitary sewage lines into the storm drains—the source of the high bacteria levels.

The classroom program continued at Huron High School for the following two years during 1985 to 1986, while the program expanded to two other high schools and communities on the Huron River, above and below Ann Arbor. All three communities conducted their two-week program simultaneously and the students shared results of their water-quality monitoring, thus gaining a perspective on the changing water quality in the river.

In 1985 and 1986 the three high school classes convened at a congress at the end of the monitoring period. They shared their test results, collected aquatic macroinvertebrates as indicators of water quality, and evaluated and recommended ways to improve the educational program. Many students continued to show their commitment by working with the city to post areas of questionable water quality; requesting the city to lower water levels to allow river clean-up activities; preparing letters to government officials regarding the results of river monitoring; and making presentations at national and international conferences.

In 1987 Friends of the Rouge, another Michigan river, expressed an interest in transferring the Huron River monitoring model to their region. The Rouge Program was developed so that students from diverse socioeconomic classes—from rural areas through wealthy suburbs to inner city Detroit—could exchange information on the progressively deteriorating water quality of the river that connected them—and in the process learn about one another as well. The program was initiated with sixteen high schools in 1987, and has expanded to fifty-five high schools as of 1992.

During the five years that the Rouge Program has been in existence, the following new components have been added to the Huron River model:

- establishing a Rouge River Advisory Committee, made up of educators, community leaders, and natural resource professionals
- linking classrooms with community organizations and citizens by an interactive computer conference program
- staging an extensive youth congress at the end of the program to bring together students from all participating schools
- developing a social studies simulation game on watershed management
- initiating a heavy-metals testing program
- involving selected schools in cross-cultural partnerships

The student congress was a particularly exciting part of the watershed program. Students gathered on a Saturday to share their results and make specific recommendations to improve the water quality. In

Figure 10.2. Basic Elements of the Original Interactive Water-Monitoring Program for Schools

1. Simple, reliable tests that measure the nine parameters in the National Sanitation Foundation's Water-Quality Index are performed at all sites on the same day to collect meaningful data about the river's quality. Tests are taught to teachers in workshops, and many schools are assisted by trained resource people.

2. The data are compared and shared along the watershed through a computer conference system and/or a student conference. From this joint analysis and interpretation, students generate questions and concerns about their river. The data may also point to issues regarding local land-use patterns.

3. The students use their concerns as a springboard to identify particular problems, collect additional information, and then plan their actions to improve the state of their river.

the afternoon, students chose one of a series of skill-developing sessions—writing public service announcements (PSAs); developing a video about the river; preparing a newspaper article; creating posters to educate others; constructing a clay watershed model; staging a dramatic production-street theater; organizing for political change—all based on educating the community on river ecology and pollution issues.

In 1986 the first edition of the *Field Manual for Water-Quality Monitoring: An Environmental Education Program for Schools* (Mitchell and Stapp 1992) was published to record the model that had proven so successful on the Huron River. The book has been revised six times and is widely disseminated around the world. It is largely through the *Field Manual* that new watershed programs have developed.

As the water-quality program expanded to other communities in Michigan and the world, other elements were added to the educational program. These included testing for heavy metals; shifting to a more comprehensive interactive computer program—EcoNet; creating Hypercard packets for watershed programs; developing international, cross-cultural partner programs; and extending the program to other curricular areas, such as art, computer studies, English, video classes, and history. This project has inspired the establishment of similar watershed programs in schools in all fifty states and in fifty-five nations (figure 10.2).

Watershed program resources and constraints. As the water-monitoring model has become more sophisticated, the constraints to developing

University students in India monitoring a local river (*photo by W. B. Stapp*).

the programs have become more complex. As a simple classroom project in monitoring local surface waters, the logistics are more basic. Teachers need the financial resources to purchase testing equipment and to transport their students to the local river or lake. This type of hands-on project can be more demanding on a teacher's already overcommitted curriculum that must meet state assessment standards. Some educators have to overcome institutional barriers in the form of unsupportive school administrations.

The question of the validity of data is a large concern and, for some programs, a true constraint. It is difficult to guarantee the quality of the data that the students collect unless the equipment is calibrated exactly and unless teachers are vigilant with the students during the monitoring. In many cases this is challenging for teachers with a full course schedule. Many educators see the data collected as an educational experience in experimental science. If any extreme results signifying pollution problems are uncovered, teachers and students are encouraged to contact natural resource professionals who have the time and equipment to follow up on the data by conducting more thorough and extensive testing.

When a watershedwide program is the goal (an area that transcends single school districts), usually an outside agency is required to act as the coordinator, fund-raiser, and logistical organizer. Teacher-training workshops, preset monitoring dates, and river sites are planned, and equipment must be prepared and calibrated. If a student computer conference is created, the complications of telecommunications in the classroom are introduced. Teachers are challenged to expand their curricula beyond the science of water into the sociology and politics of water management. In some cases teachers are allowed the freedom and luxury of time to work collaboratively as interdisciplinary teams within schools to enhance the cross-disciplinary nature of the project. Though, unfortunately, this is the rare case in most schools where teachers' free time is a limited resource.

The Next Step: GREEN

The very fact that constraints and resources exist for water-monitoring programs is actually an incentive for a network of programs to be developed so that the successes and failures of the individual programs can be shared. After extensive experience with a variety of water-monitoring programs and school scenarios, the concept of an international community of such programs was a natural, if not ambitious, step for the School of Natural Resources. The concept of GREEN was crystallized in 1989, as the result of a seminar of graduate and undergraduate students led by William Stapp in the School of Natural Resources at the University of Michigan.

IMPLEMENTATION

A program as extensive as the Global Rivers Environmental Education Network should be considered in its evolution of phases. The scope and potential for GREEN lends itself to short-term and long-term goals.

Phase 1. The Initiation of GREEN

Under the guidance of William Stapp, a committee of twenty-six university students with backgrounds in environmental education and international issues was organized as an advanced-level Environmental Education class in January 1989. Discussion about the vision and goals of GREEN took priority in creating the project. The students within the class then divided themselves into separate committees to organize the tasks that lay ahead in planning the international workshops in the summer.

Initially, letters were sent to selected environmental educators in twenty-eight nations. These letters invited educational and environmental leaders to form host committees to bring educators and others together for a workshop to exchange ideas on watershed programs. One of the aims of the workshops was to discuss educational approaches designed to provide students with an experiential, interdisciplinary program. These approaches integrate water issues into the social and natural sciences with the information that the learners collected. Each water-study program would also support the educational goals of each nation.

Twenty-two workshops were hosted in eighteen nations in Africa, Latin America, Europe (Eastern and Western), Asia, the Middle East, and Australia, bringing together teachers, school administrators, students, citizens, resource specialists, university personnel, and representatives from government and nongovernment organizations. University of Michigan representatives participated in training and facilitating at each session. The workshops were fruitful in stimulating ideas and plans, highlighted by the following points.

1. *Water quality varied.* Rivers varied in quality from very pristine to highly polluted rivers that contained, at midday, 0.0 ppm dissolved oxygen, 1.2 million colonies of fecal coliform per 100 milliliters of water, 138 ppm biochemical oxygen demand, and high concentrations of heavy metals and toxic organics. Nitrogen levels in some estuaries had increased by 200 percent since the 1950s. One bay has received 600 tons of inorganic mercury since 1953.

2. *School structure was a factor.* School curricula vary greatly throughout the world. Some nations are decentralized and flexible in permitting interdisciplinary water-quality programs into the curricula. However, other nations have highly centralized school programs where students are prepared for passing rigorous national examinations. One such nation permits students to substitute an independent study project for the national biology exam. In this case, students could petition the government to be assigned advisers for an individual river study.

Meeting with the assistant director of Taiwan Environmental Protection Agency to solicit a river to be a part of a cross-cultural program (*photo by W. B. Stapp*).

3. *Enthusiastic reception shown by participants.* Participants in many workshops expressed great interest in water-monitoring programs designed for students to link education to real-life experiences; work between disciplines; share information through computer networking; and take action on information collected. Other participants expressed concerns that science is pure and value-free, thus students should not take action on data collected; leaving the school grounds without armed security guards was not permitted; and water-monitoring kits and computer networking were too costly. To reduce expenses, some participants suggested that the study of benthic macroinvertebrates might be used to determine water quality and that the postal service, instead of computers, be used to share information.

4. *Access and interest in computer use varied.* Some schools already use powerful computer-networking systems to share data and information on water programs and have access to a national data base on rivers. These schools are interested in making better use of international computer-networking opportunities. Teachers in

some of the other international workshops, however, view computers with some hostility or skepticism. They believe that computers overshadow less "high-tech" activities, and are more costly, time-consuming, and impractical. Some concerns were expressed by educators who do not even have the means to contact other schools in their community by telephone.

5. *Local steps taken to begin water studies in schools.* Following the GREEN workshops, some nations committed government funds to developing river-monitoring programs. Teachers volunteered to organize and coordinate river projects, and computers were donated to link schools and communities to the GREEN computer network. Committees were formed to prepare teacher and student curriculum guides for water monitoring. Several countries appointed national directors to coordinate GREEN activities and prepare major articles for teacher journals. In addition, funding from private and public sectors was allocated to develop programs and obtain equipment and supplies.

Initial resources and constraints. The development of GREEN can be largely attributed to a sound environmental educational model and a vision of transcending cultural boundaries with global environmental issues. The committed work of the students and faculty at the University of Michigan have propelled the project to realization. This perseverance is complemented by the international community of environmental education leaders in close touch with the School of Natural Resources. In addition, the willingness of GREEN workshop leaders to travel on a low budget and GREEN workshop hosts to organize the seminars and share their homes and kitchens with the GREEN representatives significantly lowered the costs of the entire venture.

Certainly some constraints to the initial development of GREEN existed, such as minimal funding and the fact that GREEN was only the barest skeleton of a network. In truth, the infrastructure for the network was only developed following that first summer and is still in the process of evolving. More significant, the variety of school resources available globally are extreme in their differences. The model that was developed in Michigan for water monitoring was not completely appropriate throughout the world. Schools in Germany found the tests too simplistic for their high school students, whereas schools in Ecuador found the equipment needs too technical and inaccessible. Instead, the

Ecuadorean educators chose an alternative model of monitoring based on a biological index. Educators in different corners of the world have proved that, with minimal resources, students can collect real-world environmental data, share this data with others, and work to improve their local environment.

Phase 2: The Creation of the Infrastructure and Networking

Many of the nations that hosted workshops that first summer have initiated their own school-based, water-monitoring programs. Taiwan initiated two programs monitoring rivers; schools in Germany have created an environmental monitoring network; and Israel is incorporating river studies into their new national senior high school curriculum. The *Field Manual for Water-Quality Monitoring* has been translated into Bengali, Chinese, Czech, German, Hebrew, Hungarian, Italian, Japanese, Russian, and Spanish.

It has been clear that there is significant interest around the world to learn more about student water monitoring and networking. Consequently, GREEN has focused its next phase of development on creating a sound network accessible around the world and on the dissemination of relevant materials and resources for participants.

Components of the GREEN network. Using communication to solve environmental issues and empower students to undertake these challenges is the backbone of GREEN's philosophy. The network presently disseminates a semiannual, international newsletter to more than twenty-one hundred educators, ministry officials, and other resource persons in 125 countries. A series of GREEN International Computer Conferences has been established on EcoNet, an international communication system within the Institute for Global Communications that serves participants working for environmental preservation and maintenance. In addition, GREEN has created the Partner Watershed Program to link classrooms between nations so that they might share their cultures, water data, and land issues.

The GREEN Newsletter. The *GREEN Newsletter* is the most extensive communication tool of the network owing to the accessibility of the

American and Japanese students discussing water quality in Japan (*photo by W. B. Stapp*).

mail system. Each newsletter focuses on a particular theme of interest, such as how to start a water-monitoring program, low-cost monitoring techniques or models, and methodologies for student action. In addition, each issue highlights exciting programs that serve as examples for local water monitoring and student problem solving for different parts of the globe.

The GREEN International Computer Conferences. The GREEN conferences have established an international database of student-collected, water-quality data and the exchange of ideas and concerns among students, teachers, and other professionals. Participants from a range of different nations are able to communicate their experiences and receive almost instantaneous responses from international participants.

The GREEN International Computer Conferences are hosted by EcoNet, an interactive computer network based at the Institute for Global Communications in San Francisco. The network has more than three thousand active participants in more than eighty countries. In addition, the GREEN conferences are networked through EcoNet into the international Association for Progressive Communication (APC), a

Figure 10.3. GREEN-EcoNet Computer Conference Discussion

Topic 3   High Total Solids Readings   1 response
St. Joseph's College, Australia gr.issues   8:32 P.M. November 11, 1991

In some tests we carried out the other day, we obtained values for total solids of 1,960 mg/L and 1,700 mg/L. These are considerably higher than those obtained in other parts of the world. Has any other school had values this high?

All the best from Geelong, Australia.

Topic 3   High Total Solids Readings   Response 1 of 1
Detroit Country Day School, Michigan
gr.issues   9:14 P.M. November 13, 1991

The readings that you obtained for total solids indicate that your river must have a great deal of sediment moving in the system. What is the turbidity of the water like? Do you have a great deal of erosion into the system? Has there been a recent rain or series of storms that could have affected the results of your testing? Generally, the tests that have been conducted in the Rouge River watershed have been done during periods when not much rain had occurred. However, I am certain that if samples were taken after a series of storms or a single large rain that we would find much higher results for total solids in our samples as well.

consortium of computer nodes on each continent. Thousands of users in other nations can access GREEN because of APC's extensive networking system.

In addition, through GREEN and EcoNet, individual watershed programs use the networking capabilities to host local computer conferences. GREEN anticipates a significant number of watershedwide computer conferences opening up on EcoNet throughout the United States (and corresponding watershed conferences on the other APC networks) as more programs develop their telecommunication abilities. These conferences allow students to enter their data and communicate interactively between schools within the same watershed, as well as to access the international GREEN conferences (figure 10.3).

The Partner Watershed Program. The Partner Watershed Program has sparked remarkable interest within the network. In the pilot program in the spring of 1991, GREEN matched schools involved in watershed projects in different countries in order to develop the cross-cultural sharing inherent in the network. The pilot student-to-student links were hosted by watersheds in the United States, Canada, Mexico, Hungary, Australia, New Zealand, and Taiwan. Using local water-quality issues as a medium for discussion, students exchanged personal cultural perspectives and environmental concerns, along with ideas for ways to improve their environment. Students communicated by mail and computer to share their thoughts.

The goals of this cultural exchange program are to stimulate greater international awareness in students, while at the same time motivating students to develop concern for improving their local waterways. GREEN is presently expanding the program to other nations and developing research strategies for evaluating the program's impact on the participants.

The dissemination/clearinghouse role of GREEN. GREEN not only acts as a network but as a clearinghouse. The international GREEN office provides materials in both English and Spanish. Participants can join GREEN as an individual school involved in water monitoring or as a watershedwide program that involves schools within the same region. The GREEN office has made an effort to document the successes of these programs and to incorporate innovative activities into curricular materials for dissemination.

International participants are encouraged to contact active GREEN programs near them to create local networks. GREEN supports collaborative work among educators with similar resources and water-quality conditions. One example of this is the work of one educator/organizer, Rob O'Donoghue, in South Africa. Rob has taken the challenge of low-technology monitoring and developed methods for creating "homemade" equipment with fairly reliable results. This provides a model for educators with similar conditions.

Budgetary considerations. The funding for GREEN has been incremental and quite small considering the scope of the program. The initial international workshops were funded from a variety of foundations, corporations, and the University of Michigan. After the program's initial summer, the bulk of the funding was received from the General Motors (GM) Foundation. To date, the GM Foundation continues to sponsor the infrastructure of GREEN, while other proposals have been accepted for the development of specific programs within the network. Other funding sources continue to be cultivated.

GREEN is also working to become more self-sufficient through the sale of curricular material, subscriptions, sponsoring workshops, and consulting fees. Many of the watershed programs that exist are funded by local businesses or foundations; these programs occasionally sponsor GREEN workshops to enhance their teacher training.

PRODUCT

GREEN as an integrative educational program will always be in the process of evolving and developing. However, the structure of the basic network has been created and is currently actively growing.

Scope of GREEN

Both the national and international response to GREEN has been truly phenomenal. In January 1989 GREEN was merely a vision. By the summer of 1990 programs had been initiated in most of the original 18 nations as well as 12 others, while 35 states in the United States had developed watershedwide programs. Groups in 125 nations, as well as all 50 states, the District of Columbia, and Puerto Rico, have requested the *GREEN Newsletter* and information on how to initiate local watershed programs in their schools. Countries as disparate as Bangladesh, Czecho-slovakia, and Argentina have joined GREEN to develop educational programs and to share their experience with others around the globe. In total, 55 nations have initiated long-term, water-monitoring projects with students.

Variety of Programs within GREEN

GREEN has truly become a network of schools and communities around the world. In Europe, the network has linked older, established educational programs with other innovative ones. The skills and expertise of Northern Italian students, whose program is funded by their local government, complement the ingenuity of the nationwide Ecuadorean program that has already created a national linkage of schools monitoring for aquatic insects.

In the Rio Grande Watershed Program in the spring of 1991, the telecommunications component incorporated a cross-cultural dimension that linked students from Mexico and the United States. Students from Mexico were so enthusiastic about communicating with their American counterparts that they would travel to the local university computing center after school and on weekends—a rare example of motivation on the part of most students.

Future Needs and Directions

There are a plethora of programs that GREEN could develop under the concept of student environmental monitoring. Currently a student-based Heavy-Metals Monitoring Program is in the early pilot stages at the University of Michigan. An Air Monitoring Program was initiated in 1991, with the assistance of the Technical Education Research Committee in Boston, Massachusetts. Students are learning to monitor ground-level ozone within this project. Groundtruthing from satellite photographs is another hands-on approach to classroom science for which GREEN has been developing curricula with the Aspen Institute for Global Change. Soil monitoring is yet another dimension of environmental assessment that GREEN could research and support. Brackish water monitoring is another area in which participants have expressed an interest. A further development within GREEN is the proposal for a River Jordan Project to link the different cultures in the Arab-Israeli region to recognize their common resource of water.

One significant project to develop is extensive research into low-technology monitoring. Most nations within GREEN do not have the resources or access to the field kits that are available in the United States, Europe, and Australia. However, the components in these field kits can be substituted with chemistry lab equipment, given the proper instructions. GREEN wishes to focus more intensively in this area to better meet the needs of all participants.

Research

The diversity of programs within GREEN offer a rich resource for research in environmental education; telecommunications within the classroom; cross-cultural communication between students; changes in teaching practices; and school support of interdisciplinary educational projects. Student action is another area within the scope of education that has received little attention. GREEN will strive to find further resources for research into the effects and changes that environmental monitoring programs encourage in the educational field.

Regional Development of GREEN

Truly, the value of a network is its relevance to local participants. Over the long term, GREEN plans to establish regional offices throughout the world to strengthen its international network. Experience from other international organizations shows that developing a decentralized regional infrastructure is the most productive and culturally sensitive way to achieve GREEN's goals. Each office will identify regional needs and resources. It will set the priorities of the region and commit to using local expertise and resources to help resolve local water-quality issues.

Presently GREEN has selected country coordinators in each of the 125 nations in the network. These coordinators are chosen to assist in the dissemination of the *GREEN Newsletter*. But more important, these individuals will determine their basic needs and priorities for water-quality monitoring and draw on local resources that can enhance their nation's programs. They may also initiate local GREEN workshops for teachers within their nation, thereby further disseminating and strengthening their programs.

Training Development

GREEN intends to offer a selection of training sessions for its participants. International workshops and congresses provide opportunities for teachers and students to discuss directly their educational practices and concerns about rivers and water quality. For students, such interaction may be the most powerful experience in raising their cultural awareness and environmental sensitivity. At the workshops, teachers and students may not only share their monitoring data but also develop action strategies and design future cooperative projects.

The concept of student environmental monitoring is an exciting one. The prospect of students, teachers, researchers, and other professionals communicating about their local environmental concerns nationally and internationally is significant. It is GREEN's vision to reach this potential so that students can be empowered to become active learners and problem solvers through a successful networking system incorporated into their educational process.

Through the broad response that GREEN has received, it is clear that educational systems around the world are ready to incorporate real-world topics into their classrooms and encourage their students to get actively involved in learning. On a deeper level, GREEN participants appear to be ready to dissolve the cultural boundaries between nations in order to open up a greater sense of understanding, cooperation, and respect, especially as these attributes relate to environmental issues. GREEN hopes that this will help create more beneficial concerns today and into the future.

Acknowledgments

We thank Thomas I. Ellis for contributing material used in preparing this chapter.

For more information about GREEN, contact The GREEN Project, School of Natural Resources, University of Michigan, 430 E. University, Ann Arbor, Mich. 48109–1115.

To order copies of the *Field Manual for Water-Quality Monitoring: An Environmental Education Program for Schools,* contact William Stapp, 2050 Delaware, Ann Arbor, Mich. 48103.

11

Engaging Students in Wildlife-Focused Action Projects in Florida: A Thirty-five-Year Perspective

■■
■■

William C. Hammond

Through the past thirty-five years the author has worked with students, teachers, and public and private institutions interested in the implementation of "action-focused" learning in an environmental context. The instructional program models and component skill modules developed during this time (many using wildlife issues) have formed the core of the internationally recognized Lee County Schools Environmental Education Program, the action element of Project WILD, and a variety of other wildlife-related projects in the United States and Canada.

PLANNING

The planning efforts described in this case study have been of an evolutionary nature in the pattern of what today is called "action research." This instructional strategy is derived from the tenet that students "learn by doing" or build a knowledge framework from their own experience to which they can then attach theoretical concepts.

Their knowledge and understanding expand as they reflect on an experience in order to be more effective in the next action. The model is conceptualized as a learning cycle with an *action phase* followed by a *reflection phase,* which in turn informs the next action steps.

The environmental problems addressed in this program fall into two different but related categories. First is the effective instruction of students in a manner "bonding" them to the democratic process by empowering them to understand that they can change and improve the system if they maintain a positive attitude and master the appropriate skills and knowledge. Second is the "bonding" of students to natural systems. These two planning components are the core for program development, which through the years has led to many environmental action projects for students in the primary grades through grade 12. This case study will focus on the relationship of instructional delivery, student knowledge, skills, and understandings of taking action as developed through projects primarily focused on wildlife and wildlife habitat-related problems and issues. Wildlife projects served as a vehicle for empowering students to work within the democratic framework.

This study describes the application of the program components of wildlife-related projects successfully initiated or supported by student actions. The projects were conducted in Lee County, Florida, and include the Sea Turtle Research and Conservation Program, the Six-Mile Cypress Slough Acquisition, the Florida Manatee Protection Act, Manatee Park, the Bald Eagle Habitat Protection Ordinance, and the Lee District Schools Creating Wildlife Habitat on School Sites as a Component of the District LEESCAPES Program.

The most significant problem concerning wildlife conservation in southwest Florida is habitat loss. This condition is closely related to the "hot topics" of comprehensive land-use planning, private-property rights, government intervention and regulation, and species-specific wildlife management issues.

Another significant problem this program has addressed over the past thirty-five years is to demonstrate the instructional power and benefits derived from implementing instructional experiences for learners in a community-based problem-finding, formulation, and solutions framework. This contrasts to providing instruction through traditional didactic lecture, recitation, and lock-step field trip delivery systems. The program has challenged the assumptions of the "industrial era" mode of instruction as the most effective means of teaching and learning. Wildlife issues have served as a powerful theme and context for applying this model.

Project Goals and Objectives

The primary goals of the program were to

1. sensitize students to functional interactions within ecological systems
2. develop student knowledge and understanding of wildlife biological relationships in southwest Florida's ecological communities
3. empower students to be proficient, within the bounds of the democratic system, at implementing positive solutions to wildlife-related issues by engaging elected and appointed decision makers in informed decision-making actions
4. complete a wildlife-related project or a significant project component that directly engages students with elected public officials who have the authority to change public policy

The program component objectives were to

1. engage students in firsthand interactions with wildlife, key resource people, wildlife researchers (in the field and lab), wildlife-management problems and regulations, and wildlife issues in southwest Florida
2. develop students' knowledge, skills, and understanding fundamental to effectively engage public officials in changing policy concerning wildlife
3. provide support systems by facilitating, coaching, and teaching students according to their needs and wants to enable them to successfully engage and complete a significant wildlife project

Target Audience

The primary target audience engaged in this project were high school students in grades 11 and 12, representing nine high schools within Lee County, Florida. Students elect to participate in the program as an additional elective Environmental Science Seminar—"Action" or "Applied Environmental Investigations." These credit courses meet for seven hours every other Monday with additional weekend camping trips and evening and weekend sessions. Students provide their own transportation to and from their high schools to the Calusa Nature Center, which is the base of operations and instruction for the Lee District Schools Environmental Education Program. This year-long school program has been operating continuously since 1970, serving nearly twenty-five hundred students in the two "Monday Group" Classes. The secondary audiences are school administrators, teachers, and non-participating students, as well as potential adopters who are interested in transferring the program model.

Project Resources

The unique resources available to this program's planning, organization, and implementation included the Lee District school system staff of seven environmental educators and four support positions, six school buses assigned to environmental education, classrooms at the Calusa Nature Center, and a wide variety of environmental education-related instructional equipment and supplies. Two teachers, and in some years three, have team-taught and facilitated each of the two program courses. Between twenty-five and seventy-five students enroll for the full school year in each program option.

Project Historic Perspective

The author developed the program based on personal experience as a student and then as a teacher. Guiding interests were science, ecological systems, political change, and leadership within a democratic framework. The focus of the program was on understanding marine coastal systems and wildlife-related problems in the rapidly developing southwest Florida community. The decade of the 1960s provided intensive experience working with students of all school ages, especially students in grades 7 through 12. The 1960s was also a decade of great challenge in engaging students to learn to effectively change the very system and "establishment" they were confronting. The challenge was to encourage students to work within the system rather than advocating acts of rebellion toward the system.

During this time the author recognized that students typically would become excited and engaged when studying and conducting field and laboratory research on marine species and habitats. One project in particular, called Caretta Research, a sea turtle conservation and research program that focused primarily on the Loggerhead (*Caretta caretta*) on nearby Sanibel Island, held a great deal of interest for students. It was created by a National Wildlife Service biologist. Observation of the students' attention to this project's activities reinforced the belief that wildlife conservation projects held a powerful attraction to students. This attraction was the key to engaging students in learning and contributing meaningful community service and conservation action work. In early 1969 the author sought and received a federal Health, Education, and Welfare Title III, Elementary, Secondary Education Act Innovations Planning Grant to develop a comprehensive environmental education program for school systems. The planning grant included a proposal to develop and pilot test an expansion of the student research and action program to the entire district. The Title III Grant was funded as a full three-year operational grant, and the program was formalized and implemented as a component of the District Comprehensive Environmental Education Program. Through the years a wide variety of teachers, community leaders, resource people, environmental education staff members, and participating students, primarily in Lee County but also nationally and internationally, have greatly contributed to the program's evolution. From the program roots in the 1960s, a set of operating principles was formulated that serves as a basis for the program planning each year. There are three planning tenets:

1. Each year the selection of an action project must be the exclusive responsibility of participating students rather than a staff-directed or a significantly staff-influenced decision.
2. A primary staff role is to introduce and expose students to a wide variety of local problems and issues and to the people who are primary players in addressing these problems and issues.
3. The primary staff instructional role is to facilitate learning and the development of student "action skills," to provide students with specific affirmations relative to their learning and growth, and to be role models as effective citizens who exhibit a sincere love of the planet, an understanding of ecological systems, and a commitment to working to solve community problems and issues within the bounds of the democratic system.

Alternative methods considered in the planning of the program and related projects focused on two sets of design conditions and strategies. The decision had to be made either to (1) design and implement the program as an integral component of each secondary school's course offerings, operated within the restrictions and resource limitations of each school, or (2) design and implement the program as a centralized school district model environmental action program that pulled students from their schools to a central instructional meeting location. Owing to a multitude of constraints, coupled with a lack of teacher experience within schools with this type of community-based learning approach in 1969, we decided on a centralized model. The premise was to find a way to institutionalize what in 1969 were very different approaches to teaching, learning theory, and role relationships among students, teachers, and established school practices. Once the elements of the model were proven to be feasible and successful in the centralized context, we felt that they could then more easily be adapted into the methods and strategies of each individual secondary school.

The option selected was a "pull out" program that brought students from their individual school environments to a central, "neutral" site. This served as a venue for program-based experiences and a springboard for community-based studies and projects. A "retired" school cafeteria in the downtown area of Ft. Myers, Florida, was converted to Environmental Center offices and classrooms and functioned as the program site for the first seven years. When a new community nature center was opened in a park setting at the edge of the city, the program moved there along with the staff and offices of the Lee County Schools Environmental Education Program.

Another set of decisions centered on methods of providing instruction to students. One option was to use direct teaching strategies. This approach would provide students with all the knowledge they needed of wildlife, ecological systems, and leadership and action skills, and then guide them through a set of community-based action activities and highly staff-structured and supervised action projects. This strategy would prepare them in the second semester or fourth quarter to actually design and implement a community-based action project. The second option was to take an action-research, skill-development-and-mastery approach. This would provide direct teaching only when students were ready to learn specific information and skills through an inductive instructional approach. This method places a high locus of control for

Local biologist briefing Monday Group students on southern bald eagles (*photo by Hammond*).

teaching and learning on the participating learners. Both options were tried. The second method was the preferred approach and is the current practice.

The power of the preferred approach derives from students taking responsibility for their own learning. As they work on their chosen action-research project, they recognize the need for additional knowledge and skills in order to progress. In this context, direct teaching offered by the staff is far less abstract and thus more relevant to the learner. This approach enhances student mastery and minimizes "re-teaching."

IMPLEMENTATION

Program Operational Strategy

The primary Environmental Science Seminar Class, Monday Group Program, brings together students from nine countywide high school centers (eight public and one parochial) who elect in their junior or senior year (grade 11 or 12) to take the full-year elective science credit course. Students must either be nominated by their school principal, a teacher, or by themselves as a leader interested in improving their community environment. Since the first year of the program, school administration and staff have been encouraged to nominate at least half their student participants from the ranks of students referred to as "negative leaders." Negative leaders are those students who are often in disciplinary difficulty, are poor school attenders, or frequently lead other students into negative behaviors. In general, they tend to demonstrate leadership qualities often in direct conflict with social and political norms at school.

Since the program's inception, two Monday Group classes have been offered. The Environmental Science Action class has been offered continuously. For the first eighteen years, the Environmental Applied (Construction) Seminar class was offered. The Environmental Science Investigative class replaced the Construction class five years ago. Although there are no prerequisites other than grade level, many students take the Investigative class in their eleventh grade year and the Action class in their twelfth grade year. Typically, five or more eleventh graders will elect to take a second year of the course they participated in their initial year. In these cases a higher level of project performance is required.

The organization, particularly the title and "slant" of these courses, has changed over the past twenty-four years. New standards and requirements of the district and state for certification of teachers and official course descriptions have required the redefining and alteration of the courses. For the most part, this has been a repackaging and new labeling exercise rather than dictating any significant change in the core programs. The lesson to be learned is to creatively and rapidly adapt and conform to the new requirements, rather than resist or give up in the face of seemingly insurmountable regulatory and political changes that are bound to be encountered by any program over a twenty-four year lifetime. The evolution from the "Construction" Monday Group, which facilitated students in the designing and building of outdoor classrooms, screen or "slat" houses for plant propagation, miles of boardwalks, and trails and pavilions on school grounds and other public lands to an "Investigative" Monday Group resulted from rethinking priorities for the implementation of environmental education. This modification was triggered by changes in teacher certification requirements by the State Department of Education and by changes in the needs of the community and the students. The conclusion was that a field-based investigative experience that positioned students working with field biologists, water-quality surveyors, and other field-oriented environmental investigators was a more effective use of limited staff and program resources. The alternative was to expend significant time and resources to reorganize and sustain the construction class strategy in the face of changing state rules and legal concerns.

The Investigative class often engages students in working with professional wildlife biologists conducting field activities, such as alligator censusing, bird banding, habitat analysis, and wetland jurisdictional determinations. This approach not only connects students to the direct application of basic biological concepts but also exposes them to the excitement and realities of wildlife and other environmentally related careers.

The Action Monday Group Class

This program is limited to eleventh and twelfth graders. Most students have taken a minimum of two science courses (generally, at least basic biology) and two social studies courses, but some will have taken four science classes and three social studies classes, or even more. The content of the Monday Groups is designed to reinforce the basic school curricula by providing intensive opportunities for students to apply their knowledge to solving practical "real-life" problems within an everyday community context. A strong emphasis is placed on students viewing the world and the relationships of matter and energy in an ecological context. Systemic perspectives, systems models, ecological principles, and government concepts dominate the program's content. The emphasis for the course content is derived from the focus of the project, which the students select each year. In addition, a set of core values adopted in 1985 after fifteen years of evolution by the Instructional Development and Environmental Education Department of the Lee District schools and published in their Environmental Education Curriculum Charts are fundamental. These environmental values and attitudes, which form the foundation for all other curriculum and instructional initiatives, are the following:

- Part of Nature—recognizing the self as an integral part of nature, not separate from it

- Natural Models—utilizing nature as a model for responsible life and living on the planet
- Everything Is Connected—understanding that one action may instigate many reactions when interacting with the environment
- Independent Agent for Change—viewing oneself as an independent agent for positive change
- Opening Options—choosing actions that expand one's options in the universe
- Future Options—carefully balancing long- and short-term consequences of one's actions, while maintaining options for future generations
- Balanced Decisions—balancing a wide range of viewpoints and alternatives in the process of making environmental choices
- Responsibility for Life—feeling responsible for maintaining or improving the quality of life on the planet for all living things
- Finite Resources—maintaining a life-style that ethically responds to the planet's limited resources

Equally fundamental is the course's set of guiding principles, which have become known as the "Monday Group Commandments." These include the following:

- take only positive positions: be for something rather than against something
- do your homework, become informed, become an "expert" on your special area of interest
- treat everyone as an individual of high moral worth and avoid stereotyping anyone or any group or agency
- analyze the "forcefield" of those who support your position and those who do not; make an extended effort to know firsthand the basis and interests of those who disagree
- "recycle" if you do not succeed in reaching your goal on your first try; you will start from a more informed position with each new cycle
- never give up on a project that is worth doing; if you cannot succeed at the whole project, find an element that you can complete (Hammond 1978)

A key element of the action program's course content is the mastery of a set of skills by all participating students. These skills are initially presented through student participation in simulations and interactive skill module exercises. They are then reinforced with discussion and refresher exercises when students need further honing as they apply them in their community action project. These skills center on

- effective communication by phone, letter, public speaking, mass media, interpersonal interactions
- strategies and techniques for becoming an expert by compiling and conducting effective research on the subject of interest
- techniques for effective lobbying
- techniques for strategic planning and organization of a group to achieve a project goal
- techniques for team building and cooperation
- techniques for public presentations and media (brochures, slide programs, videos, exhibits)
- techniques for conflict resolution

The instructional strategy is an integration of course elements that focus on

- team building through core initiatives and group problem-solving activities
- acquisition and development of knowledge and understanding of ecological systems, institutional systems, and political processes
- development and refinement of the aforementioned process skills
- mastery of skills for the action research process
- connection to mentors from a wide variety of sources
- bonding students to natural systems and the democratic process

These major elements are tailored each year to the make-up and experience of the class participants. Each year's class operates differently, but uses the same basic central core of objectives and instructional strategies. Typically the first quarter of the year emphasizes team and group-community building (often including a three-day weekend camping trip) and an introduction to local ecological systems and environmental problems and issues. The second quarter focuses on the development of problem solving and strategic planning skills, as well as the basics of each of the other skill areas. All learning takes place within a community context. In the second quarter the students make a decision and commitment to the nature and plan of action for their action research project. The second semester focuses almost entirely on the students working to implement a solution to their chosen environmental projects. The students' strategic planning elements for the project undergo continuous revision as they assess progress toward their goal. As students recognize the need to further develop specific skills in order to succeed at their tasks, teaching staff or peer groups present appropriate skill modules.

Staffing

Teachers assume the roles of coaches and facilitators of learning and problem solving. They provide support materials, access to information, and positive reinforcement and affirmation of student progress for each student during every class with informal, personal feedback. Teachers try to connect students to mentors who can help them succeed at their tasks and project. Students co-plan each class session with teaching staff and take the lead role in planning during the second semester of intense student project work. The relationship between students and teachers is open and informal. It is based on a common set of class, facility, and program rules and policies, all of which have been agreed on. All participants have contributed to formulating and reviewing these guidelines within the context of School Board policy.

Budget

The school system operating budget for the class is primarily based on the salaries of four teachers and the operation of the environmental education vehicles. Because these classes use only a small component (20–25 percent) of each staff member's time, and because the two buses, which are driven by staff members, are included in the program budget, the costs to the district are minimal. Additional costs include art supplies, printing and photocopying, and some subsidy of the weekend camping trips (typically less than $500 per year). Students and staff raise funds themselves for any special projects or for elements of their own projects that require additional cost, which itself is part of the learning and project experience each year.

PRODUCT

In a rare demonstration of the program's ability to sustain itself and transfer leadership, it has continued successfully beyond the retirement, after twenty-three years, of its founder and head teacher. Furthermore, two former Monday Group students now teach full-time in the program.

The program objectives have not been systematically assessed quantitatively but rather have been reviewed based on the students' accomplishments. The key criterion is whether students succeed in producing a tangible product by either accomplishing a significant community project that involved elected decision makers or at least successfully achieved completion of a critical element necessary for their project's ultimate success. Other vital information, such as student attendance, student drop-out rate, student critiques of program operations and activities, student journals, and cognitive testing on the relevant "content of the year" all contribute to the assessment of student and program strengths and of the need for improvement each year.

In the past twenty-four years of the program, the attendance rate has typically been over 90 percent. This is considered excellent for a voluntary, supplemental program with often more than half the students considered to be "negative leaders" and generally poor school-attenders. Every year there are students whose overall school attendance is poor, yet who never miss a class in this program. In some cases students who have not attended regular school classes in weeks inevitably show up for their Monday Group session. In at least five years of the class, we have had students either officially drop out of school or graduate in January, yet continue to participate in the Monday Group for the remainder of the school year. In the program's twenty-four years of operation, we have never had a group of students fail to achieve the implementation of a significant component of the project they chose. Nonetheless the full completion of the entire selected project has occurred only nine times in the program's existence. The message is that it is not easy to solve complex problems quickly and that perseverance is the key to success.

Approximately 875 eleventh- and twelfth-grade students have participated in the Action Monday Group over the past twenty-four years with about a fifth of them "reporting back" to the instructors over the years. In addition, approximately 540 students have participated in the

Monday Group students conducting a public press conference at the proposed
Manatee Park site as a part of their media campaign (*photo by Hammond*).

Environmental Construction and Investigative Monday Group classes,
with about 15 percent of them reporting back. Unfortunately no systematic follow-up of students who have participated in this program
has been conducted. The anecdotal evidence that does exist indicates
that for hundreds of students who have reported back, the experience
was one of the most important in their schooling and shaped not only
their attitudes toward the environment and government, but also led
them to environmentally related careers and environmentally sensitive
life-styles. At least ten of the "negative leader" nominees recommended
to the program by their school principals have earned doctoral degrees
in environmentally related fields.

Representative accomplishments of the major student-generated
wildlife and wildlife habitat action projects follow.

*Caretta Research Project: Saving loggerhead sea turtles on Sanibel
Island.* During our initial project (1962–70), students worked the
beaches assisting principle investigators in tagging, measuring, and
weighing nesting turtles; collecting information and mapping nesting-
beach vegetation; digging eggs and transplanting them to a predator-

and flood-resistant compound; and collecting data on hatchlings before their release. Students also assisted in a research effort to rear hatchlings for a year before their release in order to reduce mortality, and conducted community multimedia programs about the sea turtles of southwest Florida. Although the Caretta Research Project still continues in a modified form and some students volunteer as participants, the school system no longer participates as a major component of environmental education programs.

Six-Mile Cypress Slough Acquisition Program. Over a period of years beginning in 1967, small groups of students explored, by wading and hiking, a 2,500-acre cypress slough system in a more than 5,000-acre watershed just to the east of Ft. Myers, Florida. In 1971–72, Monday Group students worked with professional biologists and conducted a biological inventory of the flora and fauna of the Six-Mile Cypress Slough. The slough contains the northernmost record for at least four semitropical orchids and a wide variety of other tropical hammock plants. Fauna include a variety of species of special concern—threatened and endangered mammals, birds, reptiles, and amphibians. In 1970 permission from private-property owners was secured to systematically wade school students into the swamp. By 1972 more than three thousand students per year were exploring the swamp as part of the school district's environmental education program. In 1973 a forester of the Florida Division of Forestry announced that a contract to log the second growth timber in "Six-Mile" was being negotiated. Students and informed community leaders searched for a means to protect the slough system. Because the slough had originally been proposed as a state park in 1967, students approached the Division of State Parks but subsequently became convinced that it would not be a priority project for state park acquisition. Students then approached the Nature Conservancy, which agreed to cooperate and even to lend the local government the 2.5 million dollars needed to buy the area at the 1975 appraised value. Unable to secure a commitment for funding reimbursement, students searched the alternatives and decided that the best solution was a public referendum. The proposal was for local taxpayers to vote to pass a tax (.02 mills for two years) to raise the funds needed to purchase the slough and wildlife buffer areas. Funds also would be used to build interpretive facilities and water-management structures to ensure future management as projected urbanization surrounded the system.

The 1975 Monday Group Action class lobbied county commissioners and other community leaders and, after two attempts, were successful in getting the commissioners to vote to place a referendum for the tax initiative to purchase the Six-Mile Cypress Slough on the 1976 fall ballot. The 1976 Monday Group class (in an economic recession year) campaigned to convince the community of the importance of raising taxes to buy a slough that in fact most of them would never experience. Students conducted an intensive news media campaign by creating news stories three or four times a week and produced "spots" for community radio and television. They also created a two-projector, multimedia slide and music program which they presented morning, noon, and evening to more than twenty-five thousand people in a variety of community organizations and groups. They strategically analyzed and worked voter precincts to gain support where they predicted the greatest opposition. No politician in the community held any hope that the referendum would be voted in. In fact, however, the referendum passed by the largest margin that any tax referendum had ever gained in Lee County. Students helped to negotiate a final land appraisal, and the Nature Conservancy became the contracting agent to purchase lands on behalf of Lee County.

As no county park planner was employed on park staff, students in the 1977 class took the rough conceptual plan that the previous Monday Group students had drafted for the management and interpretation of the slough and adopted it to draft a master interpretive and management plan for the park. They expanded the management plan to include future purchases and land-use management of tributary sloughs and wetlands as wildlife corridors. They also added the design and implementation of a twenty-five-mile "bike path/park-wildlife" habitat corridor that used the Six-Mile Cypress and the Ten-Mile Canal systems as the anchors for the plan. It took sixteen years (owing to local politics and bureaucratic difficulties) to fully acquire the Six-Mile Cypress Slough and to build the basic interpretive boardwalks and facilities, but it has been accomplished. The slough that no one but a few visionaries and teams of high school students thought could be saved is now a critical urban wildlife and public recreation resource serving all of southwest Florida. It now serves as a model for even larger wildlife habitat acquisition projects, and it all came about because students did not heed the overwhelming adult pessimism.

Florida Manatee Protection Act. The seed for the passage of the Florida Manatee Sanctuary Program had its roots with Lee County students. Two students collecting water-quality data in an attempt to prove that the Florida Power and Light Power Plant was polluting the Orange and Caloosahatchee rivers noticed a much larger population (than previously recognized) of West Indian manatees gathering at the plant's discharge canal. When the students notified the author regarding the circumstances, arrangements were made with a pilot to fly over the water system and investigate. Instead of the previous estimates of fifteen to seventy-five individuals, more than two hundred were counted.

Soon afterward, the Environmental Protection Agency (EPA) placed an injunction on the power company to create a new discharge canal into the Caloosahatchee River to reduce a thermal block rather than into the existing Orange River discharge. Monday Group students were asked to support the power company's opposition to the changes. After meeting with officials from the company and from the Atlanta EPA office, students decided that both sides of the disagreement had validity. Students felt that the EPA injunctive action was inappropriate after going up the Orange River estuary with a U.S. Fish and Wildlife Service (USFWS) biologist who conducted the original government assessment of the impacts of the power plant. They learned from him that most of the critical habitat needed for the species that were of concern to the EPA (e.g., snook, blue crabs, and other species that used the estuary's inland marshes for nursery habitat) had already been eliminated or seriously degraded. Thus the actions required would have only minimal benefit to the concerned species while it would further endanger the manatee by encouraging them to gather in the warm discharge waters in the Caloosahatchee River. This river is also the intercoastal waterway and is thus frequented by numerous large power boats that present a real physical threat to the manatee population. Students testified at an administrative hearing, and EPA waived the injunctive order with certain stipulations.

During this time the students also conducted an intensive community awareness campaign with slide programs, television spots, and large warning signs posted in all local marinas and on the banks of canals frequented by manatees. These efforts described the plight of the manatee, penalties for harassing and harming them, and the potential for boat impacts. They lobbied county officials to set speed limits in the Caloosahatchee and Orange rivers. Officials agreed at first and then found out that they had no jurisdiction. Limits could only be set at the state and federal levels. Our local state senator had worked with students and was familiar with the concerns. As a result he co-introduced the nation's first Manatee Sanctuary Program with the Caloosahatchee, establishing one of the first designated manatee sanctuaries with strict boating speed limits.

Manatee Park. In 1988 another class of Monday Group students lobbied Florida Power and Light and Lee County commissioners to create a park on the banks of the power plant discharge canal and the Orange River so that local people and tourists could safely observe manatees that gathered in the warm waters of the power plant each winter. Students worked for three years to get approval for the park. Their efforts included development of a master management and interpretive plan, and a fund-raising and donations commitment. The plan was adopted by the Lee County Commission and, although delayed because of serious budget cuts, is scheduled for construction during the 1994 fiscal year.

Bald Eagle Habitat Protection Ordinance. In 1978 students became engaged in understanding the rapid decline of the endangered southern bald eagle in Lee County. This decline was primarily the result of habitat loss owing to rapid land-development practices. After working with individuals who were local experts on the southern bald eagle, the class decided that eagles needed additional protection in order to "plug the loopholes" in the Bald Eagle Protection Act and the Endangered Species Act. These acts were not being effectively enforced in southwest Florida at the time. Students drafted a Bald Eagle Habitat Protection Ordinance for Lee County to create an enforceable protection system for critical eagle habitat surrounding nesting trees and feeding areas. After three years, seventeen public hearings, and twenty-three drafts of the ordinance, it finally was passed by the Lee County Commission and, still in place today, serves as a model ordinance. It is unique in that it provides landowners financial incentives to protect the habitat of southern bald eagles. The students' initiative changed the status of nesting eagles from being a "developer's curse" to being a valuable asset to their property. The shift from punitive approaches to incentive-driven ones has become a pattern for subsequent ordinances and regulations in the comprehensive planning process.

LEESCAPES. The lessons learned from these and other Monday Group class projects led to the establishment of a school district landscape and playground improvement project by the school board. The landscape project, known as LEESCAPES, has four basic objectives, which are to (1) beautify and enhance school grounds through "best practices" xeriscaping plantings; (2) improve instructional opportunities on the school site; (3) reduce maintenance effort and costs; and (4) enhance wildlife habitat on school sites (Hammond et al. 1984). This approach offers firsthand experience with the decisions and dilemmas associated with wildlife habitat management. Students, staff members, and parents must address fundamental questions, such as whether we should manage the habitat toward native ecological communities or manipulate habitat for the benefit of certain preferred species. It is in this context that students from even the most urban settings begin to understand the basics of wildlife management and the science underpinning it.

Program Dissemination and Effects

As described, the basic approach of the Monday Group class has been used in an adapted form in British Columbia, Ontario, Colorado, Arizona, Oklahoma, Indiana, and in other Florida communities. More limited adaptations have also been used in many other communities throughout North America. The primary dissemination has been through Project WILD. The author's Monday Group article in both the elementary school and secondary school teacher's guides over the past ten years has been the primary "action" model disseminated (Project WILD 1992). The author's publications, conference workshops, and seminars (featuring the Monday Group action approach) on behalf of the North American Association of Environmental Education have also contributed to a broad dissemination throughout North America. These, in turn, led to many follow-up workshops and presentations at local levels.

The program's basic premises have proved to work well with even the youngest of schoolchildren. The efforts of the Ft. Myers Beach Elementary third-grade students demonstrated this well. They were the instigators and catalyst for a state and local law that limits the collection of live mollusks and echinoderms to two live specimens in any twenty-four-hour period unless a special scientific permit is obtained. This is the only county law of its kind in the state.

Another example of an adaptation to a different locale is the Water Stewardship Program of the central Okanagan Region of British Columbia. This program focuses on action-research projects on fisheries, wildlife habitat, land-use practices, and stream improvement in local watersheds. The project engages students and teachers in more than thirty school districts and utilizes the Monday Group program model as its base for engaging students in action research.

The key elements of success in carrying out the programs have been to place a high trust and sense of responsibility in students; expect a high level of performance from students and continually nurture each student's ego and personal growth; pay attention to the interests, wants, and needs of students; mentor and help assure their successes in the small first steps of their project initiative; persist and be tenacious as a model while being a very frank communicator who recognizes the students as the project leaders and decision makers; be unafraid to let students make mistakes and help them process their failures in order to learn from them and move on without repeating their errors; let go of the illusion of "control" and let students run the program operation; and "bond" students to wildlife and natural systems through direct experiences.

Acknowledgments

The author wishes to acknowledge the support and vision of the Lee District school system, the school board and all its staff members, and students for their openness to innovation and exploration of new and more effective ways of educating students. A special acknowledgment goes to the members of the Environmental Education Department who co-created this program and continue to nurture it for the benefit of students. The international network of Project WILD and its coordinators has also greatly shaped the thought and practices described in this chapter.

For additional information about the currently operating Monday Groups, contact Randolf Tully, environmental education resource teacher, Lee County schools Environmental Education Office, 2055 Central Avenue, Ft. Myers, Florida 33901. Information on the Monday Group model, skill modules, and transfer location sites can be obtained by contacting the author at Natural Context, P.O. Box 07461, Ft. Myers, Florida 33919. The author is publishing a *Guide to Student Action in the Context of Schooling* in 1994, which provides an expanded overview of the details and strategies of establishing and operating an environmental action program within schools. A share of the proceeds from the sale of these books will be used to establish an Environmental Education Trust Fund to provide operating funds, scholarships, and travel funds for southwest Florida students participating in environmental action work.

12

A Zoo with Class in Victoria, Australia

■■

Greg Hunt

Is there anyone who would not look forward to a trip to the zoo? Zoos attract, worldwide, 600 million visitors annually, about 10 percent of the world's population (The World Zoo Conservation Strategy 1993). Australasian zoos have 6 million visitors annually, or about 14 percent of the population, and the Zoological Board of Victoria's three zoos—Healesville Sanctuary, Royal Melbourne Zoo, and Werribee Zoological Park—attract 1.36 million visitors, equivalent to about 30 percent of the population.

The World Zoo Conservation Strategy (1993) states, "the future of humankind greatly depends on extensive and effective environmental and conservation education. The zoos of the world have a unique role to play in the global efforts to educate people." Further, the composition of this visitation is important. Zoo visitors represent a diversity of ages and educational levels, and of social, ethnic, and cultural backgrounds. Thus zoos provide unmatched opportunities to raise issues of conservation throughout the community.

For many people zoos exist for recreation, something they are willing to pay for. The Zoological Board of Victoria (ZBV) includes recreation as just one of its purposes, along with conservation, research, and education. This chapter relates the ZBV's role in its efforts to educate the public.

PLANNING

The mission of the Zoological Board of Victoria is *to create positive attitudes toward wildlife and conservation of the world's natural living resources.* Education, inextricably linked to conservation, is fundamental to the achievement of this mission. The plight of species and habitats must be understood if their conservation is to be successful, while the conservation efforts themselves must be the focus of an educational program. Community support for species and habitat survival must be based on a prevailing attitude that values the world's living natural resources.

The challenge is to provide a conservation message which does not preach and which acknowledges that "the visitor's susceptibility to educational information exists because of the attraction to the living animal" (The World Zoo Conservation Strategy 1993). The zoo's educational program provides knowledge and understanding of these animals, builds on the curiosity of the visitor, and develops attitudes and motivation toward an involvement in conservation.

An essential feature of the educational program is the aim to motivate learners to act. Conservation education programs will count for naught if they do not lead to life-style changes that reduce environmental impact or impel learners to take part in environmental protection and improvement. Zoo educational programs are planned to feed the mind with knowledge and understanding of animal habitats, interrelationships, ecology, and behavior, and then to extend into programs based on the heart, to see value in nonhuman life forms and show care and concern for them.

Zoological Board of Victoria Education Service (ZBVES)

The ZBVES carries a large part of the work of providing innovative, engaging educational programs that will leave visitors not just satisfied with the visitor experience but motivated to take part in environmental protection and improvement. The educational service complements the roles of keepers and gardeners, groups that also provide formal and informal educational programs, and is also involved with volunteer groups to provide holiday programs for the general public. The ZBVES has a teaching staff of fourteen, provided by the state education system's Directorate of School Education (DSE) and three teachers provided by the Catholic Education Office. These teachers provide services across the three facilities of the ZBV. The ZBVES provides services to schools and the public, through formal class sessions, print and audiovisual materials, and public education programs. The teaching staff are supported by a booking officer, a receptionist, an administration officer, and an audiovisual and technical services officer. Further, the ZBV provides three keeping staff members to care for the animal collections in the seven classrooms and for the grounds that make up the zoo school.

Environmental Education Policy

Principles and practices of environmental education in schools occurs within advice given in *Ministerial Policy for Environmental Education,* where the knowledge, skills, values, and action components of environmental education are discussed for the benefit of schools throughout Victoria. The policy clearly recommends that schools should take a whole-school approach to environmental education, where all aspects of schooling— the curriculum, facilities management, and processes—provide a consistent message. This requires that classroom lessons about recycling are supported by the school's recycling program, and that efficient energy management is not just a topic for academic discussion but can be seen in practice in the school. This approach has implications for school grounds management, and thereby extends to local flora and fauna.

Whole-Zoo Approach

Responsibility for policy implementation is vested in schools, but considerable resources are provided by the directorate to support them. One such source of support is the Zoological Board of Victoria Education Service. The environmental education task is assisted considerably by the philosophy of the Zoo Board of Victoria, which is to take a whole-zoo approach to the management of its animal collection and associated facilities. The abundance of recycling bins, the placement of interpretive signs regarding conservation of biodiversity and possible sources of wildlife entrapment, and even the merchandising policies in the catering and souvenir sections support a conservation message. For

The Australian bushland room, one of the seven activity rooms of the Zoological Board of Victoria Education Service (*photo by Anton Proppe, ZBV*).

example, french-fried potatoes are purchased in edible containers that are made from a potato base. The ZBV has adopted a policy that no rain-forest timbers will be used in its facilities, while the energy management of the reptile facility has been determined in conjunction with Energy Victoria, a government agency that promotes wise use of energy resources.

IMPLEMENTATION

ZBVES Programs

One means of realizing the educational opportunities, particularly with the school population, is through the work of the Zoological Board of Victoria's Education Service, which enjoys an exceptionally high degree of support from the community. Thousands of students per year pass through the activity rooms and take part in its educational programs. For many citizens of Victoria, their first wildlife experience was while sitting in a zoo school activity room feeling a carpet python encircling their wrist or the pulsing of a bearded dragon's heart against their palm. The development of positive attitudes that occurs through such experiences is a fundamental component of successful environmental education.

Environmental education programs consist of knowledge, skills, values, and action. The ZBVES contributes to the knowledge base of students through programs in mammal classification, adaptations of birds, and the genetics of small populations. Observation and recording skills are called for in animal behavior programs, and skills of expression and communication are required for poetry and sculpture programs based on the animal collection. The area in which the ZBVES is particularly prominent is in the development of positive environmental values.

Staff of the ZBVES had face-to-face contact in 1993 with 102,000 students from preschool and the preparatory level—children around the age of four—to tertiary students. Most student visitors are in primary or elementary schools and in secondary schools. The process begins when a teacher decides to supplement a year-level program or a program in science, art, or English (or psychology, chemistry, or media studies) with a zoo excursion. They then ring the ZBVES and book their class for a one- to three-hour lesson, typically some weeks in advance. Close to the visit, the ZBVES staff member assigned to the class will contact the teacher and ask for details of the school program within which the zoo excursion will occur. The class teacher and the zoo teacher will negotiate the program to be taken at the zoo and appropriate materials will be forwarded to the school in preparation for the visit.

At the zoo, students are usually taken into one of the seven activity rooms, which are decked out in themes of a rain forest, an Australian bushland, or an urban environment, or are decorated in various colors and patterns. Another room, with feathery strips of carpet hanging from netting stretched below the ceiling, is a simulated rain forest and is darkened when the students enter. Back-lighting is used to create a mysterious atmosphere. With students' susceptibility thus enhanced, they are prepared for a more intense experience with the rain forest animals that are in the room—a pair of baby boas, tree frogs, possums, turtles, and fish.

In each of the rooms, students take part in sessions of animal handling focused on the particular program they are taking. Zoo teachers take particular care to demonstrate the responsibility they feel in the way they introduce the animals to the students. Each of the rooms has five to six animal species, cared for by the three keeping staff members. Animals in the other rooms include tree frogs, newts, skinks and dragon lizards, turtles, pythons and colubrid snakes, and marsupials, such as possums and gliders (flying possums). If the students have come for a lesson on classification, they can contrast the texture of scales with that of moist, uncovered skin. If the lesson is about endangered species, students are invited to examine the hand-held specimen extremely closely and work out how its features and characteristics enable it to meet its needs. Human environmental impacts that might prevent those needs from being met are then considered. Meanwhile the student is holding another life in his or her hands, looking eyeball to eyeball, feeling the scratching of small claws and the pulse of a heartbeat.

This experience is unashamedly designed to provoke a personal response in the learner. The intention is that students will more highly value wild animals and thereby wish to care for them and their habitats as a result of the lesson. To accompany this change in attitude, students are invited to consider ways to act that would reduce their impact on wildlife and habitats. Action, in this context, involves the student's personal, domestic, and local environments. The media might be over-fond of depicting environmental action as being a confrontation between preservationists and developers, but for students of ZBVES programs, action means, for example, minimizing home energy consumption, re-cycling paper, and purchasing wisely in supermarkets. Action means building and placing nest boxes, and planting tree habitat and ground cover on their school grounds. It means planning and conducting displays for conservation in their local community centers.

Props are used extensively. The rooms contain a number of artifacts confiscated by customs agencies, such as stuffed marine turtles, python-skin boots, crocodile handbags, fur coats, and elephant-foot umbrella stands, that are now used in the program to persuade students of the threat to endangered species. Mounted specimens of birds and mammals that lived their entire lives in the zoo continue to live on as classroom aids: armadillos to explain the difference between reptilian scales and the mammalian adaptation of horn-covered bony plates, and penguins to show the variation in feather structure to provide certain birds with greater insulation in marine environments. Teachers may borrow kits of animal artifacts for up to a month to prepare students for the zoo excursion. These include activity sheets based on the artifacts and are available for a number of topics. Teachers pay only a nominal handling fee for this service.

The role of humans in the demise of our fauna and a discussion of practical, and practicable, actions we can take is an integral part of many of the lessons. Much anecdotal evidence exists to suggest that such programs are effective. For example, follow a parent and child on a family shopping trip as they negotiate their way through a supermarket. Eavesdrop on the decision-making process and be heartened as the child lectures the parent on the need for environmentally responsible purchasing. As the poet Wordsworth wrote, "The child is father to the man," and so conservation education aimed at large-scale community change that is delivered to significant percentages of the state's school students offers the promise of success.

Teachers' Professional Development

The ZBVES is an increasingly significant provider of professional development for teachers in Victoria. The programs conducted by the ZBVES range from introductory ones that market our educational services to those with a practical, action-research orientation that aim to change teachers' classroom practices. An example of the latter is Environmental Education Programs in Classrooms (EEPIC). It consists of seven weekly two-hour sessions, is highly structured, and requires a minimum of two participants from each school. In a typical session preassigned reading is discussed, and then participants explore ways to present environmental topics, such as developing an environmental ethic, teaching an integrated curriculum, or teaching values and controversial issues. Participants then take part in teaching activities based on the particular principles they have discussed, which will then enable them to carry out the lessons in their own classrooms. A discussion of resources that may be used for support might follow, with participants volunteering information.

Between sessions, teachers are expected to carry out the teaching activity with their own classes, with the support of the other participant from their school. This allows for instant feedback, constructive criticism, and reinforcement of the last program session, all in the school context where it can have the maximum benefit.

At the next session the first item on the agenda is to report on the activity. Was it successful? Why or why not? What variations on the activity proved useful? What traps should be avoided? Teachers become their own critics, with the credibility that close peers bring. The sessions then proceed as described, with another teaching principle explored and the teaching activities that develop it. EEPIC is designed to build teachers' confidence in offering instruction in environmental education and to develop strategies for exploring ideas and issues in the teacher's practice.

Another action-oriented program is called Grow Me a Home, and is carried out in conjunction with Greening Australia (Victoria), a community group that aims to involve all community sectors in habitat-restoration programs. Grow Me a Home meets for up to ten sessions and enables teachers and parents to explore such issues as environmental education, ecology, and wildlife shelters. The program makes use of the zoo's enclosures to demonstrate ways to meet animals' needs; the zoo's gardening staff also takes part, instructing program participants in horticulture. Skills sessions are interspersed with theory, with participants studying plant identification, collecting seeds from local plants, practicing propagation techniques, and building nest boxes. While participating in the program, teachers and parents work together to revegetate the school grounds.

The ZBVES is involved in the zoo's conservation role in other, broader ways. For example, it considers the needs of its educational programs, as well as those of the animals, in the design of the zoo's enclosures. The layout of zoo paths and shelters ensure adequate space to accommodate groups of learners yet still allow public access. Further, the zoo enclosures and landscaping are designed to support an educational message about the species exhibited.

Statewide Role

The zoo is also involved in conservation on a state and regional basis. The eastern barred bandicoot (*Perameles gunnii*) provides an example of this. This small, rabbit-sized marsupial inhabited open woodland over much of Victoria before European settlement. Unfortunately this habitat was easily cleared and was readily convertible to farmlands, where bandicoots had little refuge from the introduced predators that were another feature of European settlement. There is now a relic colony of some hundreds of individuals remaining on the Australian mainland, on the outskirts of a rural town of about twenty thousand inhabitants.

The ZBVES is involved in the statewide recovery program for the bandicoot. A captive breeding program has been established, and the zoo is now providing animals for release in two secure fauna reserves in localities inhabited by this species in recent history. A public education and awareness committee has been established, made up of three ZBVES representatives, professional researchers, and such luminaries as the local newspaper editor. This group carries out programs and activities to persuade residents to maintain local habitat for the marsupials, and to curtail the nocturnal depredations of their cats and dogs.

PRODUCT

When the ZBVES was first implemented in 1994, built into its five-year plan was the recognition that the value of the schools' service must be measured by an evaluation of all activities. Internal evaluation is the chosen process whereby the ZBVES, using staff members with "first-hand knowledge of the organization's philosophy, policies, procedures, products, personnel, and management" (Love 1991), sets out on a program of accountability and improvement.

Less formally, evaluation of the success or failure of the ZBVES programs has been occurring at a number of levels. At the most obvious level, programs are judged to be successful each time a teacher requests a repeat booking. Each year about two-thirds of all bookings are repeat bookings, but teacher mobility into and out of the profession, changes in socioeconomic circumstances, and school curriculum changes all require a constant marketing program.

The work of the ZBVES is demand-driven. Schools must be aware of the services offered and must value them sufficiently to overcome the impediments of a zoo visit. Excursions, for which parents must pay and from whom permission forms must be collected, require that teachers reschedule class programs, perhaps inconvenience their colleagues, and become financial managers and experts in logistics. It is easier to stay at school.

The ZBVES does its utmost to encourage teachers to participate in its programs. Measures to maintain demand include comprehensive advertising within the professional press, direct school mailing of programs and events, and appearances by ZBVES staff at professional gatherings to present papers and conduct seminars that sell the service. The close association between the ZBVES and the DSE is of immeasur-

Activity kits for use in schools for preparing students for a zoo excursion
(*photo by Anton Proppe, ZBV*).

able benefit. Teaching staff all have school backgrounds and are selected
for their exemplary records in teaching and environmental education
curriculum development. They understand the needs of teachers and
are able to tailor comprehensive programs to meet those needs. However, the bottom line will always remain: no amount of marketing will
sell an inferior product to a discerning audience. Repeat bookings are a
cogent reminder that the service is meeting teachers' needs.

At a more precise level, the ZBVES assesses its effectiveness in the
context of the teachers' objectives for the program. Were these objectives for the excursion met? Was program delivery directed at the
students' level? Was the information given to the teachers before the
outing relevant? This information is relatively easy to collect. Teachers
are a critical audience and are generally willing to make their opinions
known, so useful feedback is gained from questionnaires handed out
immediately after a session.

Responses to a questionnaire were gathered from eighty-one teachers
in primary and postprimary schools who had brought classes to the zoo
for a range of programs, from those on diversity and classification to
sessions on endangered species. Most lessons occur within the activity

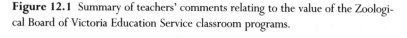

Figure 12.1 Summary of teachers' comments relating to the value of the Zoological Board of Victoria Education Service classroom programs.

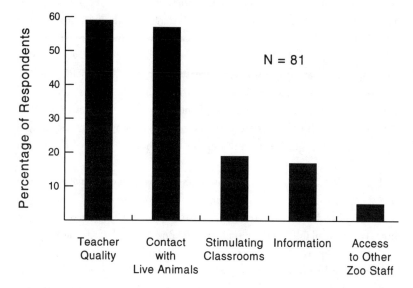

rooms of the zoo school. Some programs explored animal movement through dance, and all programs featured contacts with animals.

The knowledge and expertise of the ZBVES teachers was frequently commented on: "I liked how the teacher related animal handling to the topic of observation"; "friendly and enthusiastic teacher—he was clear and interesting." The teachers value the children's contact with the animals: "the kids' interest, involvement, and satisfaction was high"; "high level of student interaction and participation." Other comments include "balanced presentation—preserve endangered species and educate underdeveloped countries [where the species may be endangered],"; "loved the idea of the darkened room, and the ideas projected through visualization and movement." Figure 12.1 summarizes the positive comments of teachers who had participated in the program and were asked to comment on their entire interaction with the ZBVES—before, during, and after their zoo visit. Positive comments regarding the quality of the ZBVES teachers include their expertise on the topic, their emphasis on conservation, their competence in relating the session to the school program, knowing how to present stimulating activities, their ability to relate to students, and their use of a wide range of teaching skills.

Thirteen responses contained constructive criticism: two teachers said that there should have been a more direct relationship between basic classification and animals, which the kids could have actually seen at the time; three teachers pointed out that the one-hour lesson was too short; another complained that not all the animals listed in the materials were on display; three others thought that there was insufficient access to animal husbandry areas; another teacher said that the lesson was "a bit chalk and talk," that they could do that at school; the teacher of a dance/drama class complained that there were no warm-up activities to acclimate students preceding the lessons exploring animal movements through dance; and another said that the level of the lesson was too basic.

Feedback from visiting class teachers is monitored regularly in staff meetings. A number of their comments require a response. The length of lessons can be varied. Access to husbandry areas for many species is not always available, and animals are taken off display at short notice for many reasons; both are out of the control of the education staff. Lessons should not be "chalk and talk"; direct experience with animals and their habitats should be the major focus of the zoo visit. Communication with the class teacher before the visit is fundamental to the success of the visit. The teacher's purpose for the zoo visit, whether it is to introduce or conclude a unit of class work, must be clear, as this would call for quite different approaches in the zoo lesson. Furthermore, warm-up activities are essential in classes involving movement.

This still does not address the central purpose of environmental education,which is to produce an action or a behavioral change that protects or improves the environment. Education necessarily takes effect over a long period of time. When an educational program aims to bring about long-term behavioral change, a follow-up evaluation is needed sometime after the program has ended to determine if the intended change has been realized. Have students altered their management of their school environment? Did they go back to their schools and cultivate plants on the school grounds that would attract birds and animals? Is there a better recovery rate of aluminum soft-drink containers sold at the school stores? Do they now read the labels on containers before making a purchase? Do they now keep their pet cat inside at night?

Of course the best way to know the answers to these questions is to go to the school and find out. In one evaluation activity conducted in

1993 a graduate student did just that (Pickering 1993). Some months after the zoo excursion, Pickering visited eight schools and conducted interviews with teachers and students. At a primary school that had specifically requested a program based on school-ground habitat regeneration, the researcher was told that "students . . . now think it is good to have birds around to enjoy and that birds need trees to live in" and that "students have planted trees to attract birds to the area." These same students could not "remember a great deal about the zoo trip because it was at the end of last year." The program at the zoo had escaped their memories, but its effects lived on in their school grounds, which they have planted with indigenous species. A postprimary school teacher commented that "the trip to the zoo was not just a day out but was an important part of the curriculum." For her, the best aspects of the zoo program were "looking at live animals and handling them and having somebody from the zoo [available] with inside information." However, she also said that the "worksheets needed improvement—the material was a little confusing." The curriculum materials have since been revised and reprinted in a common format.

Future Directions

The ZBVES is currently exploring a number of options for future development, including expanding the preschool program; increasing the range of programs for non-English speakers, in recognition of the cultural and ethnic diversity of its users; placing teaching areas in the exhibits themselves so that program discussions can involve all visitors to the zoo, not just the school students; increasing use of the arts to deliver messages of concern about animals and their habitats; and developing curriculum materials and methods that exploit the possibilities of interactive telecommunication technologies.

In all that we do, however, we must not lose sight of what the ZBVES does best: educating students about their environment through direct experiences with animals.

PART FIVE

Involving Community Groups

■■

13

Multilevel Conservation and Education at the Community Baboon Sanctuary, Belize

██

Robert H. Horwich and
Jonathan Lyon

We have developed a community-based, low-cost, and low-technology land-use conservation program for privately held tropical lands. The program merges traditional subsistence land-use practices with long-term maintenance of species diversity. We have worked to integrate conservation biology, agricultural ecology, natural resource education, and locally controlled ecotourism in a package tailored to local farmers and their community. This holistic approach can be utilized by any person, organization, or government body concerned with the effects of subsistence agriculture on natural-resource conservation and the promotion of community-based conservation.

PLANNING

Project Target and Objectives

Tropical deforestation is occurring on unprotected lands at such an accelerated pace that national parks and protected areas alone will not achieve adequate protection of tropical forest lands for either wildlife or sustainable development. Focusing improved land-use planning, conservation, and educational efforts on traditionally unprotected lands remains a vastly overlooked option. These lands represent an enormous opportunity for the creation of uniquely tailored conservation/education programs aimed at, and designed for, the benefit of those persons who are now using and altering tropical forest lands and will be doing so in the future.

Economic development programs for unprotected lands historically have demonstrated little regard for local cultural institutions and legal rights, sustainable agricultural development, or long-term conservation concerns (Moran 1983; Gregg and McGean 1985; Dasmann 1988). Additionally, many tropical education programs have been centered around protected forests, pristine environments, or zoos, and have not addressed the topic of partially degraded or unprotected lands. In many tropical regions, fully or partially utilized forests and/or otherwise "damaged ecosystems" represent the most common type of land cover. The rural dwellers and subsistence farmers using these nonpristine forests are also commonly and unjustly saddled with the image of being primitive and peripheral to the general culture of their respective societies. This cultural separation and the lack of appreciation of the potential role of rural dwellers in protecting the environment has been inadequately addressed by both educators and conservation planners.

Linking scientific research to community-based agendas requires a retooling of perspectives on pure research, hypothesis testing, and experimentation. The researcher must accept the burden of conducting appropriate research in order to provide conservation solutions that are workable in the local community. Too often within the scientific community, researchers remain in isolation and work solely to collect and analyze data to publish in the journals of their academic fields (Boom 1990). In its worst form, this pattern of research and publication is scientific colonialism, in that it exploits the resource data of a given nation and exports the final research product in a form unusable to the vast majority of citizens in the host country. Connecting scientific and conservation research efforts to rural lands and their inhabitants, however, can produce enormous benefits. These benefits include limiting pressure to clear additional undisturbed forests (Cairns 1986; DuBois 1990), promotion of nontraditional crops adapted to marginal lands

(National Research Council 1989), protection of plant genetic resources (Cohen et al. 1991), promotion of extractive resource utilization (Allegretti 1990; Daly 1990), and an empowerment and bolstered identity of the small-scale subsistence farmer (Alcorn 1990; Horwich 1990).

The Sanctuary Region

The Community Baboon Sanctuary (CBS) project was initiated in north central Belize in 1985, along a 30-kilometer stretch of the Belize River (figure 13.1). The framework of the CBS is based on voluntary land stewardship and collaborative resource management. Detailed accounts of the development of the CBS have been discussed elsewhere (Horwich 1988, 1990; Horwich and Lyon 1987, 1988, 1990). The primary goal of the CBS is to protect the threatened black howler monkey (*Alouatta pigra*), known locally as the baboon, by protecting its habitat: the seasonally dry, semideciduous tropical forests along the Belize River. Our management target is the protection of privately owned or leased lands being used for subsistence agriculture. In Belize, land ownership is approximately half private and half government-controlled; of the latter half, the majority is open to use by logging concerns and farmers (Everitt 1987).

The CBS is located in a predominantly Creole ethnic region of Belize. The local Creole population has a mixed African ancestry and uses an English Creole dialect (Bolland 1986). Individual land holdings in the area are small (ranging from 1 to 130 hectares), but the land in composite represents a core of critical howler habitat. The indigenous farming system is small scale (0.1- to 1-hectare plots) and uses a slash-and-burn practice. Clearings are typically used for two to three years, then left fallow for fifteen to forty years. The area also supports some small-scale cattle operations (herds of five to twenty head). The targeted landscape is thus a mosaic of small, slash-and-burn clearings, pastures, and successional forests of different ages over which various forms of ownership are superimposed (figures 13.1 and 13.2).

The mosaic of different eco-units (Oldeman 1983) within the CBS poses both research and management challenges. It requires an understanding of forest successional processes and their relationships to land-use patterns, soil fertility, soil erosion, and howler habitat. Our research priority has been applied research on the ecological pressures placed on

Figure 13.1 Composite map of the Community Baboon Sanctuary (CBS) indicating main roads, the Belize River, and landowner boundaries. The broken line indicates the area covered by the aerial photograph in figure 13.2, showing the mosaic pattern of forest cover found on these lands.

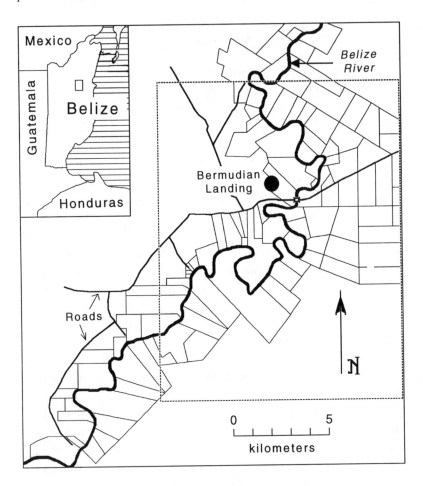

howler habitat by local peoples. Our applied-research goal has been to find habitat protection solutions that factor in the limitations and restrictions facing local farmers, namely, limited labor supplies, low technology, and little available capital. Before the CBS was formed, research on howler feeding ecology, forest succession, and local farming practices was conducted with local persons being hired to assist in most research efforts.

Figure 13.2 Aerial photograph of the central portion of the CBS taken in 1988 (*photo by Horwich and Lyon*). Note the Belize River running through the heart of the CBS and the mosaic landscape of forest and clearings.

Focal Species Approach

Initial planning of the CBS centered on the black howler monkey as a focal conservation species. The howlers were locally abundant and were not hunted by local people. One of the unique features of the sanctuary was that the target lands, privately owned or leased, were currently used for subsistence farming and small-scale cattle ranching, as they had been for several generations. The planning challenge was to develop a howler protection program that could be woven successfully into the local farming culture. It was not a viable or desired approach to enforce howler conservation through the traditional avenues of legal protection and human exclusion. Rather than working contrary to the traditions of land users, we decided to integrate the planning, development, and functioning of the sanctuary into the very community where the conservation was to take place.

Community-Based Planning

The first phase of the project involved extensive local contacts and discussions with area landowners and local political bodies—the Village Councils. A key to the initial phase was the hiring of a local liaison to field our inquiries and translate and interpret the project's aims to the local populace. It was crucial to state from the outset that the proposed sanctuary was to be voluntary and that land ownership and land use would remain under individual autonomy. We believed it was our obligation to present the community sanctuary proposal in an open, nonintimidating forum and respect the ability of the local villagers to accept or reject the merits of the proposal as presented. Recognizing the local public as rational, intelligent persons concerned about the issues affecting them engendered the support and endorsement of the local villagers (Winterbottom and Hazelwood 1987; Doyle 1991). The community sanctuary concept parallels ideas emanating from the biosphere concept (UNESCO 1984): the CBS is analogous to a biosphere without a core area (Hartup 1989). Unlike biosphere reserves, however, the CBS has focused complete attention on human land use and ecosystem interactions in a specific local context.

During the planning and implementation phases, we emphasized our role as "transient catalysts" who would provide management advice and expertise to the project; but it was always understood that ultimate control would rest with the local populace. Land-management plans were to be jointly developed with each farmer or farming family, and sanctuary membership would involve the signing of a nonbinding, symbolic pledge to uphold the management plan. This local-control approach is analogous in many respects to the participatory management concepts of social forestry and social agro-ecology (Korten 1980; Train 1988; Alcorn 1990). The CBS takes participatory management a step further, however, by giving ultimate veto power to the landowners themselves, thus yielding control of the project to the local community. Although this approach runs contrary to mainstream managerial codes, its implementation was, and continues to be, the key component of the sanctuary's success.

IMPLEMENTATION

Our primary concern was to provide a concrete and locally palatable framework to implement land-management plans for the landholdings coinciding with howler populations. The implementation strategy centered on promoting forest corridor establishment and maintenance along property boundaries and riverbanks. The minimal management objective was to secure, even under intensive land-use scenarios, a continuous and connected forest corridor system centering on the riverbank forests. Our research had shown that from these protected corridors, howlers could acquire adequate forage from the mosaic of successional forest patches. While the ecological benefits of forest corridors have been discussed in various contexts in the ecological literature (e.g., Harris 1984; Hobbs et al. 1990), we needed to translate concepts of corridor protection into the local agricultural culture. This translation served to protect both key howler habitat and improve agricultural land use by limiting soil erosion along riverbanks.

Community-Based Integration

Working to understand the local culture—its institutions, language, and ethics—was an essential first step in promoting the community sanctuary concept. It was crucial to develop an open and equal dialogue between us, the foreign initiators of the program, and community members. Although this approach is a simple building block to facilitate interactions, it is often constrained by superior or inferior feelings engendered by academic degrees or having come from an urban area or large technological nation. We worked to overcome these potential obstacles by living in the village and sharing duties, social events, schools, birthdays, and funerals. This gave us needed insight into the local culture and allowed us to become at least part-time members of the community.

Our involvement also decreased the threat some villagers felt from us as outsiders and gave us ample opportunity to describe and define the project's objectives, as well as respond to local reactions. Local farmers proved to be a vital source of information about the forests and wildlife, and also provided essential feedback on planning and implementation aspects of the sanctuary. Understanding local knowledge aided us in translating a local, informal understanding of land use into a more formal context. Enlisting the local government agricultural extension officer in our planning and research efforts was also helpful.

Program Operation: Local Participation in Management Planning

Our initial planning involved landowners, Village Council members, and other sympathetic villagers. We first circulated a petition requesting that we be allowed into the village to begin our investigations of the experimental program. After all villagers had signed the petition, we physically mapped the lands of twelve landowners in the central village (Bermudian Landing) using existing survey records and markers, natural landmarks, and recent aerial photographs. Landownership maps were rechecked and revised via landowner interviews (figure 13.3). We then developed and presented individual management plans for each landowner. After these plans were reworked to the landowner's satisfaction, we obtained their nonbinding, signatory pledge to abide by the management plan.

Once all lands surrounding Bermudian Landing were pledged to the program, we had the project placed on the agenda of the annual village meeting, which was also attended by the national representative for the district. Despite the area representative's reticence about the project because of a concern about the jurisdiction of the project, our emphasis on the voluntary nature of the program was embraced by the villagers, and the CBS project was unanimously and formally approved. With this

Figure 13.3 Lyon (*far right*) discussing land-ownership boundaries with participating sanctuary landowners (*photo by Horwich and Lyon*).

success, we expanded the CBS to include additional landowners in seven
other nearby villages, using the same procedure outlined above. In order
to counteract conflicting misinformation circulating in other villages as
to the voluntary nature of the program, Lyon spent time living in each
of these villages and explaining the program to the residents. It should
be noted that we stressed to residents that no initial economic gains or
incentives would be given for participation in the CBS; landowners
initially received only property maps of their lands, copies of the
management plan, howler T-shirts, and a formal certificate of participation.

An important aspect of all the management plans created is that they
are not static. We recognized from the outset that long-term viability
of the plans would require constant input and awareness of the resources at hand, and the relationships between these resources and
human land usage. In this vein, yearly aerial photographs and land-use
status studies have been used to maintain a quantitative input into the
constantly evolving management formula.

Budget

Obtaining initial grants from conservation organizations was difficult because of the experimental nature of the CBS project. The project thus began on volunteer money and labor (and has maintained some of that flavor to date). Once established, the sanctuary developed slowly. There were no initial staff members other than the occasional hiring of villagers to assist researchers, and no financial gain was imparted to the participating landowners. Sanctuary budgets were small, both out of necessity and intention. With the CBS, we wanted to emphasize that meaningful conservation work could be accomplished without large budgets and top-heavy administration. We set budgets for ourselves, other researchers, and hired staff in accordance with local labor standards; all received stipends comparable to the local Belizean pay scale and conforming with the rural village life-style. Except for foreign research volunteers, whenever possible all paid labor and supplies were obtained locally. The steady flow of research volunteers living, working, purchasing, and hiring within the community also helped catalyze village interest in future tourism.

In terms of specific finances, we obtained an initial $3,000 World Wildlife Fund (WWF)-U.S. grant for setting up the sanctuary in 1985 and $5,000 for its continuation in 1986. In 1987, on the basis of our commitment to set up a formal management structure, we received an additional $15,000 WWF grant for two local staff salaries and for construction of a museum building. During this period we enlisted the full-time participation of a nongovernment Belizean organization, the Belize Audubon Society (BAS), to act as both a repository of the grant monies and a consultant. The BAS oversaw the transfer and distribution of outside monies but had no authority to direct or dictate land use within the CBS.

In 1988 WWF continued support with an $8,000 grant to maintain CBS staff. Since 1988 the Zoological Society of Milwaukee, Wisconsin, has maintained the sanctuary with a $10,000 annual budget. With local management in place, support for foreign consulting dropped out of the budget and now occurs on a voluntary and individually funded basis. Additional grants from WWF and the Lincoln Park Zoological Society of Chicago, Illinois ($2,000 each) supported construction of museum exhibits in 1989. In the same year an Inter-American Foundation grant for $11,000 was awarded to the BAS to administer low-interest loans to CBS villagers for tourism facilities. Also in 1989 WWF granted $7,000 for printing the book, *A Belizean Rain Forest: The Community Baboon Sanctuary,* for free use in Belizean schools and for fund-raising. With a major increase in CBS visitation in 1989 (particularly by school classes), a 1990 grant for $16,000 from WWF was given to increase the CBS staff and to purchase a vehicle and radio equipment.

Administrative and Management Structure

The CBS was initially created with no formal, localized management structure; the land-management plans were the sole basis for sanctuary management. The formal management and administrative apparatus was developed when grants for salaried positions were obtained. The overall structure of the CBS is illustrated in figure 13.4. Although this basic structure has been in place since 1987, the actual functioning of the different management bodies have undergone constant evolution. The

Figure 13.4 Administrative and management structure of the CBS.

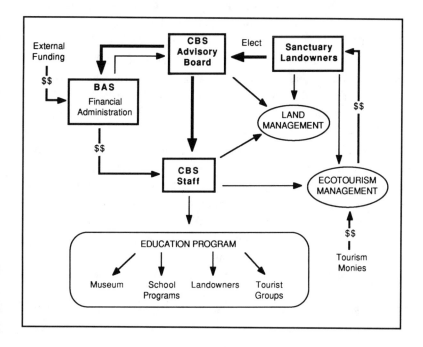

BAS remains an umbrella organization involved principally in the holding and distribution of outside funds. The CBS Advisory Board consists of eight board members—one elected landowner from each of the eight participating villages. The advisory board has grown in importance and function, and is currently being set up as a formal legal body that will oversee all components of the CBS, including staff hiring, tourism development, budget management, and museum operations. The CBS staff members are responsible for various educational duties in the CBS and throughout Belize, and for encouraging landowners to adhere to land-management plans. Regardless of the evolving management structure, voluntary landowner participation remains the essence of the CBS; landowners are free to leave the CBS at any time and even prevent CBS staff and tourists from trespassing on their lands. Of the more than 120 CBS members, to date none have sought separation from the CBS.

PRODUCT

Rural Conservation Consciousness

The CBS project has extended beyond its original scope: howler habitat protection. The main extension has been the inculcation and nurturing of a conservation consciousness and ethic within the local populace. Some of it is genuine and some is tied to the economic benefits of the project, but in all cases the idea of the value of wildlife and other natural resources has pervaded the area in dramatic new ways. This change is reflected in the topics discussed in the village and the increased protective attitude toward the monkeys. Our recent targeting of the exploited Central American river turtle (*Dermatemys mawii*) for research has also resulted in increased dialogue about the turtle's status and protection, as well as the potential for sustainable harvesting. To quantify local attitudes, Hartup (1989) conducted a study of the ecological views of the landowners. Hartup found that the success of the CBS has come about through the engendering among villagers of local community pride in their lands, villages, and in their sanctuary, which has brought about national and international interest and acclaim. The local community also expressed that the promotion of the CBS led to an increase in ethnic Creole consciousness, partly the result of a yearly festival at the sanctuary museum which features Creole folksinging, storytelling, and bushcrafts (Horwich et al., in press).

Sanctuary Education

The CBS educational program has four components: landowner education, Belizean school education, Belizean adult education, and foreign ecotourist education. The most visible educational product is the CBS museum, which was created to serve as a focal point for administration and an orientation and educational center for visiting classes and tourists. The museum gives the CBS a tangible face for what was a mostly abstract conservation concept. The low-cost museum was built on community-owned lands with local labor and materials (despite funding agency reticence to set up a museum in a remote rural location). Inexpensive displays were produced by laminating posters with photos and illustrations arranged with computer created text (figure 13.5). The museum exhibits emphasize important ecological, conservation, and cultural themes, some of which are indigenous to the sanctuary (figure 13.6).

A second CBS educational program product is the textbook *A Belizean Rain Forest: The Community Baboon Sanctuary*. The book has grown from a small, locally distributed informational pamphlet to a text/guidebook on local natural and cultural history and the CBS conservation program. Presently this is the only extensive discussion of Belize's rain forests available to a mass audience. The book has been given to many school libraries and is being used by Belizean schoolteachers (and CBS staff) as a reference book. The text includes a guide to an interpretive trail system running through part of the CBS (figure 13.7). The text and trail guide are the primary basis for field lectures given by the sanctuary staff with supplemental information coming from their own knowledge of the bush. An additional educational program has been the tutoring of sanctuary staff by visiting volunteers and researchers. Fallet Young, the first sanctuary manager, was tutored extensively on basic ecological concepts and how they related to his personal knowledge of the bush. Young, in turn, has helped to train most of the current staff and has imparted his considerable knowledge and teaching skills to national park managers throughout Belize.

Information Dissemination

Information about the CBS program has been extensively disseminated both in professional journals and the public media. The CBS has been

Figure 13.5 A typical poster exhibit in the CBS Museum.

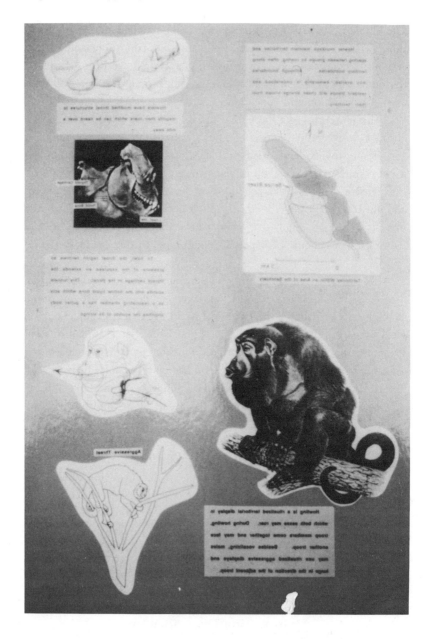

Figure 13.6 A CBS Museum exhibit room (*photo by Horwich and Lyon*).

covered in newspapers, magazines, and radio and television programs both in Belize and throughout the world. Consequently, some of the community conservation ideas are being adopted in other areas. Within Belize, three conservation programs are being developed based on the CBS (figure 13.8). In the first, CBS methods are being used to coordinate foreign landowners on Ambergris Cay to abide by management programs to protect the nesting beaches of sea turtles on privately owned lands. In the second, the effort by local people, stimulated by the success of the CBS coupled with some CBS staff consultation, has led to the formation of a nature preserve at Monkey River. In support of this effort, the government of Belize has dedicated some public lands to the program. A third program, the Manatee Community Reserve, is being developed by the authors and others to create a multiple land-use program for a 70,000-hectare tract of land along the central coast of Belize. The manatee program will integrate the community sanctuary and biosphere concepts (Horwich et al., in press). Additional efforts to create similar programs in the United States are in the early stages of development.

Figure 13.7 Fallet Young, the CBS's first manager (*second from left*), and Reuben Rhaburn, the first assistant manager and present committee member (*center*), lecturing on a section of the CBS interpretive trail (*photo by Horwich and Lyon*).

Future Improvements

When we first began the CBS project, we were unsure as to where the experiment would lead and had a limited view of its potential success. We were not fully prepared for some of the results. Our most serious error was failure to create, immediately after the CBS was formally established, a legally recognized local group to oversee, advise, and protect the sanctuary in its everyday running. Eventually a local CBS advisory board was formed, but until very recently it has had limited power outside the CBS. This oversight was not detrimental early on because we had very competent staff and the financial administration of the BAS was more than adequate. However, when the BAS's funding was abruptly cut by a U.S. conservation group in 1988, the administrative capacity of the BAS was decimated and CBS staff were ill-equipped to fill the void. Formation of a legal advisory board or cooperative during the initial phases of CBS operations would have enabled local villagers to develop the administrative expertise to limit such problems. A formal advisory board also could have been involved with the initial

Figure 13.8 Community conservation sites in Belize.

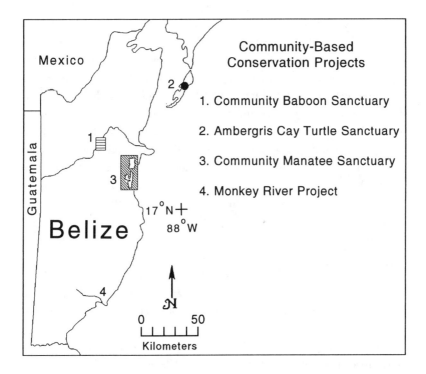

hiring of CBS personnel. Forming the board once staff roles were established has proved more difficult.

Another unexpected outcome was the degree to which the CBS became popular as an area for tourism and education. The initial popularity was stimulated by Belizean and international media publicity and further increased with the creation of the CBS museum. Construction of a bridge across the Belize River in 1988 and road improvements also stimulated increased traffic to the CBS. Annual celebrations of the museum opening have become popular social events, further publicizing the area. With the rapid growth of tourism, we should have encouraged immediate steps to control foreign tourism agencies and their accompanying tourist groups. Many foreign tour guides began circumventing sanctuary rules and ignoring sanctuary staff authority. We could have worked with the villagers and CBS staff earlier to develop better tourism management in order to prevent sidestepping of the tourism land-use rules decided by landowners and Village Councils.

Because both land-management and ecotourism decisions are constantly evolving to meet the changing physical and cultural landscape, the very dynamic nature of the CBS is essential to its past and continued success. We cannot overemphasize that the landowners and villagers who live and work in the eight CBS villages are responsible for the sanctuary's continued functioning. Yielding control of conservation and land-use decisions to rural farmers and communities has been shown by CBS members to be a new and effective tool in the arsenal of planetary protection. The CBS's nontraditional, community-based approach to conservation and education addresses both short- and long-term concerns. In the short term, the CBS approach focuses immediate attention on land-use planning for the people who, because of socioeconomic pressures, are on the frontiers of forest destruction. With the onslaught of apocalyptic predictions of tropical forest destruction, the CBS approach also addresses the long-term conservation needs predicted under the worst-case scenario: little or no pristine forest left intact, with remaining lands degraded or being utilized in a nonsustainable fashion.

To be truly effective, conservation and environmental education programs must be tailored to the realities of local people and communities. Many developing nations, like Belize, have emerging but limited capacities to rigorously confront conservation, sustainable development, and environmental education questions. We believe that local efforts like the CBS are much more likely to be able to adapt, respond, and produce results in those areas where infrastructure is weak or nonexistent. Localized community projects also can provide various avenues of direct economic and social benefit to the very people and communities pursuing the conservation effort. These benefits include monies generated from tourism and society's long-overdue respect for rural people and their crucial role in protecting the planet. Monolithic approaches to conservation show little promise in a world where the people using, destroying, and protecting the forests are as diverse as the forests themselves.

Acknowledgments

We owe our position to the more than one hundred landowners and other villagers of Bermudian Landing, Big Falls, Double Head Cabbage, Flowers Bank, Isabella Bank, Saint Paul's Bank, Scotland Half Moon, and Willows Bank. Special thanks and appreciation go to Fallet Young, the first CBS manager, who did so much to further the sanctuary goals. Thanks also go to Clifton Young for help during the beginning sanctuary stages. We greatly appreciate all the help of the Belize Audubon Society and their Board of Directors in administering the sanctuary and helping it to grow, especially Mick Craig, Dr. Victor Gonzalez, Dolores Godfrey, Janet Gibson, Lydia Waight, and Philip Balaramos.

A Belizean Rain Forest: The Community Baboon Sanctuary, by R. Horwich and J. Lyon, can be purchased from Howlers Forever, Inc., RD 1, Box 96, Gays Mills, Wis. 54631 ([608] 735–4717) for $14 postpaid, with wholesale prices for the purchase of more than ten copies. Sale proceeds are used for a trust fund for the CBS.

14

Les Mielles: A Conservation Opportunity in the United Kingdom

■■
■■

Michael Romeril

The year 1978 was a conservation watershed for Jersey, Channel Islands, when its government designated a significant part of the island as "a special area." Until then, the island had not been noticeably conservation-minded; yet the success of the project would depend on its acceptance by the community. Although no formal educational program was envisaged, good public relations activities and education would clearly be a major influence in achieving conservation goals. The need to overcome certain prejudices on a small island community provided an interesting challenge.[1]

PLANNING

Jersey is an island of about 115 square kilometers, lying approximately 185 kilometers south of England and 25 kilometers west of France's Normandy coast. Although still essentially a rural community, Jersey is a crowded island with a population of more than eighty thousand.

---

[1] The views expressed in this chapter are the author's and do not necessarily imply a departmental view.

While some of its valleys support extensive woodland, the greater part of the island is open farmland divided by banks and hedges, although Dutch Elm Disease has taken its toll on the latter. The western part of the island, more exposed to Atlantic gales, is open, with large areas of sand dunes and heathland.

Because of its island status, Jersey enjoys a mild climate for its latitude. This, together with its geographical position and the fact that it was once joined to mainland France, has resulted in an extremely rich and varied wildlife, with a unique mixture of typically temperate and Mediterranean species. This is reflected in the number of British rarities, such as sand crocus (*Romulea columnae*) and Dartford warbler (*Sylvia undata*) that occur on the island in significant numbers.

On the reverse side of the coin are the pressures and demands of a densely populated, affluent island. The per capita car-ownership level, for example, is one of the highest in the world. Meeting the demands and needs of housing and recreation creates ever increasing development pressure on undeveloped and seminatural areas.

The Jersey Planning Law, in effect since 1964, has done much to control the spread of development into the countryside. However, specific, directed conservation measures date from a more recent time. Events of 1978 are seen as a particular watershed.

The coastal area of the western part of the island is especially well endowed with wildlife; the landscape, even in 1978, remained relatively undeveloped. This fact prompted the government to approve, in that year, the "special" designation of the area now known as Les Mielles (figure 14.1). *Les Mielles,* the Norman-French word for sand dunes, has close parallels with the U.K. and European national park designation, though obviously on a smaller scale. It is a populated area, very popular for recreation, with a significant agricultural dimension complementing the important wildlife and landscape character. The object of the designation was to focus attention and action on this important area in order to safeguard existing wildlife and their habitats and to restore those areas that had become derelict or degraded.

The designation of Les Mielles was a unique first on Jersey, marking the culmination of much political pressure, and becoming an historic milestone, especially for nature conservation. Its strategy was underpinned by a land-use zoning policy, directed toward nature conservation, agriculture, and recreation (Romeril 1983). An important aspect of this zoning policy was that no land-use designation was exclusive.

Figure 14.1 Les Mielles development plan (Romeril 1983).

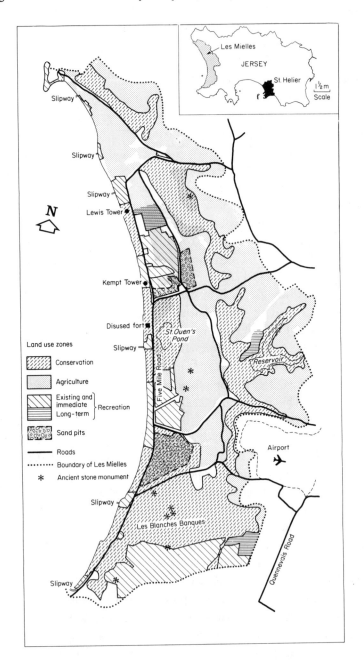

Indeed the opposite was true. Considerable emphasis was placed on the interrelatedness of the activities, especially with respect to nature conservation goals. Thus the land-use designation operates to confer an order of priority in the decision-making process, and, where possible, compatible activities are accommodated in specific areas.

This integrated, multiuse approach was particularly important, and reflects the prevailing global attitude that sympathetic activities can and should be accommodated in environmentally sensitive areas. To a significant portion of the island's population, nature conservation was seen as an elitist activity that pursued negative protectionist policies. Additionally, it was viewed as being excessively concerned with safeguarding a few rare species even at the expense of human requirements.

Given these prevailing attitudes, the need to build support for conservation policies was paramount both within the designated area and within the wider island context. Les Mielles provided a vehicle to communicate nature-conservation priorities and values islandwide. On an island the size of Jersey, with its historical background, the whole population was seen as the target audience to whom environmental awareness should be directed.

The appointment of a conservation officer to implement the proposals was another first for the island. Based within the island's Planning Department, the conservation officer spent much of his time, in the first few years after the designation of Les Mielles, "in the field." This was essential and valuable in those early days since much needed to be done to gain the support and cooperation of the public and, indeed, some politicians who were still not wholly convinced of the value of the designation.

Many of the approaches used were not new or original. However, they were "new" in the local context and needed to overcome much prejudice in some specific cases. Nevertheless, Les Mielles is now judged a success and provides further evidence of the efficacy of basic conservation principles, particularly the involvement of local people and good communication. Of particular value was the high degree of personal involvement and motivation by conservation staff. In this respect the implementation of Les Mielles's policies paralleled the approaches successfully adopted with the U.K. Heritage Coast projects (Department of Environment 1972). The main feature is the integration of traditional planning controls with an on-ground management presence. The key factor is a project officer who acts as a link between various local authorities and as an interface with both landowners and user groups.

IMPLEMENTATION

Communication with all sectors of the community and direct, on-site contact with farmers and landowners provided the main thrust in building support for the scheme. The presence of a ranger "in the field" was critical so that one could respond quickly and practically to a problem. It was important to explain the "why," as well as the "what," of practical tasks, and this was particularly vital with issues involving the restraint of specific activities, especially if they had become unofficially established.

On occasion, a public meeting, advertised in the local press, would have special value. This would normally be called to discuss a particular issue, but also to provide a forum for general discussion. Views could be aired and conservation staff could respond. In this way, any suspicion of an air of secrecy could be quashed. This approach proved especially valuable in dealing with problems posed by horseback riding activities. Some routes previously used for horseback riding were inappropriate or destructive of valuable wildlife habitats and had to be eliminated. Where possible, alternative routes were created to compensate for the loss of established bridlepaths. A public meeting with horseback riders led to the formation of a representatives' liaison group, which acts as an "early warning system" and avoids some of the earlier situations that tended to become confrontational. The liaison group consists of three horseback riders, and meetings are held with conservation staff when the need arises.

With the future in mind, young children were a special focus for environmental education. Local schools have been encouraged to visit the area and undertake studies there as part of their school core curriculum. The recent appointment of an interpretive officer within the Conservation Section of the Planning Office has considerably facilitated this particular exercise. Educating teaching staff introduces a multiplier effect. Because of other pressures, conservation staff have to put a limit on the time spent in direct contact with school parties. For that reason, a number of short courses have been organized to acquaint teachers with the educational opportunities of Les Mielles and the possible study methods to be adopted. Attendance at such courses is

Figure 14.2 A Les Mielles Visitor Interpretation Center in a converted and re-stored nineteenth-century Martello tower (*photo by Romeril*).

voluntary; although they have been mostly successful and well sup-ported, there remains a reluctance among some teachers to involve themselves directly in outdoor teaching.

"Fun days" are particularly popular. During the summer holidays, young children can spend a day at Les Mielles, organized and supervised by conservation staff, enjoying a variety of games and exercises, all with an environmental theme. The "fun days" are always oversubscribed, demonstrating their popularity. "Fun days," as well as all other youth activity in Les Mielles, have a particularly useful by-product in their feedback to parents. Many a visiting adult will admit that his or her first realization of what was happening at Les Mielles came from tales related by their children.

Schools and youth groups also participate in practical conservation work, which increases their involvement in local community activities. Their contribution may be a one-time activity or students may attend regularly, undertaking a range of tasks. A major litter clearance exercise can be undertaken by a large number of students spending a single day in the area. In other instances, several students, undertaking a community project one afternoon per week throughout the school year, can tackle more long-term maintenance projects.

A Visitor Interpretation Center, created in a converted and restored nineteenth-century Martello tower (figure 14.2), is a valuable focus for visitors to Les Mielles. An audiovisual theater, various displays, and information leaflets raise the visitor's awareness of events and notable sites in the area. These all enhance the visitor experience. Phone cards carrying a wildlife conservation message are the latest idea for extending this educational process.

The obvious attraction of the Interpretation Center (and of Les Mielles) to tourists, as well as locals, provides a most useful opportunity to point up the indirect economic value of nature conservation efforts. Tourism is a major industry in Jersey accounting for about 30 percent of its gross domestic product (GDP). With its increasing global popularity, so-called green tourism is seen as especially promising on an island such as Jersey with its fine coastal landscapes and rich and varied wildlife. The change in marketing emphasis, which now seeks to capitalize on the island's natural heritage, has generated new, and sometimes unlikely, support for nature-conservation initiatives.

Harnessed in a positive manner, the media can be a valuable public relations tool. On a small island such as Jersey, the media play a particularly significant communications role. Through interviews, features, and a local radio lunchtime chat show, full use has been made of the local newspaper, television, and radio services to inform the public of activities and progress in Les Mielles, and to explain the rationale behind various initiatives, both regulatory and promotional. Such activities were generally organized as the need arose but, given the extent of personal contact on this small island, could be arranged at any opportune time. With a different emphasis, the local television company, in the early groundswell of feeling for the environment, provided a year's sponsorship and encouragement of conservation schemes.

PRODUCT

Evaluating success is not easy, but it is now generally agreed that considerable progress has been made in Les Mielles. Clearly the majority of the community now accepts and has respect for the conservation work undertaken there. This is evident from political comment, positive editorial comment in the local media, and direct positive feedback from members of the community. Visitor surveys at the Interpretive Center provide further evidence of support and satisfaction. Even outright critics of earlier years now sing its praises. Because of Les Mielles's visibility, nature conservation islandwide has benefited through increased public support and a willingness to cooperate in conservation schemes.

Tangible measures of success came with the winning of national awards. In 1984 landscape restoration work within the Les Mielles area won a Civic Trust Award (a Great Britain environmental improvement award scheme)—one of only twenty-three out of more than a thousand entries. Of particular significance, in view of the original objectives for the scheme, was the wording of the citation. It especially praised the fact that the project "was an inspiring example of countryside management which has ensured that nature conservation interests and public enjoyment are not mutually exclusive." In 1987 the Kempt Tower conversion won a Civic Trust Commendation—a second tier award, but still prestigious.

A key element in the success story has been the promotion of the positive side of nature conservation and its benefits to the public, as well as to wildlife. Staff involved at Les Mielles have endeavored at all times to promote this aspect and erase the negative image that had dominated local conservation issues until recent years. Although this has been successful in many ways, aspects of nature conservation still remain that give rise to unwarranted criticism. To some, whose attitude of conservation is to "let nature take its course," certain management tasks, such as the removal of scrub trees and shrubs on sand dunes, are seen as the antithesis of conservation.

This lack of understanding of the more subtle aspects of nature conservation is often at the root of problems involved in reconciling the myriad demands made on limited land space, such as exists on Jersey. A balanced approach that seeks to be sympathetic to as many of those demands as possible will still inevitably fail to please everyone. Only those with real understanding and compassion will accept the limitations imposed on them in the pursuance of a policy that insists on the right of wildlife to exist alongside the human species.

The close involvement of school groups and other youth organizations has had significant benefit. It engenders an attitude of stewardship on the part of students and generates a greater respect for, and understanding of, conservation initiatives.

Because of its status as a global financial center, Jersey enjoys a favorable economy and its inhabitants are oriented toward a materialistic outlook on life. As such, that difficulties would be encountered with a project such as Les Mielles was perhaps inevitable. Direct benefits are not readily tangible in an economic sense, although the current appreciation that tourism can be a beneficiary of conservation initiatives is an encouraging sign.

Certainly some major setbacks occurred. It is not unreasonable to conclude that the time scale of achievement was too long, which, in no small measure, can be related to equivocal political support. A major government decision in 1991 to allow a golf course extension contrary to the original zoning policy and philosophy highlighted the fact that too many remain who fail (or do not want) to understand the subtle relationship between nature and landscape conservation and our own (human) quality of life. There are no easy environmental causes and Les Mielles has been no exception. Nevertheless, despite setbacks, considerable progress has been made, and this has provided a valuable means of building support for conservation.

15

Conservation and Local Naturalist Guide Training Programs in Costa Rica

■■
■■

Pia Paaby and
David B. Clark

Conservation areas in the tropics are receiving increasing world attention. This interest has led to a marked increase in ecotourism to these areas. We describe a mechanism to integrate the population living in or near these conservation areas into the ecotourism activities and economy by providing training for local naturalist guides.

PLANNING

The pilot project we describe was conducted at the La Selva Biological Station of the Organization for Tropical Studies (OTS). La Selva is located in the Sarapiqui region, in the Atlantic lowlands of the Republic of Costa Rica (figure 15.1). The 1,550-hectare private reserve borders Braulio Carrillo National Park, a 47,000-hectare area that spans a 2,800-meter altitudinal gradient and protects a spectacular sample of Central American lowland, premontane, and montane rain forests (Hartshorn and Peralta 1988; Pringle 1988).

The training of local naturalist guides developed in response to

Figure 15.1 Location of La Selva Biological Station in Costa Rica.

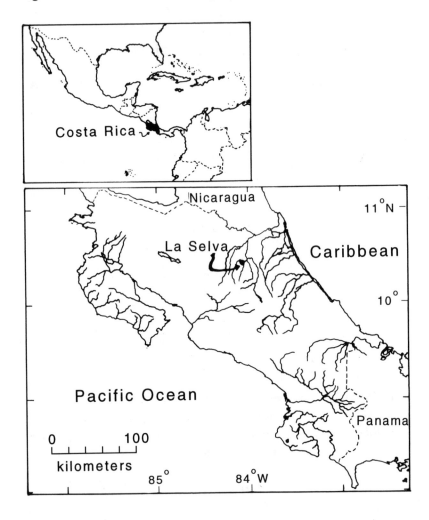

increasing numbers of natural history visitors to the Sarapiqui region, including La Selva. We were seeking a mechanism to increase the economic returns of ecotourism to the local level and also to increase the capacity of local sites to receive these visitors in an environmentally benign fashion. To do this, we organized a program focused on training local residents as naturalists, that is, someone able to accompany, entertain, and, it was hoped, educate visitors interested in natural history. In addition, our program aimed to increase the environmental awareness of local residents by providing the rationale of conservation issues and an understanding of ecological concepts pertinent to terrestrial and aquatic systems of the region.

We decided to target local residents who were currently either underemployed or unemployed, and therefore most in need of alternative sources of income. To become a participant an individual had to be able to read and write (as proof, an application form had to be filled out); to be at least sixteen years old; to have had no university or technical education; to have no business ownership; and, if possible, to be in a position to get involved in conservation, environmental education, or ecotourism activities in the future. The participation of women was also a factor in the final selection of eighteen men and eight women (applications were received from sixty-three men and thirty women).

Planning, organizing, and teaching the course were carried out by two ecologists (Paaby and Clark). Most of the logistics were provided by the OTS San José office or the La Selva Biological Station (LSBS). Our close contact with OTS and the University of Costa Rica (UCR) meant that many academic resources were easily accessible. To provide students with up-to-date techniques and information on specialized subjects, we invited resource people from the UCR, the Universidad Nacional, the National Museum, the Costa Rican National Park Service, OTS staff and researchers, and Costa Rican biologists working as full-time nature tour guides. This institutional support and the volunteer participation of collaborating specialists significantly increased the quality and quantity of course activities.

Because visitation pressure in the Sarapiqui region is constantly increasing, and because many of the natural history and tourist groups are mainly interested in birds, we could have designed the program to concentrate on bird-watching and the English language. Instead, we decided to develop a program to provide participants with tools that would allow them to work in several environmental fields, for example, ecotourism, environmental education, and as assistants for ecological research. Thus a variety of themes were included in the teaching program (table 15.1). English, the language of most visiting tourists, was covered only superficially.

IMPLEMENTATION

Most of the teaching and field activities were carried out at La Selva. Trips to neighboring ecotourist installations and Braulio Carrillo Na-

Table 15.1. Organization of the Local Naturalists' Training Course at the La Selva Biological Station, Puerto Viejo, Costa Rica

1. Introduction to fundamental ecological concepts: individuals, populations, communities, food chains, forest ecology
   - Use of binoculars and field guides
2. Conservation and environmental education
   - System of protected areas in Costa Rica (Costa Rican National Park Service)
   - Introduction to scientific nomenclature
   - Introduction to plant diversity: common plant families of the area (researchers at La Selva)
3. Plant structure and function, emphasizing aspects of interest to tourists
   - Plant-animal interactions
   - "Tourist" plants, that is, those most interesting to visitors
4. Economically valuable plants, especially medicinal and timber species (La Selva researchers, local medicinal plant co-op)
   - History of deforestation in Costa Rica
5. Introduction to ornithology and the hundred most common birds of the region, taught at a local ecotourist lodge, Selva Verde (University of Costa Rica)
   - "In search of the lost bird"—field practice in finding and describing birds
6. Ecology of birds (University of Costa Rica)
   - Field practice in observing bird behavior
7. Introduction to mammals and mammals of special interest to tourists (National University)
   - Field practice in identifying mammal signs, such as tracks, scat, burrows, and so forth (taught by local ex-hunters)
   - Introduction to insects (National Institute of Biodiversity)
   - Common, spectacular, and interesting local insects
   - Field practice in locating and identifying insects
8. Amphibians and reptiles, basic identification and ecology; poisonous and nonpoisonous snakes (University of Costa Rica)
   - Field practice in locating and identifying reptiles and amphibians
   - Night walk to observe amphibians and reptiles
9. Aquatic ecology, including common plants and animals of tourist interest along streams and rivers
   - Field practice in aquatic ecology from boats
   - Archaeological history of the Sarapiqui region (National Museum)
   - Visit to local archaeological site
10. Ecology of tropical premontane forest; three-day field trip to nearby Rara Avis Lodge, ending with an eight-hour hike through Braulio Carrillo National Park to La Selva
11. Scientific research and its application to tourists (researchers at La Selva)
    - Basic first aid
    - Field guiding and group management techniques
12. Field guiding techniques taught by professional biologist guides
    - Field exam: students guiding "volunteer" tourists
    - Evaluation of students' guiding performance (written evaluations by tourists)
13. Presentation of Certificates of Participation
    - Postcourse party

Note: Each number refers to topics covered in a one-day session. Written materials for each unit included a glossary of scientific words, basic English vocabulary, and a list of questions commonly asked by tourists about topics covered in the session. Institutions in addition to the Organization for Tropical Studies that supplied collaborating staff are given in parentheses. Adapted from Clark and Paaby (1990) and Paaby et al. (1991).

Costa Rica's lowland tropical rain forest (*photo by S. K. Jacobson*).

tional Park also were included so that participants could learn the access, facilities, and natural history of these sites.

The course was taught once a week, all day on Saturdays. We decided against Sunday because it is a family day. The one-day-a-week format gave participants a week to read, digest, and understand the new concepts introduced. In addition, this allowed students with jobs to participate without affecting their current employment, as well as enabling women with families to participate. The drop-out rate of courses in Costa Rica's rural areas is usually high. We believe that allowing adequate time for the family and for studying contributed to the zero drop-out rate in this course.

Although all participants could read and write, taking notes in a class requires practice. Because we wanted the students' complete attention, all written materials were delivered a week in advance of their discussion in class. When a specialist was invited, we asked that individual to provide a written form of the lecture ahead of time, so that we could search for technical jargon and check that the common species names were those used in the region. The participants had little access to books or staff between classes. By receiving all the materials in written form, students were able to prepare for each session. In addition, the written lectures have proven useful for post-course review by the graduated naturalists.

Saturday classes started at 7:00 A.M. with announcements and comments regarding the previous week's activities. This was followed by a talk by one of us or an invited specialist. At approximately 8:30 we had a coffee break (for some students this was breakfast) and prepared for the field work, which lasted until noon. In the field we split the group into two to increase student-teacher interactions. We did not use slides but rather concentrated on the forest as our main audiovisual aid. For the amphibian and reptile session we offered an optional night walk in which all students participated. At 1:00 P.M. we regrouped in the classroom to practice oral presentation skills. Each participant had to briefly explain something they had seen in the field in the morning, describing color, smell, natural history, and other attributes. This activity was followed by a short lecture, after which we returned to the field. At 4:30 we met again for a written quiz. This schedule was tiring but effective. Students took the course very seriously, in part because they were presented with a constant flow of activities.

The course was organized into twelve sessions (table 15.1). The field activities took place regardless of the weather. When it rained, we discussed how to entertain groups who did not want to get wet. Even though each session had a main theme, past material and guiding techniques (especially learning to be spontaneous) were constantly practiced. The course resulted in a 143-hour teaching-learning experience (40 hours in the class and 103 hours in the field). One of the sessions involved a three-day field trip to another biological station in the region. From there we walked 24 kilometers to La Selva through Braulio Carrillo National Park, covering an altitudinal gradient of 650 to 35 meters above sea level. The goals of this trip were to integrate the students as a group, to expose them to living in close quarters, to introduce them to another type of recreational activity (i.e., nature hikes), and also to introduce them to this part of the national park.

We had to face the issue of how to best integrate the students' existing knowledge with the material we were presenting. Our approach to this was not by planning traditional classroom lectures with a speaker dominating the teaching. Instead we integrated the cultural and field knowledge of the students in every activity through question-and-answer exercises. The experience we had with teaching at various levels and working with ecotourists, together with the fact that both of us have been involved with the people of the area for almost ten years, helped in designing the teaching methods appropriate both to the material being presented and to the students.

The original budget of U.S. $13,665 was obtained as a World Wildlife Fund grant. This budget was calculated for fifteen students. Given that we accepted and graduated twenty-six, it was necessary to obtain additional financing. This came in the form of logistic subsidies from OTS and donated professional time. If these subsidies are included, the total cost of the course was U.S. $24,614.

PRODUCT

We think that our program met the initial objectives. Twenty-six students (100 percent) finished the twelve-week course. We gave a certificate to all those who had attended twelve sessions, and, when necessary, included a make-up session near the completion of the course. Quiz grades were not used as a criterion for graduation.

Based on the results of this course, we believe the following experiences and techniques were useful and contributed to the educational success of the program:

1. Learn to appreciate the experience and knowledge that each participant already has. Learn to exploit and integrate this knowledge into the program and teach the students how to present it effectively to visitors (sometimes slight vocabulary nuances may hinder communication). For example, all students were familiar with common tropical fruits, such as banana, pineapple, and coconut. By pointing out that seeing these fruits in their tropical habitat was something new and interesting to visitors from the north, we were able to give students useful information based on their existing knowledge. The students felt involved in the teaching process because their individual experience and knowledge was being used and integrated with ours.

2. Plan a complete day with active participation by everyone. This day should not be the religious or family day commonly used by the local population.

3. Provide the written materials before classes. These will also serve for future reference.

4. Include oral practices in the field, based on local history, geography, and environmental issues of the area, and the natural history of the organisms reviewed. This activity increased students' self-assurance and observational abilities, and it sometimes helped them to understand the natural history of the area by using the ecological concepts learned in the course.

5. Use daily written exams to help increase the seriousness of the participants. We think it helped stimulate studying and practicing between sessions and paying attention. It was clear, however, that student performance was much better in the field when the questions were asked spontaneously in conversation.

6. Discuss the goals and approach of the course with resource people in advance. The vocabulary should be as nontechnical as possible. Additionally, as one of our goals was to provide participants with information that is considered "interesting" (i.e., entertaining) by ecotourists, much of the scientific knowledge has to be transformed into short and easily understandable

stories that incorporate details with which the tourists may identify (e.g., using the common term, *the coffee family,* instead of the botanical nomenclature, "Rubiaceae"). We also concentrated on common species. Although tropical biodiversity is staggering, the list of species sure to be seen by all visitors is much shorter. Our strategy was to concentrate on the common species, while at the same time teaching the techniques necessary to learn the rarer species.

7. Involve commercial tourist operators and government entities related to tourism in the process by informing them of the occurrence, development, and results of the course.

8. Limit the participation to a ratio of ten to fifteen students per teacher. This fosters a high level of interaction between teacher and students.

Four months after the course ended we interviewed twenty-two students to assess conservation awareness and their employment in activities related to the course. Twenty-one agreed that before the course they would not have been involved in conservation activities, whereas now they wanted to continue studying and working with issues related to nature.

Some unanticipated results surfaced at the end of the course. The local naturalist guides were a new and immediately available human resource. The naturalists could not only guide and educate visitors, but could also protect the La Selva sites designated for light visitation. As a result, OTS changed its policy regulating day visitors to La Selva, requiring that each group of ten employ one local naturalist. By being able to carefully control general-public visitors, OTS was able to increase the number of groups and individuals visiting the station. Future environmental education activities at La Selva also will capitalize on the local naturalists. For instance, local naturalists will play a prominent role in visitor management in the new OTS La Flaminea regional environmental education center. Additionally, OTS has hired a graduated naturalist as a full-time assistant in La Selva's Environmental Education Program.

When the course and the post-course evaluations were finished, the course material was integrated into a book (Clark and Paaby 1990) that was sent to government and nongovernment institutions in Costa Rica and to individuals working on similar issues in education, tourism, and conservation. The book was photocopied to sell at cost to visitors at the OTS offices and La Selva Biological Station. Tourists at the Monteverde Private Reserve in northwestern Costa Rica have purchased this book to use as a guide to basic tropical ecology.

In the medium term the project continues to be successful; two and one-half years later (1992), eleven former students continue working as naturalist guides, five are assisting in research projects in the area, one is involved in environmental education, two are participating in forestry conservation projects, and one is enrolled in a university degree program in biology.

On a national level, the local naturalists project has had an impact in Costa Rica. A variety of individuals, environmental associations and institutions have requested the course materials, as well as advice, regarding the feasibility and organization of similar programs at other sites around the country. For instance, other local naturalist courses now have been developed elsewhere in Costa Rica, with goals and methods designed to satisfy the region's own local requirements.

Another Approach: The Monteverde
Local Naturalist Project

The Tropical Science Center, together with the Conservation League of Monteverde, organized an intensive, daily four-month course for seven local residents of communities neighboring the Monteverde Private Reserve. The students chosen were similar to those in the La Selva naturalist program: literate local residents, twenty to thirty years old, with no college education. The main goal of this course was to satisfy the immediate needs of both institutions. The Monteverde Reserve needed naturalist guides to help handle a large and increasing flow of ecotourists. The Conservation League also needed environmental educators with enough natural history knowledge to work in primary school and artisan programs.

This course intensively covered basic biological principles in order to provide students with an adequate background for a variety of jobs. English was taught two to three hours a day. That Monteverde is one of the most heavily visited natural history sites in Costa Rica increased the odds that the naturalists would find work upon graduation. An innovative feature of the Monteverde program was the decision to pay the naturalists a modest stipend during the course period. This allowed students to participate full time during the four-month period, a significant educational advantage.

There have been interesting similarities, as well as differences, between the La Selva and the Monteverde courses. The latter course was longer and therefore produced more highly trained naturalists with a broader background in basic biology. The intensive format allowed better course integration. Compared to a once-a-week format (the La Selva approach), however, it demanded a much greater commitment from students to a new and untested idea. In addition, few rural women with families could ever participate in programs with a four-month continuous schedule. The unit cost at Monteverde (approximately $2,100 per student; Susana Schik, personal communication) was substantially higher than at La Selva ($947 per student; Paaby et al. 1991). The Monteverde course gave much more instruction in English. However, neither at Monteverde nor at La Selva was this training sufficient for the naturalists to guide effectively in English. At both the Monteverde and the La Selva sites, there were stable institutions with substantial self-interest in the success of the naturalist courses. These institutions controlled a local resource, and wished to both manage and protect it. In both cases the institutions themselves were immediate employers of the course graduates, and other employment opportunities for course graduates already were available. We consider that these points are critical to the success of any future local naturalist projects. No matter how good the training, local rural residents are unlikely to be able to successfully obtain ongoing employment and continuing education without the post-course assistance of a local institution.

Other Experiences in Costa Rica

In northwestern Costa Rica, in the area of the Guanacaste National Park, a course was organized for high-school students with the main objective of training leaders in local conservation issues. Another program is underway on the south Caribbean coast of Costa Rica, in an area that is also receiving increasing ecotourist visitation. This course will train local naturalists to work in recreation enterprises, thereby locally garnering some of the economic returns of the visiting nature-oriented groups. The aim of the course is to increase the environmental and cultural awareness of the naturalists in order to protect their natural surroundings and maintain their way of life.

Finally, in the Tortuguero National Park (TNP), the Caribbean Conservation Corporation (CCC) and the TNP, with assistance from the University of Florida, developed a program of training local tour guides. The program surveyed scientists, park managers, tour guides, hotel owners, and tourists to plan and organize the activities according to the local ways and needs. One important initial objective of the Tortuguero program was to run a ten-hour pilot training course to decrease the negative impacts visitors were having on the behavior of nesting marine turtles. This short course did result in improved control of visitors, as local tour guides were better able to manage the number of visitor groups, as well as their use of flashlights and photographic activities, which, on many occasions, had caused turtles to return to the sea without nesting. However, it was recognized that tour guides with more natural history knowledge and more guiding and communication skills would result in a more fruitful interaction with the natural history visitors. Currently, the CCC and the TNP are in the process of planning a more complete training course that will allow local guides to exploit other natural resources, for example, the canals, for the enjoyment of the ecotourists (Jacobson and Robles 1992).

Conclusions and Suggestions

In terms of intensity of training, these different naturalist courses in Costa Rica represent points along a spectrum of potential training projects. Which model is most appropriate to a given site will depend to a great extent on local conditions. The factors discussed in the following paragraphs should be considered.

First, who is the target group for potential participants, and what is their educational, social, and economic situation? Costa Rica has a very high rural literacy rate, and all students in the Monteverde and La Selva courses could read and write. However, a similar course could be developed for illiterate students based on more intensive use of audiovisual aides. The rural residents' economic condition will help determine who can participate. If the course format requires full-time attendance, this may mean that students would have to give up existing jobs. If so, a stipend for students may be necessary.

Second, what is the potential market for employment? This will greatly influence the material presented. If the target audience is national, then training in a foreign language can be eliminated. Both at

Monteverde and La Selva, the local naturalists were able to successfully guide Costa Rican visitors after the courses. Success in guiding foreign visitors will ultimately depend on mastering a second language.

Third, who are the potential employers? The course curriculum should meet the needs of these employers. For example, tourist operators will want a different kind of naturalist than will directors of environmental education programs. Both the Monteverde and La Selva projects produced broadly based naturalists conversant in tropical ecology. However, the basic idea of training local people as guides is also applicable anywhere a local institution has interests in protecting and managing a resource. Other potential sites could include national parks and wildlife reserves, areas conserving geological features (such as Costa Rica's Irazu Volcano National Park and Barra Honda Caverns Park), as well as historical and archaeological sites.

As in many tropical countries, economic development and environmental degradation in Costa Rica are proceeding rapidly. Although conservation and ecological concepts are being included in national planning (Quesada 1990), formidable problems hinder their implementation. To facilitate regional environmental management, the country has recently been divided into seven main conservation areas with one or several national parks as core areas. The success of ideas such as the conservation areas, which are similar in many respects to biosphere reserves, will ultimately depend on the active support of the populations surrounding these areas. Local naturalist training programs, such as those discussed here, can be a useful tool to mitigate some of the negative impacts caused by the ecotourism industry (Butler 1991b), as well as to generate both short- and long-term local support for conservation efforts.

Acknowledgments

For financial and logistic support, we thank the World Wildlife Fund and the Organization for Tropical Studies. We acknowledge with deep gratitude the vigorous support of Donald Stone, executive director of OTS, throughout the local naturalist project. Employees of the Tropical Science Center Monteverde Reserve and the Monteverde Conservation League, particularly Susana Schik, patiently answered our questions about the Monteverde naturalist project. We very much appreciate the time and editorial comments received from D. A. Clark; she helped us improve the first draft considerably. All opinions expressed are those of the authors and do not necessarily represent the positions of any of the organizations we mention.

References

Ahmad, Mohammad Farooq, Ashiq Ahmad Khan, and Syed Ali Ghalib. 1993. *The Cranes of Pakistan.* Karachi, Pakistan: Zoological Survey of Pakistan.

Ajzen, Icek. 1988. *Attitudes, Personality, and Behavior.* Milton Keynes, England: Open University Press.

Alcorn, Janis B. 1990. "Indigenous Agroforestry Strategies Meeting Farmer's Needs." In A. B. Anderson, ed., *Alternatives to Deforestation,* pp. 141–151. New York: Columbia University Press.

Allegretti, Mary H. 1990. "Extractive Reserves: An Alternative for Reconciling Development and Environmental Conservation in Amazonia." In A. B. Anderson, ed., *Alternatives to Deforestation,* pp. 252–264. New York: Columbia University Press.

Ali, Salim and Dillon Ripley. 1969. *Handbook of the Birds of India and Pakistan.* Vol. 2. London and Bombay: Oxford University Press.

Anonymous. 1989. Proposed rules: Endangered and threatened wildlife and plants; annual notice of review. *Federal Register* 54 (6 January): 554.

Ashiq, Ahmad and Khurshid Najam. 1991. Observations of migration and migratory routes of cranes through Baluchistan. *Natura.* Lahore, Pakistan: WWF-Pakistan (Autumn): 9–11.

Ashtiani, Mohammad Ali. 1987. Siberian crane as wintering bird in Iran. In George W. Archibald and Roger F. Pasquier, eds., *Proceedings of the 1983*

International Crane Workshop, pp. 135–137. Baraboo, Wis.: International Crane Foundation.

Audubon, M. R. 1897. *Audubon and His Journals.* Vol. 1. New York: Scribners.

Berger, J. Dhyani. 1991. *Wildlife Extension: A Participatory Approach to Conservation—A Case Study Among the Maasai of Kenya.* Ph.D. diss., University of California, Berkeley.

Berkes, Fikret. 1989. *Common Property Resources: Ecology and Human-Based Sustainable Development.* London: Bellhaven.

Blanchard, K. A. 1983. Of tinkers, turrs, and treaties. *Nature Canada* 12:44–46.

Blanchard, K. A. 1984. *Seabird Harvest and the Importance of Education in Seabird Management on the North Shore of the Gulf of St. Lawrence.* Ph.D. diss., Cornell University, Ithaca, New York.

Blanchard, K. A. 1987a. Bring on the wardens! *Nature Canada* 16:20–21.

Blanchard, K. A. 1987b. Strategies for the conservation of seabirds on Quebec's North Shore and geese on Alaska's Yukon-Kuskokwim Delta: A comparison. *Transactions of the North American Wildlife and Natural Resources Conference* 52:399–407.

Blanchard, K. A. 1987c. Tinkers and turrs. *Nature Canada* 16:14–21, 28.

Blanchard, K. A. 1989. Working together for the conservation of seabirds on the North Shore of the Gulf of St. Lawrence. In *Proceedings: Joint Conference of the North American Association for Environmental Education and the Conservation Education Association,* pp. 47–53. Troy, Ohio: North American Association for Environmental Education.

Blanchard, K. A. 1994. "Culture and Seabird Conservation: The North Shore of the Gulf of the St. Lawrence, Canada." In D. N. Nettleship, J. Burger, and M. Gochfeld, eds., *Seabirds on Islands: Threats, Case Studies and Action Plans,* pp. 294–310. Cambridge: BirdLife Conservation Series No. 1, BirdLife International.

Blanchard, K. A. and M. C. Monroe. 1990. Effective educational strategies for reducing population declines in seabirds. *Transactions of the North American Wildlife and Natural Resources Conference* 55:108–117.

Blanchard, K. A. and D. N. Nettleship. 1992. "Education and Seabird Conservation: A Conceptual Framework." In D. R. McCullough and R. H. Barrett, eds., *Wildlife 2001: Populations,* pp. 616–632. London: Elsevier Applied Science.

Bolland, Nigel O. 1986. *Belize: A New Nation in Central America.* Boulder, Colo.: Westview.

Boom, B. M. 1990. Giving native people a share of the profits. *Garden* (Bronx, New York) 14:28–31.

Brown, L. R. 1988. *State of the World.* New York: W. W. Norton.

Bruntland. 1987. *Our Common Future.* World Commission on Environment and Development. Oxford: Oxford University Press.

Bunch, R. 1982. *Two Ears of Corn: A Guide to People-Centered Agricultural Improvement*. Oklahoma City, Okla.: World Neighbors.

Bunnel, Fred and David E. N. Tait. 1981. "Population Dynamics of Bears—Implications." In W. G. Fowler and T. D. Smith, eds., *Dynamics of Large Mammal Populations*, pp. 75–98. New York: John Wiley and Sons.

Butler, Paul J. 1988. *The Saint Vincent Parrot (Amazona guildingii): The Road to Recovery*. Philadelphia: RARE Center for Tropical Bird Conservation.

Butler, Paul J. 1989. *The Imperial or Sisserou Parrot (Amazona imperialis): A New Beginning*. Philadelphia, Pennsylvania: RARE Center for Tropical Bird Conservation.

Butler, Paul J. 1991a. *The Saint Lucia Parrot (Amazona versicolor): Consolidating a Conservation Campaign*. Philadelphia, Pennsylvania: RARE Center for Tropical Bird Conservation.

Butler, R. W. 1991b. Tourism, environment, and sustainable development. *Environmental Conservation* 18 (3): 201–209.

Cairns, D. 1978. Seabird sanctuaries ignored. *Nature Canada* 7:31–32.

Cairns, John, Jr. 1986. "Restoration, Reclamation, and Regeneration of Degraded or Destroyed Ecosystems." In M. E. Soulé, ed., *Conservation Biology*, pp. 465–484. Sunderland, Mass.: Sinauer Associates.

Chapdelaine, G. 1980. Onzieme inventaire et analyse des fluctuations des populations d'oiseaux marins dans les refuges de la Cote-Nord du Golfe Saint-Laurent. *The Canadian Field-Naturalist* 94:34–42.

Chapdelaine, G. and P. Brousseau. 1984. Douzieme inventaire des populations d'oiseaux marins dans les refuges de la Cote-Nord du Golfe Saint-Laurent. *The Canadian Field-Naturalist* 98:178–183.

Chapdelaine, G. and P. Brousseau. 1991. Thirteenth census of seabird populations in the sanctuaries of the North Shore of the Gulf of St. Lawrence, 1982–1988. *The Canadian Field-Naturalist* 105:60–66.

Chin, R. and K. D. Benne. 1985. "General Strategies for Effecting Change in Human Systems." In W. G. Bennis, K. D. Benne, and R. Chin, eds., *The Planning of Change*, 4th ed., pp. 22–45. New York: Holt, Rinehart and Winston.

Clark, D. B. and P. Paaby. 1990. *Informe Técnico: Capacitación de Naturalistas Locales para Fomentar el Ecoturismo y Conservación Rural*. San José, Costa Rica: Organization for Tropical Studies.

Cockrum, Lendell E. 1970. Insecticides and guano bats. *Ecology* 51 (5): 761–762.

Cohen, J. I., J. B. Alcorn, and C. S. Christopher. 1991. Utilization and conservation of genetic resources: International projects for sustainable agriculture. *Economic Botany* 45:190–199.

Daly, D. 1990. Extractive reserves: A great new hope. *Garden* (Bronx, New York) 14:14–18.

Daschbach, Nancy. 1990. After the hurricane. *Bats* 8 (3): 14–15.

Dasmann, R. F. 1988. Biosphere reserves, buffers, and boundaries. *BioScience* 38 (7): 487–489.

Davis, Stephen. 1988. *Proceedings of the 5th National Conference, Alice Springs, 2–6 October 1988*, pp. 25–26. Australian Association for Environmental Education.

Delepierre, G. 1982. Les régions agro-climatiques en relation avec l'intensité de l'érosion du sol. *Bulletin Agricole du Rwanda* 15 (2): 87–96.

Department of Environment. 1972. *The Planning of the Undeveloped Coast*. Circular 12/72. Great Britain: Her Majesty's Stationery Office.

Dimock, Hedley G. 1992. *Intervention and Collaborative Change*. 4th ed. Toronto, Canada: Captus.

Doyle, D. 1991. Sustainable development: Growth without losing ground. *Journal of Soil and Water Conservation* 46:8–13.

DuBois, Jean C. L. 1990. "Secondary Forests as a Land-Use Resource in Frontier Zones of Amazonia." In A. B. Anderson, ed., *Alternatives to Deforestation*, pp. 183–194. New York: Columbia University Press.

Eaton, Randall L. 1978. The evolution of trophy hunting. *Carnivore* 1 (1): 110–121.

Eggleston, Richard. 1989. Satellite tracking may be Siberian crane's last hope. *The Capital Times*, Madison, Wis., February 27, p. 20.

Everitt, J. C. 1987. The torch is passed: Neocolonialism in Belize. *Caribbean Quarterly* 33:42–59.

Farooq, Mohsin. 1992. "Crane Migration Through Dera Ismail Khan (NWFP): Conservation Problems and Prospects." Unpublished thesis. Peshawar, Pakistan: Pakistan Forest Institute.

Ferguson, David A. 1982. Special foreign currency program: Opportunity for international wildlife conservation. *Fish and Wildlife News*. Washington, D.C.: U.S. Department of the Interior.

Ferguson, David A. 1986. PL-480: The Foreign Currency Program. *Fish and Wildlife News*, June/July/August. Washington, D.C.: U.S. Department of the Interior.

Fortin, P. 1866. *Annual Report of Pierre Fortin Esq., Stipendary Magistrate in Command of the Expedition for the Protection of the Fisheries in the Gulf of St. Lawrence on Board "LaCanadienne" During the Season of 1865*. Sessional Papers No. 36. Ottawa, Canada: Legislative Assembly.

Fossey, D. 1970. Making friends with mountain gorillas. *National Geographic Magazine* 137:48–67.

Fossey, D. 1971. More years with mountain gorillas. *National Geographic Magazine* 140:574–586.

Frazar, M. A. 1887. An ornithologist's summer in Labrador. *Ornithology and Oology* 11:1, 17, 33.

Fujita, Marty S. and Merlin D. Tuttle. 1991. Flying foxes (Chiroptera:Pteropod-idae): Threatened animals of key ecological and economic importance. *Conservation Biology* 5 (4): 455–463.

Government of the Yukon. 1990. *Yukon Conservation Strategy*. Whitehorse, Yukon, Canada: Government of the Yukon.

Graham, Gary L. 1989. Landmark legislation to protect flying foxes. *Bats* 7 (4): 3–4.

Gregg, W. P. and B. A. McGean. 1985. Biosphere reserves: Their history and their promise. *Orion Nature Quarterly* 4 (3): 40–51.

Groom, A. F. 1973. Squeezing out the mountain gorilla. *Oryx* 2:207–215.

Grumbine, E. 1988. The university of the wilderness. *Journal of Environmental Education* 19 (4): 3–7.

Hammond, W. F. 1978. *Acting on Action Workshop Handouts*. Ft. Myers, Fla.: Natural Context.

Hammond, W. F., C. Hortman, R. Tully, C. Bear, and J. Kessler. 1984. *LEESCAPES*. Ft. Myers, Fla.: Lee District Schools.

Hannah, L. 1992. *African People, African Parks*. Washington, D.C.: United States Agency for International Development.

Harcourt, A. H. and A. F. Groom. 1972. Gorilla census. *Oryx* 11:355–163.

Harris, Larry D. 1984. *The Fragmented Forest: Island Biogeography Theory and the Preservation of Biotic Diversity*. Chicago: University of Chicago Press.

Harroy, J. P. 1981. *Evolution entre 1958 et 1979 du covert forestier*. Brussels, Belgium: Assistance International pour le Développement Rurale.

Hartshorn, G. S. and R. Peralta. 1988. Preliminary description of primary forests along the La Selva-Volcán Barba Altitudinal Transect, Costa Rica. In F. Almeda and C. Pringle, eds., *Tropical Rainforests: Diversity and Conservation*, pp. 281–295. San Francisco: California Academy of Science.

Hartup, B. K. 1989. *An Alternative Conservation Model for Tropical Areas: The Community Baboon Sanctuary in Belize*. M.S. thesis, University of Wisconsin–Madison.

Herrero, Stephen. 1985. *Bear Attacks: Their Causes and Avoidance*. Piscataway, N.J.: Winchester Press, New Century Publishers.

Hewitt, O. H. 1950. Fifth census of non-passerine birds on the sanctuaries of the North Shore of the Gulf of St. Lawrence. *The Canadian Field-Naturalist* 64:73–76.

Hines, J. M., H. R. Hungerford, and A. N. Tomera. 1986/87. Analysis and synthesis of research on responsible environmental behavior: A meta-analy-sis. *Journal of Environmental Education* 18 (2): 1–8.

Hobbs, R. J., D. A. Saunders, and B.M.T. Hussey. 1990. Nature conservation: The role of corridors (synopsis). *Ambio* 19:94–95.

Horwich, R. H. 1988. "The Community Baboon Sanctuary: An Approach to the Conservation of Private Lands, Belize." In J. Gradwohl and R.

Greenberg, eds., *Saving the Tropical Forests,* pp. 72–75. London: Earthscan.

Horwich, R. H. 1990. How to develop a community sanctuary: An experimental approach to the conservation of private lands. *Oryx* 24:95–102.

Horwich, R. H. and J. Lyon. 1987. Development of the "Community Baboon Sanctuary" in Belize: An experiment in grassroots conservation. *Primate Conservation* 8:32–34.

Horwich, R. H. and J. Lyon. 1988. An experimental technique for the conservation of private lands. *Journal of Medical Primatology* 17:169–176.

Horwich, R. H. and J. Lyon. 1990. *A Belizean Rain Forest: The Community Baboon Sanctuary.* Gays Mills, Wis.: Orangutan Press.

Horwich, R. H., D. Murray, E. Saqui, J. Lyon, and D. Godfrey. In press. Ecotourism redefined: A view from the field. In K. Lindberg, ed., *Handbook of Ecotourism.* Alexandria, Va.: The Ecotourism Society.

Hume, Allan O. and C.H.T. Marshall. 1881. *The Snow-wreath or Siberian Crane: Game Birds of India, Burma, and Ceylon.* Vol. 3. Calcutta, India: Calcutta Central Press.

Hummel, Monte. 1988. *Endangered Spaces.* Toronto, Canada: Key Porter.

Hungerford, Harold. 1989. What we know about citizenship behavior in environmental education. Paper presented at the Joint Annual Conference of the North American Association for Environmental Education and Conservation Education Association, August 1989, Estes Park, Colorado.

Hungerford, Harold and T. Volk. 1990. Changing learner behavior through environmental education. *Journal of Environmental Education* 21 (3): 8–21.

Institute of Social and Economic Research. 1980. *Studies on Population, Development and the Environment in the Eastern Caribbean.* Man and Biosphere Project. Washington, D.C.: United Nations Educational Scientific and Cultural Organization/United Nations Fund for Population Activities/Institute of Social and Economic Research.

IUCN. 1980. *World Conservation Strategy.* Gland, Switzerland: International Union for the Conservation of Nature.

Jacobson, S. K. 1986. The development of a school programme for Kinabalu Park. *Sabah Society Journal* 8 (2): 213–223.

Jacobson, S. K. 1990. The Malaysian National Park System. In C. W. Allin, ed., *The International Handbook of National Parks and Nature Preserves,* pp. 253–272. Westport, Conn.: Greenwood.

Jacobson, S. K. 1991. Evaluation model for developing, implementing and assessing conservation education programs: Examples from Belize and Costa Rica. *Environmental Management* 15 (2): 143–150.

Jacobson, S. K. and S. M. Padua. 1992. Parks and pupils: Environmental education using national parks in developing countries. *Childhood Education* 68 (5): 290–293.

Jacobson, S. K. and R. Robles. 1992. Ecotourism, sustainable development, and conservation education: Development of a tour guide training program in Tortuguero, Costa Rica. *Environmental Management* 16 (6): 701–713.

Jenkins, D. V., F. Liew, and P. Hecht. 1976. *A National Parks Policy for Sabah.* Sabah, Malaysia: Government Printing Office.

Kellert, Stephen R. and Joyce K. Berry. 1980. *Knowledge, Affection and Basic Attitudes Toward Animals in American Society: Phase III.* Washington, D.C.: U.S. Government Printing Office #024–010–00–625–1. (Also available through National Technical Information Service, U.S. Department of Commerce, Springfield, Va. 22161, Accession #PB81–173106.)

Kellert, Stephen R. and Miriam Westervelt. 1983. *Children's Attitudes, Knowledge and Behaviors Toward Animals: Phase V.* Washington, D.C.: U.S. Government Printing Office #024–010–00641–2. (Also available through National Technical Information Service, U.S. Department of Commerce, Springfield, Va. 22161, Accession #PB83–211–474.)

Kleiman, D. G., B. B. Beck, J. M. Dietz, L. A. Dietz, J. D. Ballou, and A. F. Coimbra-Filho. 1986. "Conservation Program for the Golden Lion Tamarin: Captive Research and Management, Ecological Studies, Educational Strategies, and Reintroduction." In E. Benirschke, ed., *Primates: The Road to Self-Sustaining Populations,* pp. 959–979. New York: Springer-Verlag.

Koran, J. and S. Longino. 1983. *Curiosity Behavior in Formal and Informal Settings: What Research Says.* Research bulletin. Gainesville: Florida Educational Research and Development Council.

Korten, David C. 1980. Community organization and rural development: A learning process approach. *Public Administration Review* (September/October): 480–511.

Korten, David C. 1986. *Community Management: Asian Experience and Perspectives.* New Haven, Conn.: Kumarian.

Kotler, Philip. 1982. *Marketing for Nonprofit Organizations.* 2d ed. London: Prentice Hall International.

Lambet, F. 1983. *Report of an Expedition to Survey the Status of the Saint Vincent Parrot, Amazona guildingii.* Cambridge: International Council for Bird Preservation Study Report No. 3.

Landfried, S. E. 1980a. Siberian cranes at Bharatpur. *World Wildlife Fund-India Newsletter* (4th quarter): 7–9. Bombay: World Wildlife Fund–India.

Landfried, S. E. 1980b. Siberian crane: Going, going . . . *IUCN Bulletin* 11 (September/October): 85. Gland, Switzerland: International Union for the Conservation of Nature.

Landfried, S. E. 1980/81. Cranes of the Commonwealth—On last legs? London: *World Wildlife News* (Winter): 24–26.

Landfried, S. E. 1982a. Pakistan: New Siberian crane data. *IUCN Bulletin* (July/August/September): 72. Gland, Switzerland: International Union for the Conservation of Nature.

Landfried, S. E. 1982b. Siberian crane stamp soon a reality. *ICF Bugle* 8 (4):4. Baraboo, Wis.: International Crane Foundation.

Landfried, S. E. 1983. The threatened white crane. *Pakistan Times,* Islamabad, April 1, pp. 1, 6.

Landfried, S. E. 1984a. Pakistan acts to save rare Siberian cranes. *WWF-News* (November/December): 2. Gland, Switzerland: International Union for the Conservation of Nature.

Landfried, S. E. 1984b. Flight for survival: The Siberian cranes' winter migration to the subcontinent. *India Magazine* (March): 46–54. New Delhi.

Larsen, Douglas G., David A. Gauthier, and Rhonda L. Markel. 1989. Causes and rate of moose mortality in the southwest Yukon. *Journal of Wildlife Management* 53 (3): 548–557.

Lemieux, G. 1956. Seventh census of non-passerine birds in the bird sanctuaries of the North Shore of the Gulf of St. Lawrence. *The Canadian Field-Naturalist* 70:183–185.

Lewis, H. F. 1925. The new bird sanctuaries in the Gulf of St. Lawrence. *The Canadian Field-Naturalist* 39:177–179.

Lewis, H. F. 1931. Five years' progress in the bird sanctuaries of the North Shore of the Gulf of St. Lawrence. *The Canadian Field-Naturalist* 45:73–78.

Lewis, H. F. 1937. A decade of progress in the bird sanctuaries of the North Shore of the Gulf of St. Lawrence. *The Canadian Field-Naturalist* 51:51–55.

Lewis, H. F. 1942. Fourth census of non-passerine birds in the bird sanctuaries of the North Shore of the Gulf of St. Lawrence. *The Canadian Field-Naturalist* 58:5–8.

Lindberg, K. 1991. *Policies for Maximizing Nature Tourism's Ecological and Economic Benefits.* Washington, D.C.: World Resources Institute.

Lortie, Grant M. and John McDonald. 1976. *A 23-Year Analysis of Grizzly Bear Harvests in the Yukon.* Yukon Game Branch Technical Report. Whitehorse, Yukon: Government of the Yukon.

Love, A. J. 1991. *Internal Evaluation Building Organizations from Within.* Applied Social Research Methods series. Vol. 24. Newbury Park, Calif.: Sage.

Makin, David H. and H. Mendelssohn. 1985. Insectivorous bats victims of Israeli campaign. *Bats* 2 (4): 1–4.

Malik, M. Mumtaz. 1992. The Indus River ecosystem—A case study. In Heather Whitaker, ed., *Proceedings of the International Crane Symposium,* pp. 36–39. Rowe Sanctuary: National Audubon Society.

May, R. 1988. How many species are there on earth? *Science* 241:1441–1448.

McNeely, J. A. and K. R. Miller, eds. 1984. *National Parks, Conservation Development.* Gland, Switzerland: International Union for the Conservation of Nature.

Meinertzhagen, Col. R. 1955. The speed and altitude of bird flight. *Ibis* 97:81–117.

Miles, J. 1986/87. Wilderness as a learning place. *Journal of Environmental Education* 18 (2): 33–40.

Miller, Stirling D. 1990. Population management of bears in North America. *International Conference on Bear Research and Management* 8:357–373.

Miller, Stirling D. and Warren B. Ballard. 1992. Analysis of an effort to increase moose calf survivorship by increased hunting of brown bears in south-central Alaska. *Wildlife Society Bulletin* 20 (4): 445–454.

Mitchell, Mark K. and Stapp, William B. 1992. *Field Manual for Water Quality Monitoring: An Environmental Education Program for Schools.* 6th ed. Dexter, Mich.: Thomson-Shore Printers.

Moran, Emilio F. 1983. *Land Use: The Dilemma of Amazonian Development.* Boulder, Colo.: Westview.

Moreno, Arnulfo and Paul Robertson. 1992. "Northern Mexico Bat, *Tadarida brasiliensis,* Cave Surveys, 1991." Unpublished report. Austin, Tex.: Bat Conservation International.

Morton, Patricia. 1991. "An Educational Campaign to Develop an Awareness of Bat Conservation in Tropical America." In M. Mares and D. Schmidly, eds., *Latin American Mammalogy,* pp. 381–391. Norman, Okla., and London: University of Oklahoma Press.

Mycasiw, Len. 1981. A system to regulate commercial big game hunting (outfitting) in Yukon Territory. *Canadian Wildlife Administration* 7:40–41.

National Research Council. 1989. *Lost Crops of the Incas: Little Known Plants of the Andes with Promise for Worldwide Cultivation.* Washington, D.C.: National Academy Press.

Nettleship, D. N. and A. R. Lock. 1973. Tenth census of seabirds in the sanctuaries of the North Shore of the Gulf of St. Lawrence. *The Canadian Field-Naturalist* 87:395–402.

O'Gara, Bart, Lee Metzgar, Robert Eng, and Daniel Pletscher. 1985. *Observations on Wildlife Issues in Pakistan.* Report to Office of International Affairs, U.S. Fish and Wildlife Service, Washington, D.C.

Oldeman, R.A.A. 1983. "The Design of Ecologically Sound Agroforests." In P. A. Huxley, ed., *Plant Research and Agroforestry,* pp. 173–207. Nairobi: International Center for Research in Agroforestry.

Paaby, P., D. B. Clark, and H. Gonzalez. 1991. Training rural residents as naturalist guides: Evaluation of a pilot project in Costa Rica. *Conservation Biology* 5:542–546.

Pearson, Arthur M. 1975. *The Northern Interior Grizzly Bear, Ursus arctos L.* Canadian Wildlife Service Report series 34. Ottawa, Canada: Ministry of Environment.

Pickering, A. 1993. "Evaluation of the Zoo Education Service." Unpublished report to the Zoological Board of Victoria Education Service.

Pinkerton, Evelyn. 1989. *Co-operative Management of Local Fisheries: New Directions for Improved Management and Community Development.* Vancouver: University of British Columbia Press.

Pomerantz, Gerri A. and K. A. Blanchard. 1992. Effective communication and education strategies for wildlife conservation. *Transactions of the North American Wildlife and Natural Resources Conference* 57:156–163.

Pringle, C. M. 1988. "History of Conservation Efforts and Initial Exploration of the Lower Extension of Parque Nacional Braulio Carrillo, Costa Rica." In F. Almeda and C. Pringle, eds., *Tropical Rainforests: Diversity and Conservation,* pp. 225–241. San Francisco: California Academy of Science.

Project WILD. 1992. *Project WILD Activity Guide.* 2d ed. Boulder, Colo.: Western Regional Environmental Education Council.

Quebec Labrador Foundation/Atlantic Center for the Environment. 1986. *Conference Proceedings: Building Support for Conservation in Rural Areas,* 27–31 May, Ipswich, Mass.

Quesada, M. C. 1990. *Estrategia de Conservación para el Desarrollo Sostenible de Costa Rica.* San José, Costa Rica: Ministerio de Recursos Naturales, Energía y Minas.

Roberts, T. J. 1977. Crane catchers of the Kurram Valley. *International Wildlife* 19 (9): 398–401. London.

Roberts, T. J. and S. E. Landfried. 1987. Hunting pressures on crane migrations through Pakistan. In George W. Archibald and Roger F. Pasquier, eds., *Proceedings of the 1983 International Crane Workshop,* pp. 139–145. Baraboo, Wis.: International Crane Foundation.

Romeril, M. 1983. A balanced strategy for recreation, tourism. and conservation: The case of Les Mielles, Jersey. *Tourism Management* 4:126–128.

Sauey, Ronald T. 1976. The behavior of Siberian cranes wintering in India. In J. C. Lewis, ed., *Proceedings of the International Crane Workshop,* pp. 326–342. Stillwater: Oklahoma State University.

Sauey, Ronald T. 1985. The Range, Status, and Winter Ecology of the Siberian Crane (*Grus leucogeranus*). Ph.D. diss., Cornell University, Ithaca, New York.

Sawhney, J. C. 1981. *The Cranes.* Bombay: World Wildlife Fund–India.

Schaller, G. B. 1963. *The Mountain Gorilla: Ecology and Behavior.* Chicago: University of Chicago Press.

Schaller, G. B. 1964. *The Year of the Gorilla.* Chicago: University of Chicago Press.

Sidorowicz, George A. and Fred F. Gilbert. 1981. The management of grizzly bears in the Yukon, Canada. *Wildlife Society Bulletin* 9 (2): 125–135.

Singer, Andre. 1982. *Honors Uncompromising Code, Guardians of the North-West Frontier: The Pathans.* Amsterdam: Time-Life.

Smith, Bernard L. 1990. Sex-weighted point system regulates grizzly bear harvest. *International Conference on Bear Research and Management* 8:375–383.

Smith, Bernard L. 1991. *Hunt Wisely: A Guide to Male-Selective Grizzly Bear*

Hunting. Yukon Fish and Wildlife Branch Extension Report. Whitehorse, Yukon: Government of the Yukon.

Smith, Bernard L. 1992. *Collaborative Strategies to Promote Local Conservation of Wildlife*. M.S. thesis, Department of Rural Extension, University of Guelph, Ontario.

Smith, Bernard L. and Edward J. Osmond-Jones. 1991. *Grizzly Bear Abundance in Yukon Ecoregions*. Yukon Fish and Wildlife Branch Technical Report. Whitehorse, Yukon: Government of the Yukon.

Spain, James W. 1973. *The Way of the Pathans*. Karachi: Oxford University Press.

Strehlow, T.G.H. 1947. *Aranda Traditions*. Melbourne, Australia: Melbourne University Press.

Tener, J. S. 1951. Sixth census of non-passerine birds in the bird sanctuaries of the North Shore of the Gulf of St. Lawrence. *The Canadian Field-Naturalist* 65:65–68.

Thomas, D. W. 1982. *The Ecology of an African Savanna Fruit Bat Community: Resource Partitioning and Role in Seed Dispersal*. Ph.D. diss., University of Aberdeen, Aberdeen, Scotland.

Train, R. E. 1988. Healthy forests, healthy world. *Journal of Soil and Water Conservation* 33:438–439.

Tuttle, M. D. 1990. Return to Thailand. *Bats* 8 (3): 6–11.

Tuttle, M. D. 1991. Bats, the cactus connection. *National Geographic* 179 (6): 131–140.

UNESCO. 1984. Action plan for biosphere reserves. *Nature and Resources* 20 (4): 1–12.

Vandenbeld, John. 1988. *Nature of Australia*. Sydney, Australia: William Collins and ABC Enterprises.

Vardhan, Harsh. 1989. Refuge for Siberian cranes, *The Hindustan Times,* Delhi, February 25.

Vedder, A. 1984. Movement patterns of a group of free-ranging gorillas (*Gorilla gorilla beringei*) and their relationship to food availability. *American Journal of Primatology* 2:73–88.

Vedder, A. 1989a. Ecology and Conservation of the Mountain Gorilla (*Gorilla gorilla beringei*). Ph.D. diss., University of Wisconsin, Madison, Wis.

Vedder, A. 1989b. In the hall of the mountain king. *Animal Kingdom* 92:30–43.

Vedder, A. and W. Weber. 1980. *Volcanos National Park*. Kigali, Rwanda: Office Rwandais du Tourisme et des Parcs Nationaux.

Vedder, A. and W. Weber. 1990. "The Mountain Gorilla Project (Volcanos National Park)." In A. Kiss, ed., *Living with Wildlife: Wildlife Resource Management with Local Participation in Africa*. Washington, D.C.: World Bank.

Waak, Patricia and Kenneth Strom, eds. 1992. *Sharing the Earth: Cross-Cultural Experiences in Population, Wildlife, and the Environment*. New York: National Audubon Society.

Walkinshaw, Lawrence. 1973. *Cranes of the World.* New York: Winchester.

Weber, W. 1979. Gorilla problems in Rwanda. *Swara* 2:29–32.

Weber, W. 1981. "Conservation of the Virunga Gorillas: A Socioeconomic Perspective on Habitat and Wildlife Preservation in Rwanda." M.S. thesis, University of Wisconsin, Madison, Wis.

Weber, W. 1987a. *Ruhengeri and Its Resources: An Environmental Profile of the Ruhengeri Prefecture, Rwanda.* Kigali, Rwanda: United States Agency for International Development/Ministry of Agriculture.

Weber, W. 1987b. "Sociologic Factors in the Conservation of Afromontane Forest Reserves." In Clive W. Marsh and Russell A. Mittermeier, eds., *Primate Conservation in the Tropical Rainforest,* pp. 325–340. New York: Alan R. Liss.

Weber, W. 1989. *Conservation and Development on the Zaire-Nile Divide: An Analysis of Value Conflicts and Convergence in the Management of Afromontane Forests in Rwanda.* Ph.D. diss., University of Wisconsin, Madison, Wis.

Weber, W. 1993. "Ecotourism and Primate Conservation in African Rain Forests." In *The Conservation of Genetic Resources.* Washington, D.C.: American Association for the Advancement of Science.

Weber, W. and A. Vedder. 1983. Population dynamics of the Virunga gorillas: 1959–1978. *Biological Conservation* 26:341–366.

Wells, M., K. Brandon, and L. Hannah. 1992. *People and Parks: Linking Protected Area Management with Local Communities.* Washington, D.C.: World Bank.

Westervelt, Miriam O. and Lynn G. Llewellyn. 1985. *Youth and Wildlife: The Beliefs and Behaviors of Fifth and Sixth Grade Students Regarding Non-Domestic Animals.* Washington, D.C.: U.S. Government Printing Office.

Wilson, E. O. 1988. *Biodiversity.* Washington, D.C.: National Academy Press.

Wingate, D. 1969. *Summary Report for ICBP Meeting.* ICBP newsletter. Cambridge: International Council for Bird Preservation.

Winterbottom, R. and P. T. Hazelwood. 1987. Agroforestry and sustainable development: Making the connection. *Ambio* 16:100–110.

The World Zoo Conservation Strategy; The Role of the Zoos and Aquaria of the World in Global Conservation. 1993. International Union of Directors of Zoological Gardens—The World Zoo Organization and the Captive Breeding Specialist Group of the International Union for the Conservation of Nature/Species Survival Commission, September.

Index

Action research, 198, 225; Global Rivers Environmental Education Network, 177; *see also* Wildlife-focused action projects

Advisory committee, water quality, 183

Africa: bats, 116; mountain gorillas, 28; water quality, 187

Air quality, monitoring program, 195

Alca torda, 52

Alces alces, 157

Alouatta pigra, 237

Amazona guildingii, 98

Amazona leucocephala bahamensis, 100

Amazona versicolor, 99

American Samoa: bats, 109, 114; Le Vaomatua, 110

Anthropoides virgo, 126

Anti-poaching, Mountain Gorilla Project, 37, 41

Argentina, water quality, 194

Asia, water quality, 187

Aspen Institute for Global Change, 195

Association for Progressive Communication, 191

Atlantic Center for the Environment, 14

Atlantic puffin, 52

Audiovisual materials: Bat Conservation International, 105; bats, Costa Rica, 112; bats, for adult audiences, 116; bats. for youth audiences, 116; Caribbean Education Campaign, 97; crane conservation, 138, 143, 145, 146, 152; Golden Lion Tamarin Conservation Program, 74; grizzly bear conservation, 171; guide training, Costa Rica, 268; for illiterate audiences, 274; Les Mielles, 260;

Audiovisual materials (*Continued*)
Mountain Gorilla Project, 38; tailoring for audience, 152; value of, 152; zoo program, 221; *see also* Slide programs
Australia, 16; Junior Ranger Program, 16; water quality, 187, 192; zoo education program, 219; Zoological Board of Victoria, 219

Bahama parrot, 100
Bald Eagle Habitat Protection Ordinance, 199, 215
Baluchistan, 126
Bangladesh, water quality, 194
Barra Honda Caverns Park, Costa Rica, 275
Baseline community surveys: Golden Lion Tamarin Conservation Program, 68; Mountain Gorilla Project, 31
Bat Awareness Teams, 114
Bat Conservation International, 103
Behavioral change: crane conservation, 144, 145; grizzly bear conservation, 158, 161; introducing, 159, 230; promoting, 5, 16, 18, 21, 26, 27, 54, 57, 68, 73, 108, 168
Belize: Belize Audubon Society, 244, 245; Manatee Community Reserve, 249; nature preserve, Monkey River, 249
Belizean Rain Forest: The Community Baboon Sanctuary, A, 245, 247, 253
Belize River, Belize, 237, 251
Bharatpur Crane Conference, 128
Bibliographic database, Bat Conservation International, 105
Biosphere reserves: Belize, 240; Costa Rica, 275
Black bear, 157
Black guillemot, 52

Black howler monkey, 237
Black lion tamarin, 5
Bombay Natural History Society, 123, 132
Booklets: environmental, 101; for hunters, Yukon, 163, 168; for students, 10, 101; for teachers, 38; gorillas, Rwanda, 38; legislation, Caribbean, 101; Siberian cranes, 135
Books: activity, bats, 103, 116; activity, for adult audiences, 116; activity, for youth audiences, 116; bats, Costa Rica, 111; *A Belizean Rain Forest: The Community Baboon Sanctuary* 245, 247, 253; guide training, Costa Rica, 271; tropical ecology guide, 272; water quality, 184
Borneo, Malaysian, 5
Bradypus torquatus, 84
Braulio Carrillo National Park, Costa Rica, 263, 266, 269
Brazil: Golden Lion Tamarin Conservation Program, 66; lowland Atlantic forest, 5, 66; Morro do Diabo Park, 5; Poço das Antas Biological Reserve, 67; Rio de Janeiro State, 66
Brochures, crane conservation, 139

Cacti, Sonoran Desert, 115
Calendars: Mountain Gorilla Project, 39, 46; seabird conservation, 58
Canada, 51; Quebec-Labrador Foundation, 51; St. Mary's Islands Seabird Sanctuary, 55; water quality, 192
Canadian Broadcasting Corporation, 58
Canadian Wildlife Service, 52, 54
Canis lupus, 157
Caretta caretta, 202

Caretta Research, 202, 211
Caribbean Conservation Corporation, 274
Caribbean Education Campaign: activities, 96; attitudinal survey, 92, 98, 102; educational materials, 96; goal, 91; philosophy, 92; results in the Bahamas, 100; target audiences for education, 96
Caribou, 157
Central American river turtle, 246
Cepphus grylle, 52
CITES, 99, 113
Citizen's guide, seabirds, 58
Clearinghouses, GREEN, 193
Clubs: Bat Awareness Teams, 114; Conservation clubs, Rwanda, 40; crane conservation, 139; Golden Lion Tamarin Conservation Program, 76; Junior Rangers, Australia, 18; Junior Rangers, Kinabalu Park, Malaysia, 9; Lions, 97; Pakistan Youth Conservation, 139, 143, 146; Rotary, 97; seabird conservation, Canada, 57, 61
Commercial interests, conservation education programs for, 172
Common crane, 126
Common eider, 52
Common murre, 52
Community Baboon Sanctuary: administrative and management structure, 245; budget, 244; educational program, 247; focal species approach, 240; museum, 247; program operation, 242
Community-based planning, Belize, 240
Community involvement: conservation education programs, 73; crane conservation, 136; Golden Lion Tamarin Conservation Program, 73,

84; grizzly bear conservation program, 161; Morro do Diabo Park, Brazil, 11, 14; wildlife-focused action projects, 199
Community programs: Belize, 247; Community Baboon Sanctuary, 235; howler monkey T-shirts, 243; Mountain Gorilla Project, 38, 39
Computer conferences, water quality, 183, 190, 191
Conservation: education, types of programs, 3; educational programs, elements of success, 10; marketing the concept, 87; programs, integrated, 3
Conservation areas, Costa Rica, 275
Conservation Commission Act of 1980, Australia, 18
Conservation Commission of the Northern Territory, Australia, 18
Conservation League of Monteverde, Costa Rica, 272
Conservation marketing, 89; in the Caribbean, 92; manual, 99
Conservation organizations, 15; African Wildlife Foundation, 37; as target audience, 123; Bat Conservation International, 103; Belize Audubon Society, 244; Bombay Natural History Society, 123; Brazilian Institute for the Environment, 86; Canadian Wildlife Service, 54; Caribbean Conservation Corporation, 274; Conservation Commission of the Northern Territory, Australia 18; Ecological Society of India, 123; Fauna and Flora Preservation Society, 37; Fish and Wildlife Foundation, 115; Forest Institute of India, 123; Forestry Institute of S o Paulo, 15; Frankfurt Zoological Society, 86; Friends of the National

Conservation organizations (*Cont.*)
Zoo, 86; Fundación de Educación
Ambiental, Costa Rica, 111; Ghana
Keoladeo Natural History Society,
123; International Center for Bat
Research and Conservation, 117;
International Crane Foundation,
122; Le Vaomatua, 110; Lincoln
Park Zoological Society of Chicago,
Illinois, 244; Mammal Information
Center, Israel, 110; National Audu-
bon Society, 147; National Council
for the Conservation of Wildlife,
139; National Geographic Society,
115; Nature Conservancy, 114, 212;
Pakistan Forest Institute, 139, 146;
Program for Studies in Tropical
Conservation, 15; Quebec-Labrador
Foundation, 54; RARE Center for
Tropical Conservation, 90; Smith-
sonian Institution, National Zoologi-
cal Park, 86; Tourism and Wildlife
Society of India, 123; U.S. Fish and
Wildlife Service, 15, 63, 114, 115,
122, 139, 214; U.S. National Park
Service, 114; Whitley Animal Pro-
tection Trust, 15; Wild Bird Society
of Japan, 146; Wildlife Conserva-
tion Society, 37; Wildlife Preserva-
tion Trust International, 15; World
Wide Fund for Nature, 86; World
Wildlife Fund, 15, 37, 111, 269;
World Wildlife Fund-India, 123,
126; World Wildlife Fund-Pakistan,
135, 139, 146; World Wildlife
Fund-U.S., 244; Yukon Fish and
Wildlife Branch, 158; Zoological
Board of Victoria, 219; Zoological
Society of Milwaukee, Wisc., 244
Costa Rica: Barra Honda Caverns
Park, 275; bats, 110, 111, 116;
Braulio Carrillo National Park, 263;
community programs, 111; Conservation League of Monteverde, 272;
Fundación de Educación Ambiental,
111; Guanacaste National Park,
273; Irazu Volcano National Park,
275; La Selva Biological Station,
263; Monteverde Reserve, 272;
ational Museum, 266; National Park
Service, 266; Tortuguero National
Park, 274; Tropical Science Center,
272
Crane catching, 125
Crane conservation: attitudinal surveys, 141; audiovisual materials,
138; education center, 142; educational initiatives, 136; goals, 129;
hunter education, 139; hunter survey, 129, 132; hunting laws, 134;
hunting laws, goals, 134; hunting
laws, publicity, 135; infrastructure
building, 131, 151; institutional
base, 127; outcomes, 145; project
activities, 134; public information
campaign, results of, 125; publicity,
131; reserves, 142; restrictions on
hunting, 134
Crocodiles, 20
Cross-cultural partnerships: Partner
Watershed Program, 192; water
quality, 183, 184
Currency notes: Bahama parrot, 101;
mountain gorillas, 46
Czechoslovakia, water quality, 194

Dall sheep, 157
Dartford warbler, 255
Database: Mountain Gorilla Project,
37; water quality, 191
Decals, 167
Demoiselle crane, 126
Dermatemys mawii, 246
Desmodus rotundus, 110

Eastern barred bandicoot, 226
EcoNet, water quality, 184, 190, 191
Ecotourism: Belize, 235; Community Baboon Sanctuary, 251; Costa Rica, 263, 264, 275; ecotourist education, Belize, 247; gorillas, 37; Les Mielles, 260; Mountain Gorilla Project, 41; visitor guide, Costa Rica, 272
Ecotours, Bat Conservation International, 108
Ecuador, water quality, 189, 194
Educational materials: Bat Conservation International, 108; Caribbean Education Campaign, 90, 95, 96, 98; crane conservation, 138, 144, 152; decals, 167; Golden Lion Tamarin Conservation Program, 74; grassroots audiences, 152; grizzly bear conservation, 163, 165, 170; seabird conservation, 58; *see also specific media,* e.g., Audiovisual materials
Educational strategies: action research, 198; Australian Junior Ranger Program, 16; Bat Conservation International, 104; Brazil park program, 8; Caribbean Conservation Campaign, 89; Caribbean Education Campaign, 91; Community Baboon Sanctuary, 247; crane conservation, 121, 123, 129, 136; Global Rivers Environmental Education Network, 178; Golden Lion Tamarin Conservation Program, 73; grizzly bear conservation program, 159; Les Mielles, 258; naturalist guide training program, 270; park-based conservation education program, 6, 14; Quebec-Labrador Foundation, 54, 55; Rwandan conservation education, 39; wildlife-focused action projects in schools,
203, 208; zoo education program, 220
Educator's Activity Book About Bats, 116
Endangered species: bats, 104, 113–15; bats, Tennessee, 114; black lion tamarin, 5; golden lion tamarin, 66; in zoo education program, 224, 228; Junior Ranger Program, 20; maned sloth, 84; mountain gorilla, 28; Pacific island flying foxes, 113; Siberian crane, 149; southern bald eagle, 215; West Indian manatee, 214
Environmental education programs, as environmental marketing, 89
Environmental Education Programs In Classrooms (EEPIC), 225
Environmental educators, as target audience, 123
Europe, water quality, 187
Evaluation: Golden Lion Tamarin Conservation Program, 76, 85; grizzly bear conservation, 158, 169; Les Mielles, 260; model, 3; park-based conservation education program, 8, 10, 12; seabird conservation, 51; zoo education program, 227, 230
Extinction, bats, 113

Federal Health, Education, and Welfare Title III: Elementary, Secondary Education Act Innovations Planning grant, 202
Field Manual for Water-Quality Monitoring, 184
Field trips, Mountain Gorilla Project, 40
Films: crane conservation, 132, 138, 139, 144, 145, 152; Mountain Gorilla Project, 38; seabird conservation, Canada, 58, 63

Fish and Wildlife Foundation, 115
Flagship species, 65; in conservation education, 66, 91, 92; parrots, 91; see also Focal species; Target species
Florida Manatee Protection Act, 199, 214
Flying fox bats, 110; Pacific island, 113; plant propagation, 116; protection, 113; Samoa, 114
Focal species, 156; bats, 103; black howler monkey, 240; black lion tamarin, 5; eastern barred bandicoot, 226; golden lion tamarin, 66; in conservation education, 5, 240; manatee, 214; mountain gorilla, 29; seabirds, Canada, 51; Siberian cranes, 122; southern bald eagle, 215; see also Flagship species; Target species
Fratercula arctica, 52
French Guiana, bats, 116
Friends of the Rouge, Mich., 183
Fundación de Educatión Ambiental, Costa Rica, 111
Funding: Bat Conservation International, 106, 115; Caribbean Education Campaign, 92; Community Baboon Sanctuary, 244, 253; crane conservation, 123, 126, 128, 131, 132, 135, 143, 148, 154; Global Rivers Environmental Education Network, 189, 193, 194; Golden Lion Tamarin Conservation Program, 74; grizzly bear conservation, 158, 160, 161; guide training, Costa Rica, 269; Junior Ranger Review, Australia, 21; Morro do Diabo Park, Brazil, 7; Mountain Gorilla Project, 37; seabird conservation, 54, 59, 61, 62; wildlife-focused action projects, 202, 209, 212, 218

Geese, 55
General Motors Foundation, 193
Germany: GREEN, 189; water quality, 190
Globalization, 177
Global Rivers Environmental Education Network (GREEN): Air Monitoring Program, 195; budget, 193; cross-cultural partnerships, 184; EcoNet, 184; Heavy Metals Monitoring Program, 195; Hypercard packets, 184; Interactive Water-Quality Monitoring Program, 180; international workshops, 187; newsletter, 190; Partner Watershed Program, 190, 192; Rio Grande Watershed Program, 194; River Jordan Project, 195; Rouge Program, 183; Water Quality Monitoring Program, 180
Goals: Caribbean Education Campaign, 91; Community Baboon Sanctuary, 238; Community Baboon Sanctuary, Belize, 237, 238; conservation education, 3; crane conservation, 122, 129; crane conservation hunting laws, 134; Global Rivers Environmental Education Network, 178, 186; Golden Lion Tamarin Conservation Program, 76, 85, 86; GREEN, 178; grizzly bear conservation, 160; guide training, Costa Rica, 269, 270, 272; Les Mielles, Jersey, Great Britain, 254, 257; park-based conservation education, 6; RARE Center for Tropical Conservation, 90; seabird conservation, Canada, 54, 60; wildlife-focused action projects, 200; see also Objectives
Golden lion tamarin, 66; in pet trade, 67

Golden Lion Tamarin Conservation Program: activities, 75; attitudinal surveys, 76; baseline community surveys, 68; community involvement, 84; educational materials, 74; funding, 74; objectives, 67; reintroduction of animals, 84; target audiences for education, 73

Gorilla gorilla beringei, 29

Governmental officials, as target audience, 13, 37, 46, 54, 58, 90, 104, 105, 114, 121, 123, 125, 128, 129, 132, 134, 136, 137, 143, 148, 149, 152, 183, 212, 214, 242, 271

GREEN, *see* Global Rivers Environmental Education Network

Grenada Dove, 98

Grizzly bear, 156; harvest management, 157; hunting, 157; point-system management scheme, 158

Grizzly bear conservation program: booklet, 168; community involvement, 161; constraints, 161; decals, 167; elements of success, 171; forces favoring status quo, 169; objectives, 160; product dissemination, 172; products, 163; resources available initially, 160; results, 169; video, 163

Grus antigone, 132

Grus grus, 126

Grus leucogeranus, 122

Guanacaste National Park, Costa Rica, 273

Guano production, 112

Habitat loss, 199

Habitat protection, American Samoa, 114; Bald Eagle, Fla., 215; bald eagles, 199; bats, 104, 107, 117; Caribbean Education Campaign, 91, 96, 99; crane conservation, 142;

Golden Lion Tamarin Conservation Program, 64, 86; howler monkeys, 237, 238, 246; Jersey, Great Britain, 255, 258; manatees, 214; mountain gorillas, 37; seabird conservation, Canada, 173; Tennessee, 114; wildlife-focused action projects, 213

Heavy metals, monitoring program, 183, 195

Hubbards Cave, Tenn., 114

Hungary, water quality, 192

Hunter education: crane conservation, 131, 134, 135, 138–42, 146, 149, 152–54; grizzly bear conservation, 156, 158; guides, grizzly bear conservation, 161, 163, 165, 170–72; guides, grizzly bear conservation, 160; seabird conservation, Canada, 55, 60

Hunting laws: cranes, 134; publicity, 135; seabirds, Canada, 52

Hypercard packets, water-quality monitoring, 184

Institute for Global Communications, 190

International Center for Bat Research and Conservation, 117

International Crane Conference, 128

International Crane Foundation, 122

Interpretive exhibits: bats, 108, 111, 114; Community Baboon Sanctuary, 244, 247; Golden Lion Tamarin Conservation Program, 75; Jersey, Great Britain, 261; wildlife-focused action projects, 208, 212; zoo education, 221, 231

Interpretive trails: Caribbean Education Campaign, 99; Community Baboon Sanctuary, Belize, 247; Golden Lion Tamarin Conservation Program, 75, 76; park education, 7, 8;

Interpretive trails (*Continued*)
wildlife-focused action projects,
205
Irazu Volcano National Park, Costa
Rica, 275
Israel: bats, 110; Mammal Informa-
tion Center, 110
Italy, water quality, 194

Jersey, Channel Islands, Great Britain, 254
Jersey Planning Law, Great Britain,
255
Junior Ranger, awards, 19
Junior Ranger Program, 16, 27; Aboriginal children, 22, 26; activities,
20; coordination, 20; development,
18, 19; goals, 22; magazine, 21;
park-based education, 9, 12, 14

Keoladeo Ghana Bird Sanctuary, 122,
126
Keoladeo Ghana Natural History
Society, 132
Keoladeo National Park, 122, 128,
132
Kinabalu Park, Malaysia, 5

Land Rights Act, Australia, 26
La Selva Biological Station, Costa
Rica, 263
Latin America: bats, 110, 112; water
quality, 187
Leadership Training, 57
Leaflets: crane conservation, 139;
Jersey, Great Britain, 260
Lee County Schools Environmental
Education Program, 198; *see also*
Wildlife-focused action projects
LEESCAPES, 199, 216
Legislation enforcement, for wildlife
protection, 88

Leontopithecus chrysopygus, 5
Leontopithecus rosalia, 66
Leptonycteris curasoae, 115
Leptonycteris nivalis, 115
Leptotila wellsi, 98
Les Mielles, Great Britain, 254, 261
Le Vaomatua, American Samoa, 110
Lewis and Clark National Forest, 107
Lincoln Park Zoological Society, 244
Local naturalist guide training: Carib-
bean coast, Costa Rica, 273; Guana-
caste National Park, 273; La Selva
Biological Station, 263; Monte-
verde, 272; Tortuguero National
Park, 274
Loggerhead sea turtle, 202
Long-nosed bats, 115
Lowland Atlantic forest, Brazil, 5, 66

Magazines: bats, 108; Community Baboon Sanctuary, 249; crane conservation, 144; hunter education, 164,
172; *Junior Ranger Review,* 21
Maharini Shri University, 132
Malaysia, 5
Mammal Information Center, Israel,
110
Management plans: bat conservation,
104, 108; grizzly bear conservation,
156–58; howler monkeys, 241; land
management, Belize, 241, 242, 245,
246; Les Mielles, 261; seabird
conservation, 51, 54, 60; wildlife-
focused action projects, 213,
215
Manatee Community Reserve, Belize,
249
Manatee Park, Fla., 199, 215
Maned sloths, 84
Mass media: as target audience, 123;
Bat Conservation International,
110; Golden Lion Tamarin Conser-

vation Program, 73, 85; limitations, 82; see also specific media
Mexican free-tailed bats, 109, 114
Mexico: bats, 108; water quality, 192, 194
Middle East, water quality, 187
Migratory Bird Treaty of 1916, 52
Migratory Birds Convention, 52
Miscellaneous products: phone cards, Les Mielles, 260; soap, mountain gorillas, 46
Mobile displays, bat conservation, 111
Models: action research, 199, 200; conservation programs, integrated, 3; for conservation action, 28; content, wildlife-focused action projects, 206; environmentally responsible behavior, 22; evaluation, 3, 15; guide training, Costa Rica, 274; natural, 207; park-based education, 3; program, wildlife-focused action projects, 198; systems, for conservation education, 66; water-quality program, 180, 183, 184, 193
Monteverde Reserve, Costa Rica, 272
Moose, 157
Morro do Diabo Park, Brazil, 5
Mountain gorilla, 28
Mountain Gorilla Project, 28; anti-poaching, 37; attitudinal surveys, 31; education results, 42; interdisciplinary research data base, 37; mobile education unit, 39; target audiences, 38; tourism, 37
Museums, Community Baboon Sanctuary, 247

National Audubon Society, 147
National Geographic Society, bats, 115
National Guard, 114
National Museum, Costa Rica, 266
National Park Service, Costa Rica, 266
National Speleological Society, bats, 114
Nature Conservancy, 212
Nature preserves, Monkey River, Belize, 249
Newsletters: GREEN, 190, 196; seabird conservation, Canada, 58
Newspapers, 95, 106; bats, 108; bats, American Samoa, 110; bats, Costa Rica, 111; Community Baboon Sanctuary, 249; crane conservation, 125, 132, 144; Global Rivers Environmental Education Network, 181; Les Mielles, 260; supplements, Caribbean Education Campaign, 96; water quality, 184
New Zealand, water quality, 192
Noctuid moths, 110

Objectives: Bat Conservation International, 106; Community Baboon Sanctuary, Belize, 235; Golden Lion Tamarin Conservation Program, 67; grizzly bear conservation, 160; Mountain Gorilla Project, 41; park-based conservation education program, 6; seabird conservation, 54; wildlife-focused action projects, 200; wildlife-focused action projects, LEESCAPES, 216; see also Goals
Organization for Tropical Studies, 263
Outdoor education, benefits, 5
Ovis dalli 157

Parc National des Volcans, Rwanda, 31

Park-based conservation education program, 3; activities, 8, 14; augmentation to school curriculum, 14; Australia, 19, 20; benefit to parks, 15; community involvement, 8, 10; constraints, 6; evaluation, 10, 12; follow-up activities, 9; goals, 6; Golden Lion Tamarin Conservation Program, 67; needs assessment survey, 5; objectives, 6; resources available, 6; Rwanda, 37, 38

Perameles gunnii, 226

Photo collection, Bat Conservation International, 106

PL-480 funds (U.S. Special Foreign Currency Program), 153

Poço das Antas Biological Reserve, Brazil, 67

Pollination, bats, 103, 104, 106, 115, 116, 118

Postage stamps: mountain gorillas, 46; Siberian crane, 128, 137

Posters, 18; bats, Costa Rica, 112; Caribbean Education Campaign, 91, 92, 96, 97, 100; Community Baboon Sanctuary, 247; contest, seabird conservation, 57, 58; Global Rivers Environmental Education Network, 184; Golden Lion Tamarin Conservation Program, 75; grizzly bear conservation, 163; Mountain Gorilla Project, 39; seabird conservation, 58; water quality, 184

Preferences for animal species, 65

Program evaluation, park-based conservation education, 10

Project WILD, 198, 216

Publications: bat activity book, 116; Bat Conservation International, 105; *Educator's Activity Book About Bats,* 116; *see also specific media*

Public service announcements: Caribbean Education Campaign, 97; Golden Lion Tamarin Conservation Program, 74, 82; water quality, 184

Public support for conservation programs: gaining, 64; importance of, 64

Public surveys: Caribbean Education Campaign, 92, 98; Caribbean Man and Biosphere Program, 88; crane conservation, 129, 141; crane hunters, 129, 132; Golden Lion Tamarin Conservation Program, 68, 76; Mountain Gorilla Project, 31, 42, 48

Punjab Wildlife Research Center, 141

Quebec-Labrador Foundation, 54

Radio: bats, American Samoa, 110; bats, Costa Rica, 111; Caribbean Education Campaign, 90, 95, 97, 101; Community Baboon Sanctuary, 249; crane conservation, 138, 144; Golden Lion Tamarin Conservation Program, 73, 74; Junior Ranger Program, Australia, 20; Les Mielles, 260; Mountain Gorilla Project, 39, 46; park-based conservation education program, 10; seabird conservation, 58, 63; wildlife-focused action projects, 213

Rangifer tarandus, 157

RARE Center for Tropical Conservation, 90; Conservation Education Campaign (CEC), 91; conservation-marketing manual, 99

Razorbill, 52

Reintroduction of animals, Golden Lion Tamarin Conservation Program, 84

Research: action, wildlife-focused projects, 198; Bat Conservation International, 106, 115–17; Community Baboon Sanctuary, 237, 241, 246; community-based agendas, 236; crane conservation, 121, 122, 125, 126, 129, 131, 134, 135, 140, 141–47, 149, 151; educational, 134, 136, 140, 141; Global Rivers Environmental Education Network, 178, 193, 195; Golden Lion Tamarin Conservation Program, 64; grizzly bear conservation, 171; in guide training, Costa Rica, 277; interdisciplinary, Mountain Gorilla Project, 30, 37, 48; market, 68, 92; seabird conservation, Canada, 52; sea turtle, wildlife-focused action projects, 211; Siberian cranes, 122; wildlife, India, 127; wildlife, Pakistan, 127; wildlife-focused action projects, 202, 203, 208, 217

Romulea columnae, 255

Royal Forest Department, Thailand, 113

Rwanda, 28; Parc National des Volcans, 31; Virunga reserve system, 29

Saint Lucia parrot, 99

Sand crocus, 255

Sanibel Island, Fla., 202, 211

Sarus cranes, 132

School program, Kinabalu Park, Malaysia, 5

School programs, 221; activities, 9; Air Monitoring Program, 195; bat conservation, 112; bat T-shirts, 112; Belize, 245, 247; Caribbean Education Campaign, 90, 91, 96, 100, 101; clubs, 40, 114; Community Baboon Sanctuary, 245, 247; crane

conservation, 138, 139; curriculum integration, 14; Ecuador, 189; *Field Manual for Water-Quality Monitoring,* 184, 190; Fun days, 259; Germany, 189, 190; Global Rivers Environmental Education Network, 178; Golden Lion Tamarin Conservation program, 75, 76; Heavy Metals Monitoring Program, 195; Junior Ranger Program, 16, 18, 20, 26; Labrador, 55; Les Mielles, 258, 259, 261; Morro do Diabo Park, Brazil, 7, 12; Mountain Gorilla project, 38–40; naturalist guide training, 273; park-based conservation education, 3, 4, 10; seabird conservation, Canada, 57, 58, 63; Taiwan, 190; Thailand, 112; Water-Quality Monitoring Program, 180, 183; wildlife-focused action projects, 199, 201; zoo-based education, Australia, 223, 225, 229, 231

Scientific organizations, as target audience, 123

Seabirds, management plan, 51, 54

Sea Turtle Research and Conservation Program, 199

Sea turtles, Belize, 249

Seed dispersal, bats, 103, 104, 116, 118

Siberian cranes, 122

Simulation games, water quality, 183

Six-Mile Cypress Slough Acquisition, 199, 212

Slide programs: Bat Conservation International, 106; Caribbean Conservation Program, 97; crane conservation, 125, 131, 132, 138, 139; Global Rivers Environmental Education Network, 180; Golden Lion Tamarin Conservation Program, 75; Mountain Gorilla Project, 38; park

Slide programs (*Continued*) programs, 8; wildlife-focused action projects, 213, 214; *see also* Audiovisual materials

Social marketing, in conservation education programs, 172

Somateria mollissima, 52

Songs: Caribbean Education Campaign, 91, 96, 97, 100, 101; mountain gorillas, 46

South Africa, water quality, 193

St. Mary's Islands Seabird Sanctuary, Canada, 55

St. Vincent parrot, 98

Strategies: Community Baboon Sanctuary, 241; conservation consciousness, 246; crane conservation, 123, 129, 136; education program, seabird conservation, 55; educational, crane conservation, 135; educational, seabird conservation, 54; Golden Lion Tamarin Conservation Program, 73; grizzly bear conservation, 158; hunting, grizzly bear conservation, 158, 168–70; instructional, action research, 198; instructional, Global Rivers Environmental Education Network 178; instructional, wildlife-focused action projects, 203, 208; Mountain Gorilla Project, 37; National education, Rwanda, 40; operational, wildlife-focused action projects, 204; teaching, 16; wildlife-focused action projects, 203

Street theater, water quality, 184

Student conferences, water quality, 183

Survey, planning, 4; *see also* Public surveys

Sylvia undata, 255

Symbolic values, in conservation education, 172

Systems model, conservation education program, 3, 66

T-shirts, bats, 112

Tadarida brasiliensis, 109

Taiwan, water quality, 190, 192

Target audiences for education, 3, 4; Caribbean Education Campaign, 90, 96; Community Baboon Sanctuary, Belize, 237; crane conservation, 123, 136, 139, 150; Golden Lion Tamarin Conservation Program, 65, 68, 73, 85; grizzly bear conservation, 164; guide training, Costa Rica, 266, 274; Junior Ranger Program, Australia, 22; Les Mielles, 257; Mountain Gorilla Project, 38; park-based conservation education programs, 3; seabird conservation, 54, 57; wildlife-focused action projects, 200; *see also specific audiences*

Target species, 91; in conservation education, 5, 91, 96–98, 100, 101; *see also* Flagship species; Focal species

Teachers: bat conservation, 114; booklets for, 38; Caribbean Education Campaign, 90; Community Baboon Sanctuary, 247; crane conservation, 134, 136, 138, 151; Global Rivers Environmental Education Network, 178, 185, 186, 188, 195, 196; Golden Lion Tamarin Conservation Program, 68, 73; guidebooks for, 8, 10; Junior Ranger Program, Australia, 26; Mountain Gorilla Project, 40; park-based conservation education, 5, 7, 8, 10, 12, 15; training, 75, 123, 139, 146, 186,

225, 258; wildlife-focused action projects, 201, 202, 205, 209; zoo-based education, Australia, 221, 223, 225, 227–29

Technical Education Research Committee, Boston, 195

Television: bats, Costa Rica, 111; Caribbean Education Campaign, 90; Community Baboon Sanctuary, 249; crane conservation, 137, 138, 144; Golden Lion Tamarin Conservation program, 73, 74, 82; Les Mielles, 260; Mountain Gorilla Project, 38; seabirds, 58

Tennessee, bats, 114

Texas, bats, 114

Texas A & M University, 117

Texas Nature Conservancy, 108

Texas Parks and Wildlife Department, 108

Thailand: bats, 112; guano production, 112; Royal Forest Department, 113; school programs, 112

The Nature Conservancy: bats, 114; Six-Mile Slough Cypress Acquisition, 212

Tortuguero National Park, Costa Rica, 274

Training: bat conservation, 106, 117; crane conservation, 129, 136, 146, 153; Global Rivers Environmental Education Network, 196; guard, 75; hunting guide, 167; leadership, 55, 61; nature guide, 7, 263; resource managers, 247; teacher, 75, 123, 139, 146, 186, 225, 258; wildlife officers, 136; youth, 55, 58, 146

Treaties, Bonn Convention Migratory Bird Treaty, 146; *see also* CITES

Tropical Science Center, Costa Rica, 272

U.K. Heritage Coast projects, 257

U.S. Fish and Wildlife Service, 63, 122, 214; bats, 114, 115

U.S. Forest Service, bats, 107

U.S. National Park Service, bats, 114

U.S. Special Foreign Currency Program, 123

Uganda, 29

United Nations Conference on Environment and Development, 1992 2, 85

United States, water quality, 192, 194

Universidad Nacional, Costa Rica, 266

University of Costa Rica, 266

University of Florida, 274

University of Michigan, 177, 189, 195

Uria aalge, 52

Ursus americanus, 157

Ursus arctos, 156

Vampire bats, 104, 110–12

Videos: grizzly bear conservation, 163; water quality, 184

Virunga reserve system, Rwanda, 29

Visitor guides: Belize, 247; Costa Rica, 272

Visitor information, Jersey, Great Britain, 260

Visitor interpretation centers: Community Baboon Sanctuary, 247; crane conservation, 134, 142; Les Mielles, 260; Organization of Tropical Studies, Costa Rica, 271; park-based conservation education, 7; Poço das Antas Reserve, Brazil, 85

Water quality, 192–94
Water-Quality Monitoring Program: advisory committee, 183; computer conference, 183; cross-cultural partnerships, 183; field manual, 184; heavy metals, 183; Huron River, Mich., 180; Rio Grande, 194; Rouge River, Mich., 183; simulation game, 183; student congress, 183; two-week model program, 180
Water Stewardship Program, British Columbia, 217
Wildlife-focused action projects, 212; action research, 198; Bald Eagle Habitat Protection Ordinance, 199, 215; budget, 209; Caretta Research, 202, 211; community involvement, 199; course elements, 208; dissemination, 216; elements of success, 217; Environmental Applied (Construction) class, 205; Environmental Science Investigative class, 205; environmental values and attitudes, 206; Florida Manatee Protection Act, 199, 214; goals, 200; guiding principles, 207; historic perspective, 201; LEESCAPES, 199, 216; Manatee Park, Fla., 199, 215; Monday Group, 205; objectives, 200; operational strategy, 204; planning ten-

ets, 202; resources available, 201; Sea Turtle Research and Conservation Program, 199; Six-Mile Cypress Slough Acquisition, 199; staffing, 209; target audience, 200
Wolves, 157
Workshops: Bat Conservation International, 106, 107; crane conservation, 130, 139, 146; GREEN, 187, 188, 193, 196; for hunting guides, 163–65; for teachers, 139, 186, 187, 258; wildlife-focused action projects, 216
World Wildlife Fund: bats, 111; howler monkeys, 244; Mountain Gorilla Project, 37; naturalist guide training, 269; park-based conservation education, 15
World Wildlife Fund-India, 126

Youth congress, 183
Yukon Fish and Wildlife Branch, 158
Yukon Outfitters Association, 158

Zaire, 29
Zoo-based education, Australia, Environmental Education Programs In Classrooms (EEPIC) 225
Zoological Society of Milwaukee County, Wisc., 244